The
Chicago
Guide to
Your
Academic
Career

The Chicago Guide to Your Academic Career

A Portable Mentor for Scholars
from Graduate School
through Tenure

JOHN A. GOLDSMITH, JOHN KOMLOS,
AND PENNY SCHINE GOLD

The University of Chicago Press / Chicago and London

The University of Chicago Press, Chicago 60637
The University of Chicago Press, Ltd., London
© 2001 by The University of Chicago
All rights reserved. Published 2001
Printed in the United States of America
10 09 08 07 06 05 04 03 02 01   1 2 3 4 5

ISBN: 0-226-30150-8 (cloth)
ISBN: 0-226-30151-6 (paper)

Library of Congress Cataloging-in-Publication Data

Goldsmith, John A., 1951–
    The Chicago guide to your academic career : a portable mentor for
scholars from graduate school through tenure / John A. Goldsmith, John
Komlos, Penny Schine Gold.
        p. cm.
    Includes bibliographical references (p.   ) and index.
    ISBN 0-226-30150-8 (hard.) — ISBN 0-226-30151-6 (pbk.)
    1. College training—Vocational guidance. 2. College teachers.
I. Komlos, John, 1944– . II. Gold, Penny Schine. III. Title.
LB1778 .G63   2001
378.1′2′023—dc21
                                                    00-012565

Contents

Part Two: The Academic Profession

Preface

This book is, in essence, a user's guide to academic life, conceived for those considering taking up a career in the traditional academic disciplines—seniors in college, perhaps, or others thinking about going into graduate school—as well as those who have already started out along that path, which is to say, men and women working on a Ph.D. and those already with appointments as assistant professors at a college or a university.[1] Some of our remarks may be of interest to others as well: senior professors who are interested in other perspectives on the academic scene, confused and bewildered parents of junior academics, professional advisors, spouses of graduate students and junior faculty, and laymen interested in learning about the mysteries of academia. Foreign students who are thinking about acquiring an American graduate school education will certainly profit from reading this book.[2]

Our backgrounds are in the humanities and the social sciences, and our views naturally reflect our own experiences, observations, and what we have learned in the course of our careers. We believe there is sufficient overlap among the various academic disciplines to make valid generalizations possible. As teachers, we have often been asked to offer advice on myriad issues of both a professional and a personal nature, and we have tended to give the same advice over and over again. We've written this book in response to what we felt was a real need for information. We chose the format of an extended conversation, much like conversations that we have actually had on many occasions with those who have sought us out to discuss their aspirations, hopes, fears, and problems. The question-and-answer format emphasizes that we are speaking in this book much as we would during our office hours or over coffee in the departmental lounge. Although the questions in boldface are our constructions, for the most part they are questions we've often heard or can imagine our readers might want to ask if they could.

Could you tell us a bit about yourselves?

John Goldsmith: I'm a professor of linguistics at the University of Chicago. I have been in this business close to thirty years now, twenty-five of them as a professor, and my own views have changed—I would like to say "grown"—over this time in countless ways. I began with many assumptions about how academia worked, and what it was about, that I have since found to be grossly in error. Not surprisingly, I have found that my own preconceptions were not unique to me—not by a long shot. In fact, as I have come to see, there are a host of misconceptions about academia as a way of life that virtually all young men and women coming into the university share—misconceptions that they must slowly outgrow or else, in one way or another, pay the price. Linguistics is considered a part of the humanities at the university where I presently work, though at most other universities it is considered to be a part of the social sciences. My perspective thus leans toward the humanities, with a very strong inclination toward the social sciences. At the same time, I have had a number of contacts with colleagues in the natural and biological sciences, especially mathematics and computer science, and this has helped balance the general remarks that I have to offer. In my career, I have spent a good deal of time at two universities, quite different from one another. One was a large public state university; the other, a small private university. Both are research universities with strong graduate commitments, but there the resemblance ends. I have also had the opportunity to be a visiting professor at a number of other universities in this country and in Canada and, most recently, have spent quite a bit of time as a visiting scholar at a large software company in the Pacific Northwest.

One thing that sets the academic life in a different category, as far as I can see, is that it is the only field in which so many of the myths are perpetuated without any ready source of realistic advice to serve as a countermeasure. In the business world, there are countless "how to" books; in the medical world, there are long and rigorous periods of internship, in which medical students (or recent recipients of the M.D. degree) learn how the system works, while being overseen by doctors with greater experience. In many parts of academia, though, such as my own, there is little in the way of equivalent. In a brief two- or three-year period, the research period, the typical student learns to do research in her chosen field of study, in collaboration with a research advisor. Thereafter, she is typically thrown into an academic job, generally quite ill-equipped for the challenge. The junior academic enters the system still with the set of experiences—the mindset—of a student, and she is supposed to some-how play the part of the professor. *Sauve qui peut,* and the Devil take the hindmost.

John Komlos: My perspective also has been molded to a considerable de-gree by my association with the University of Chicago as a graduate stu-dent of both economics and history. Consequently, like John Goldsmith's, my perspective bridges the social sciences and humanities, and I've spent about as much time in academia as he. And like him, I entered the world of research, teaching, and scholarship with few expectations that, in hind-sight, I consider realistic. I thought at first that this was the case because I am of the first generation in my family to attend college, and, therefore, I had no inside information easily available to me on the workings of this world. I learned by doing. It became obvious to me, however, that this is a rather widespread phenomenon: there seems to be a need for a candid introduction to the academic career. College seldom prepares one suffi-ciently for the complexities of graduate school—as graduate school, in turn, seldom provides a balanced view of university life on the other side of the podium. This is just as true of the social dynamics within the com-munity of scholars as of the practical mechanics of fulfilling the expecta-tions of one's colleagues for acceptance into, and promotion within, the discipline. As a consequence, many of us leave graduate school with ide-alized expectations and have to piece together tediously for ourselves the puzzle of how things function. The key for success is not apparent at first. As a rule, professional groups have unspoken rules on what is considered indiscreet, and this is also true for academia. Hence, survival techniques and the meaning of rituals generally have to be learned through on-the-job training.

It was not only naïveté, but perhaps also a sensibility shared with my cohort that came of age intellectually at the end of the 1960s that led me to make the choice of profession without much soul-searching. I entered academia willy-nilly, not by some rational choice, with a weighing of the pros and cons. Money or career mattered to fewer members of this gen-eration than to subsequent ones. We were more preoccupied, it seems to me, with a sense of doing something meaningful. Success was often mea-sured in doing the best we could. I think we assumed implicitly that the world could be changed for the better, that it was in our power to do so, and that it was actually our moral obligation to rise to the challenge. Many of us chose to become an integral part of this process, even if in small ways, without necessarily being well informed about what that choice really entailed. I entered graduate school in 1971, to be specific, and have spent the intervening years in academia as a participant and as an observer from various vantage points. I advanced, in the meanwhile, from a non-tenure-track position at a tiny institution to a chaired professorship in economics at the University of Munich, a major European university. I held tenure-track and non-tenure-track jobs; I was a student, a postdoctoral fellow, a visiting lecturer, and an associate professor. I worked in Europe as well as in America. I earned two Ph.D.s along the way. Hence, I interacted with the academic world in a broad spectrum of ways. I blundered, I persevered, and ultimately I soared, and in the process, I learned and matured.

In retrospect, a deficiency in my graduate education at the University of Chicago was the faculty's avowed disinterest at the time in the practicalities of professionalization, and a candid overview of academia, such as this one, would have been extremely helpful to me. In neither economics nor in history, the two departments I knew best, was there even an oral tradition of how to approach academic life after we left the campus.[3] On the contrary, the topic seems to have been somehow taboo, and there was an ethos that rather tended to idealize its dynamics. Other universities may, of course, be different, and much has changed since I was a graduate student, but once a professor, I spent a fair share of my office hours saying the same things over and over again to students. So I decided to put my advice in a book rather than have to repeat myself. I do think that the more level-headed information a student has about the way academia functions, the better off she is. We want to describe it as viewed from the ground level—without lofty idealism and illusions, but with plenty of frankness and a good dose of pragmatism.

Penny Gold: For three people thrown together by chance, it's interesting that we all have spent part of our lives at the University of Chicago—me as an undergraduate student, John Komlos as a graduate student, and John Goldsmith as a professor. And the three of us are close in age and in the types of disciplines chosen—I am also a historian, with additional graduate training in literature and art history. A large difference among us, however, is that my teaching career has been primarily at a small liberal arts college (Knox College), an institution that puts its strongest emphasis on teaching, even while research is encouraged and expected. I'm also female and began my career during a period of time in which women were just beginning to enter academia in significant numbers; this has been a formative influence on my life in the academy and in my attitudes toward it.

I entered graduate school without a clear commitment to professional training. In the fall term of my senior year, I was suddenly caught up in my studies by a serendipitous concatenation of courses in medieval studies and cultural history, and I just wanted to keep learning. It happened that Stanford, where I chose to go, was giving full funding for four years to all entering history graduate students at that time (thanks to generous funding from the Ford Foundation, which was—unsuccessfully, it turns out—trying to speed completion of Ph.D.s), so I paid nothing for my graduate education, nor did I have to go into debt. The first year of graduate school was quite a shock, and if I had been spending thousands of dollars of my own money, I'm not sure I would have stayed in school. But in the end, I was very glad the financial support enticed me to stay, helping me through a rough transition.

While Stanford then gave its graduate students no instruction in teaching (a situation now changed), I had the good fortune to experience excellent mentoring while I was there, and unlike John Komlos and John Goldsmith, I learned a great deal during graduate school about how the academy works. My advisor was beginning his first job as a professor in the same year I began graduate school, and I learned much from him about the demands, pleasures, and precariousness of academic life. Another professor I worked closely with was denied tenure while I was in my third year; I contributed a letter to her successful appeal and learned a good deal about academic values and processes along the way. I was at Stanford in the early years of the women's movement (1969–74), and my involvement in the History Graduate Students Women's Caucus was also a crucial learning experience. The department at Stanford had only one female professor at the time, a Harvard Ph.D. who, because of nepotism rules (her husband had a position in another department), was limited to a non-tenure-track adjunct appointment. When this woman resigned, the Women's Caucus organized an effort to persuade the department to hire a woman for a tenure-track appointment. We talked, we wrote letters, and we succeeded. Another student and I were members of the search committee that resulted. I think I learned more about how the academy works, and how one can work to change it, in that one year than in many of the rest. Also, within this early cohort of women in the academy, there was a strong sense of solidarity, amongst both graduate students and faculty, within and across institutions. We knew we needed to figure out all we could about academic institutions and procedures in order to make it as newcomers, and we helped each other out as best we could. Often without access to the "old boy" networks, we founded "new girl" networks, and these have been a crucial source of support, comfort, and help to me over the years.

How do you expect this book to be used?

John Komlos: In order to make best use of our guide, you may want to read some parts less intensely than others. Yet perusing the whole should give you a pretty good indication of what academic life will be like a few years down the road, should you choose this path, and you can always return to the chapters devoted to that part of your career that lies just ahead in order to take more careful notes. You may also want to supplement our volume with others devoted to the next station in your career.

John Goldsmith: This book is an attempt to redress the imbalance between reality and perception that now seems to prevail. We do our best, first of all, to inform the reader about how academia is set up and how it works—to answer the questions you always wanted to have answered, but were afraid to ask—and we also try to give some advice about how the academic world should be viewed. We'll put our cards on the table: we like the academic world very much and have enjoyed our choices of career a great deal. We have also seen any number of friends and acquaintances suffer a great deal in this world, partly because there was an unfortunate mismatch between academia and their personal needs and gifts and partly because they carried around in their heads inaccurate assumptions about how the system functioned. These people were, without exception, bright enough to make it in the academic world, however you wish to interpret that; academics are, by and large, no more and no less intelligent than the successful people in medicine, in law, in business, or in engineering. These folk, as a rule, also had something to offer and did, indeed, have the potential to make a contribution, which for some reason could not be realized. To succeed in a profession, two things are necessary: one's goals and abilities must match those required by the profession, and one must possess a realistic understanding of how the profession works. This book is an attempt to help future academics or junior academics come to grips with those matters. We hope to provide the reader with an unbuttoned view of the academic life. We'll call the shots as we see them, and there's a lot of personal opinion that is bound up in the remarks that we offer.

**Are you speaking just for yourselves, or are you saying that your views
are representative of the profession at large?**

John Komlos: With almost a million faculty involved in the American academic world, frankly we have no way of really ascertaining the extent to
which we represent the mainstream. Nonetheless, among us, we bring
to this guide three-quarters of a century of broad experience of working
in academia, and we have seen the system function from many vantage points. We have experience working with students, colleagues, grant
agencies, and administrators. All of us have been chairs of our respective
departments. Nonetheless, we do not claim to be "representative." That
does not exist except in a statistical sense, and in the process of doing some
background research for this book, I came to the surprising realization
that there has been extremely little actual scholarly research done on academia itself. The study of education has focused almost exclusively on
elementary and high schools, with only peripheral interest in higher education. Regrettably and incomprehensibly, the field of education seems to
have completely neglected the field of graduate education as a legitimate
scientific field of inquiry.[4]

Admittedly, our distillation of our experiences reflects our own personalities, our philosophical and ethical views, and the way we view the
world. Our main experience has been in the humanities and the social
sciences, and those who are considering careers in a laboratory science
might wish to supplement our perspective with more specialized surveys.[5]
That is obviously not to say that such students will not benefit from our
book. We address concerns that, in the main, permeate all areas of academia, and our views should also be helpful to those who are still undecided about which discipline to pursue in graduate school. We obviously
enjoy what we do and would like to share that experience with you. At the
same time, we see the blemishes of the world we inhabit as well, and we
are not inhibited from discussing them, without blowing them out of
proportion.

We are quite aware of the fact that one set of guidelines cannot cover
the billions of possibilities there are: following our advice does not guarantee success by any means. Excellence is hard to quantify or define, and
careers always develop in a unique and highly contingent manner. Values
are disparate, and advice on specific issues ought not overlook these con-
tingencies or the context in which they unfold. Nevertheless, it is surprising that no broad overview exists for a profession that engages nearly a

million employees in the United States alone![6] There are any number of
guides aimed at certain segments of the market, such as minorities and
women, while others are devoted to some aspects of the academic career,
such as applying to graduate school, or to certain disciplines, such as engineering.[7] Our hope is that this introduction to the main features of academic life, that is to say, to the possibilities it has to give meaning to one's
life, will enable students to make a more informed decision about whether
to wager entering this world. We hope that there will be more fulfilling
lives as a consequence: fewer mistakes made, fewer regrets, fewer students
changing their minds in midstream, fewer denials of tenure, and more
people in careers they find most rewarding. We will have also succeeded if
we attract some people who would otherwise not have ventured the journey or if we can persuade many others to realize that the academic career
is not the right one for them. We do not carry our dialog much beyond
promotion to tenure because by then, we expect, mature academics will
have learned to navigate the seas without our compass.

Ours is not a politicized view, with open or hidden agendas.[8] We do,
nonetheless, present the unpleasant aspects along with the exhilaration of
belonging to a subculture with high moral standing and very substantial
intellectual accomplishments. Yet unfortunately we are not all reincarna-
tions of Socrates. The system of higher education happened to evolve on
earth and not in heaven. And I believe that contrary to theological teach-
ings, even if it had been created in heaven, it would still be imperfect. We
are human, after all, and though some of our colleagues will vigorously
disagree, we are fallible. Compared to other institutions, though, American academia deserves a very high rating, and in the international arena,
it is certainly equaled by none. Though we are critical, we refrain from
proposing solutions to its problems and challenges.[9] Rather, our aim is to
open a window for the reader to see into this world through our eyes. So
do join us on this personal journey through this fascinating and, in many
ways, mysterious world.

How did this book come into being?

John Goldsmith: A few years ago I began writing a manuscript discussing
what the academic career was really like, for those who were thinking
about taking that road. I showed it to Geoff Huck, not only a colleague
and a friend, but also an acquisitions editor at the University of Chicago
Press. He encouraged me to continue, and a bit later, due to a kind of

fortuitous happenstance, he put me in touch with someone who, completely unbeknownst to me, had a similar idea. It just so happens that Geoff had published a book edited by John Komlos some years ago, and when John turned to Geoff for advice about his new project, Geoff brought us together. Thanks to the Internet, John and I could exchange our manuscripts almost instantaneously and saw that there were lots of reasons to merge them. With authors thousands of miles apart, it would never have worked without the Internet. Some time after that, Geoff came across an op-ed piece in the *Chronicle of Higher Education* by a historian named Penny Gold. She had terrific things to say about the academic career, and what's more, she was on sabbatical that year at the University of Chicago. Wouldn't it be nice to add a third perspective to our conversation? I walked over to the Divinity School, where she was (merely fifty feet from my building), and invited her to join the project. After giving it some thought, she agreed to contribute, and the result is the book that you hold in your hands.

Penny Gold: Our voices are distinct from each other, and not always in agreement. While the voices are usually complementary, sometimes they are discordant, and you will have to decide whose advice to follow. We did not attempt to smooth out such disharmonies because they are, in fact, illustrative of the differences of opinion through which you will have to navigate during your career in the academy. It's always a good idea to seek advice from more than one person, and here you have the three of us conveniently in one package. We hope that listening to our three voices and considering our suggestions will help you in deciding on your own path through the complex and rewarding world of academia.

John Goldsmith: We've asked a few colleagues with special kinds of experience to give us some brief remarks that could be helpful. These we have included under the title "The Inside Track."

Acknowledgments

Our deepest thanks go to Geoff Huck, our editor at the University of Chicago Press, without whom this book simply would not exist. This observation is truer than the reader can imagine. Geoff brought us, the authors, together and worked with us step by step in the maturation of this project. We give a small indication of the work that he did in the preface to this book, but Geoff did much more all along the way than we can possibly say. He is the consummate professional editor, and we are extremely grateful to him.

John Goldsmith: This book has grown out of many experiences that I've had during my academic career—most, but not all, happy ones. I'm especially grateful to the teachers I've had, of whom seven stand out: Lila Gleitman, Bernie Saffran, Jim England, Richie Schuldenfrei, Morris Halle, Noam Chomsky, and Haj Ross. Morris Halle was my dissertation advisor, and as such, he set a personal example for me (and countless others like me) that is hard to live up to and that has left many traces for the better in the discussions in this book. I've also learned a great deal from students in my department over the years, too numerous again to mention, but I would like anyway to thank Diane Brentari, Manuela Noske, and Yukari Hirata. Svetlana Soglasnova went over the manuscript in great detail and contributed many very helpful suggestions. I've also learned a lot from working with the administration at the University of Chicago during the more than fifteen years I've been here, most notably from my colleagues who have been chair before and after me, especially Jerry Sadock and Salikoko Mufwene, and our deans during this time, Stuart Tave, Phil Gossett, and Janel Mueller, as well as Tom Thuerer. I've learned a great deal about these subjects from discussions with my wife, Jessie Pinkham, and with other friends, including BC Black-Schaffer, Ami Kronfeld, Bernard Laks, and Pierre Laszlo.

John Komlos: Good teachers are so important all along one's intellectual development, from kindergarten through graduate school—not necessarily for the transmission of knowledge perhaps as much as for the transmission of the spirit of inquiry, which is difficult to foster without a nurturing environment. I was rather fortunate to have such inspiring teachers throughout my youth and subsequent years of maturation. So many of them are now gone, yet their influence lives on. Is it not amazing what long-range impact we educators have on successive generations, without even knowing about it perhaps? This book could not have come into existence if I had not experienced those nurturing environments along the way. In a sense, my contribution to this book is dedicated to fostering this spirit of the academic enterprise. I also thank Brian A'Hearn and Timothy Cuff for their detailed comment on the manuscript and Peter Coclanis and Peter Salamon for always being interested listeners. I dedicate the book to my two sons, Stefan and Simon, in the hope that they, too, might benefit from it.

Penny Gold: I have come to be in the position of contributing to a book such as this one only with the encouragement, support, advice, and generosity of a wide variety of people. It is a pleasure to have the opportunity to thank them here.

Thanks to Alan Bernstein, the best advisor imaginable; to Suzanne Lewis, my first guide through the challenges of being a female in academia; to Michel Dahlin and Glenna Matthews, in fond recollection of our work in the History Graduate Students Women's Caucus; to Carolyn Lougee Chappell, for showing me how one might be an academic and a mother, vetting my clothing for job interviews, and—not least—inspiring me with her love of doing history.

Thanks also to my colleagues at Knox, who have made this college such a satisfying place for me to work. My special gratitude to those who have supported and encouraged me, pushed me along, comforted me when I was in despair, listened to my stories, and told me theirs—the echoes run throughout this book: Robin Behn, Larry Breitborde, Rodney Davis, Nancy Eberhardt, Brenda Fineberg, Joanne Finkelstein, E. Inman Fox, Mikiso Hane, Harley Knosher, John McCall, Rick Nahm, Wilbur Pillsbury, Natania Rosenfeld, Don Torrence, and Lewis Salter.

And for specific help on this manuscript, thanks to Brenda Fineberg for her reading of chapter 10 and to David Amor, Larry Breitborde, Carolyn Lougee Chappell, and Natania Rosenfeld for their careful reading of my parts of the book.

And, finally, to David Amor, who's been my interlocutor on academic, and all other, matters for twenty-eight of my thirty years in academia.

Part
One

Becoming a Scholar

1 | Deciding on an Academic Career

How should I decide whether to try for an academic career?

John Goldsmith: One of the odd characteristics of academia is how many people manage somehow to slide into it without ever making a serious and conscious decision to become academics. In the present day and age, a student who does very well in college gets a good deal of encouragement to continue an education in graduate school. Why not, after all? Those in a position to advise these young students—their professors—have themselves all gone through graduate school, and many of them did so directly from college. Unless economic pressures, such as the need to support parents, a spouse, or a child, intercede, continuing in school—graduate school, now—will often appear to be the course of least resistance. It may even seem to be a way to avoid choosing a job, and perhaps thus a career. What an irony, to be sure! Having chosen to go on to graduate school, the student is quite likely to have chosen a particular career track, having hoped to avoid making any decisions at all! As we'll see, it doesn't really work that way. Academia is a very specific career choice, with its pros and cons, its ups and downs, and its ins and outs. One would think that since it's quite difficult to get a successful academic career up and running, those who perform well in the enterprise have given the matter serious thought and carefully considered alternative career paths. I'm not at all convinced that that's the case.

John Komlos: Our message is that before embarking on this path, you should give it some serious thought and consider if this is really the right career for you. It is not a good idea at all to just stumble into it willy-nilly, although, in fact, many people do. Unless you enjoy the kind of life we are about to describe, it does not make much sense for you to pursue an academic career. Are you willing to take the risks?[1] What happens if you find out six years into graduate school that you have lost interest in your dissertation research and are not able or willing to complete it? Will you feel it was worth giving it a try anyway, or will you be embittered? Does your strategy include a back-up? Will you be able to find a way to bail yourself out? Are you focused enough to complete the thesis, or will you be easily distracted by friends asking you to accompany them to the movies? After completing your doctorate, will you be willing to put up with a couple of years of part-time teaching before you land a tenure-track position (see table 1 in appendix 3), or will you be impatient and start another career? You will then have reached an age when it is no longer easy to switch to another promising endeavor, especially if further schooling would be called for.

These are just some of the reasons why it is helpful to make an informed decision before you choose this profession. It is indispensable for you to spend some time gathering basic information on what your prospects are likely to be five years from now in the discipline you are considering.[2] Of course, many of the growth fields are common knowledge, but it is less well known perhaps that in 1993 those with a bachelor's degree in pharmacy earned (on average) a third more than those with a degree in chemistry ($49,000 versus $35,400) and those with a degree in English earned almost $20,000 less ($28,500) than those with a pharmacy degree.[3] It is also not widely known that 7 percent of Ph.D. recipients in political science last year were unemployed. Such information might well help you to make up your mind whether or not to enter a particular discipline.

There is a wide range of possible outcomes in an academic career, and it is difficult, particularly at the beginning, to predict where you will end up. Note the travails of a full-time teacher in part-time status, Paul Ton, at Metropolitan State College in Denver, which has an enrollment of about 18,000 students. According to his letter to the editor of *Perspectives*, Paul teaches three classes and earns $1,800 for each. He reveals openly that his before-tax annual income averaged $8,000 per annum for the last ten years. "Why do I teach?" he asks himself. "Because I enjoy teaching and because the people at the department . . . are among the best friends I have ever had."[4] Contrast this with the eulogy of Lawrence Stone by

Robert Darnton of Princeton University, published in the same issue of the newsletter, from which one gets a very different view of the academic experience: "No historian since World War II, except Fernand Braudel, has written history so authoritatively on so large a scale. . . . The audacity of [his arguments] energized us all. We left the seminar or the last page of a paper or even a department meeting with a dizzying sensation: Lawrence had clarified things so radically."[5] So the range of possible outcomes in an academic career is enormous.

Note, moreover, that, by and large, financial considerations do not speak for an academic career. You can expect a secure and comfortable middle-class existence with a full-time job, but probably not commensurate with either your learning or your intelligence. There are very few professors earning in what might be described as an opulent salary (see table 2 in appendix 3). And a detailed breakdown reveals that business employment is much more lucrative (see table 3 in appendix 3). A math major with a master's degree starting out in private business can expect to earn more than twice as much as his counterpart in academia. The advantage with a doctoral degree is similarly skewed in favor of a business career. Moreover, your income will not increase meaningfully by obtaining a doctorate. A person in his forties with a master's degree in the social sciences can expect to earn $40,000 per annum in academia, whereas if he were to obtain a doctorate, his income would increase by only $10,000 per year.[6] Obviously, he would have to save all his incremental salary for an extended period of time to make up for the more than $100,000 that it might cost him to earn a doctorate after the master's. Furthermore, someone with a master's degree working in the business sector can expect to earn much more than his counterpart with a doctorate working in academia: for a math major, the loss in income is $10,000 at the beginning of one's career and rises to $15,000–16,000 subsequently.[7] Hence, the decision to work toward a doctorate and remain in academia becomes much more of a choice of a lifestyle, of the quality of life you want to achieve, because the investment in effort and monetary expenses coupled with the risks associated with doing so (say, four to five years beyond the master's degree)[8] can hardly be justified in pecuniary terms alone. In summary, if you are interested in a life full of material amenities, with your talents and achievements, well, you are much better off going to a professional school or working in the private sector after you earn an advanced degree.

What's more, faculty salaries essentially have not changed during the past quarter century (see table 4 in appendix 3), in keeping with economy-wide trends. In the meanwhile, however, the incomes of wealthy professionals have just skyrocketed. For example, in 1994, there were 1.1 million individual tax returns reporting an adjusted gross income of $200,000 or more. Measured in constant dollars, the number of such high-income individuals is 3.6 times greater today than it was in 1977. This is merely one indication that academic salaries have not kept pace with those of other high-achieving groups in American society.[9]

In addition, the purchasing power of your salary will not increase substantially over your lifetime. You can expect modest annual increases, so-called merit pay increases; they are of mere symbolic value and will barely keep up with inflation. The chances are that the two more substantial pay raises you can expect—upon receiving tenure and upon being promoted to full professor-will not increase your salary by more than 50 percent (combined) over your lifetime (see table 4 in appendix 3). So unless you can generate an outside offer from another university, your living standard is not likely to keep up with that of the Joneses.[10] Academia has no stock options either, and even the most successful academics, such as Paul Samuelson (who sold between three and four hundred thousand copies of his textbook annually for many, many years), do not come close to earning as much as the Bill Gateses. Samuelson did receive the Nobel Prize, to be sure, but the CEOs of the major corporations earn the multiple of its worth every single year.

Academia is hardly a rapidly expanding field either. The number of professorial positions will grow modestly in the near future (under 2 percent per annum)—so we will continue to produce too many Ph.D.s. Though you are certainly going to find a job after the doctorate, it may not be in academia, and it might not be in the field you prepared for. Unemployment of 1996–97 Ph.D.s in science and social science was only about 2.5 percent in the fall of 1997, and as low as 0.7 percent in psychology, but as high as 7 percent in political science, as I have noted.[11] Yet the substantial increase in the number of part-time faculty is a disturbing trend. In history departments, their numbers increased by 5 percent just between 1996 and 1998, to reach 12 percent of the total. At the same time, the number of full professors declined by 7 percent![12] Moreover, these data are reported by the departments themselves, and according to a survey, they are downwardly biased: "62 percent of the part-time faculty were not listed" in the departmental directory.[13] Accordingly, the Bureau of Labor Statistics (BLS) predicts that the job market for college and university faculty will continue to be tight: "Applicants for full-time college faculty positions face keen competition, because many colleges and universities, in an effort to cut costs, will hire more part-time faculty." "Keen" is a bit of an understatement. Competing in a field of several hundred for a particular junior position is what "keen" can mean in some cases. The BLS report continues by noting that "job prospects will continue to be better in certain fields—computer science, engineering, and business, for example—that offer attractive nonacademic job opportunities and attract fewer applications for academic positions."[14]

To be sure, academics know in advance that their pecuniary rewards over their lifetime will not be commensurate with their merit, but actually experiencing it can still cause a fair bit of job dissatisfaction, typically once one is well into the career. This can contribute to a phenomenon known as burnout. We will not discuss this issue—because posttenure issues are, in the main, outside of the scope of our volume—beyond speculating that perhaps the frustration with income gains (in an era of conspicuous consumption) induces academics to be more conscious of the symbolic rewards that academia is able to offer by way of prestige. Consequently, the competition for such rewards is keen and their display exaggerated.

Can you recommend academia as a career choice?

John Komlos: Perhaps we have succeeded in talking you out of an academic career already, and if so, you do not need to read on. Good luck; we're glad to have been of service! We might have saved you a fair bit of consternation. Consider the purchase of this book a wise investment for finding out early that this is not the right career choice for you.

John Goldsmith: Seriously, as with any other career track, the person and the job have to fit, or there's bound to be friction and trouble. But if the fit is right, then becoming a professor is an excellent choice. What are some of the good points? First of all, there is a good deal of flexibility in the scheduling of your day: for most professors, there is nothing like the 9-to-5, stay-in-your-office, stare-out-the-window life that many of our friends know.[15] You'll have hours when you have to be in the classroom teaching, scheduled times when you have to be in your office to meet with students, and hours meeting in committees; but the rest of the time is yours to schedule. Don't get the impression, however, that being a professor is like being a preacher, who only works one hour a week, on Sunday mornings—because it's not true about the preacher and it's equally not true about the professor. I haven't said anything about the number of hours spent working—there will be many of them. Still, there is a good deal of flexibility concerning when you're going to spend those hours, and where.[16]

The second good point about an academic job comes about seven years into it, for those fortunate enough to get tenure. A professor with tenure is guaranteed a job for life, subject to various conditions regarding moral turpitude and the like. It has happened that a tenured professor has been fired, but it's extremely rare. For most practical purposes, a tenured professor has a secure job for as long as he wants to keep it. For life, in short. Third, there's the summer break.[17] Most professors use that time to work, mind you—and devote the lion's share of it to rekindling, as necessary, their love affair with their research area. But a lot of us like the freedom to do that work where and when we like. By and large, a professor is free from specific responsibilities for about three months during the summer. That's a good long time. Finally—let's not lose sight of the fact that if the job fits right, then the professor has the chance to do something that he really loves: doing research in the chosen field and teaching that material to other people who care about it.

Penny Gold: I agree that the flexibility of work time is a major benefit of academic life. The summer is, indeed, a special "perk" because of the extended break from teaching, committee, and most administrative (e.g., department chair) duties. Yet it's also true that even during those months, I rarely take more than two weeks of actual vacation, since this is the time when I can work most intensively on my research, as well as do extended background work on any new courses I may be offering in the upcoming year—never mind catching up on journal reading and filing. I've generally managed to carry on with my research during the regular school year, but this is harder to do at a primarily teaching institution, and the summer is precious work time for that reason.

John Komlos: Another great thing about being an academic is that after finals we can simply pack up and—even if we don't call it vacation—let's say, continue our work in another place, and that place is often interesting, even exciting. I find that the change of pace can be quite invigorating. One can genuinely, and without any feelings of guilt, combine conferences or research visits to archives in exotic places with a little sightseeing. If you join academia, you will no doubt see the world.

Penny Gold: Academic work is both flexible and all-consuming. One can read a book or journal article anywhere, and so it's a challenge to keep work from creeping into every available space. Sometimes I think wistfully of a 9-to-5 job, where I would come home at the end of the day and be done with it. So why is it worth it? For me, it's the personal gratification and the sense of making a contribution to the lives of others. On the personal side, I feel enormously privileged to have a job in which I'm paid to be continually learning. I love reading, observing, and figuring things out, and this is what I get to do for large chunks of my day. In midcareer, I changed my research field from medieval European history to modern Jewish history, and as part of my job, I delved into a whole new body of historical material and language learning. I often offer new courses in areas in which I want to extend and deepen my own knowledge—teaching to learn, I think of it. So my own continuing learning is part of my job, which I like very much. The range of things I've been able to (and sometimes had to) learn in the course of teaching is extended by my being at a small, teaching institution. For example, right out of graduate school, with training limited to medieval European history, I was expected to teach the history of Western civilization from the ancient world to the present. This was a daunting, humbling challenge, but I also learned much that helped me put the medieval world in sharper perspective and that later served as a helpful, general base when I moved into modern Jewish history. And there have been things far afield that I've chosen—and been allowed—to teach, courses like "Writing by Women on Women" or "Gay and Lesbian Identities," only possible in an institution not crowded with specialists in most imaginable fields. The satisfaction I get from writing and publishing also, for me, falls mostly in this category of the gratification of extending my own learning—it's an enormous feeling of accomplishment to reach the point where I understand enough about something to feel it merits communication to the wider world of academia. If others learn from what I write, so much the better.

It is in my teaching, the center of my professional life, that I most directly feel that I contribute to the learning and growth of other people. When I was a teenager, I taught swimming in the summers, and it was very gratifying to help kids go from being scared of the water to swimming across the pool. There are fewer concrete signs of progress when I teach the skills involved in historical analysis, but the reward is the same: I am helping people gain skills that will help keep them "afloat" in life—help them to better understand the complexity of the world around them, to see beneath the surface of words and other phenomena to the hidden motivations and agenda that produced them. It's my hope that this increased understanding can then contribute to the remaking and repair of that world. That I am paid quite well to do this work (in comparison to jobs like secondary school teaching or social work, which would have been my other choices) is another privilege of the job.

John Komlos: In other words, there is potential for lots of job satisfaction, to give one's life meaning. It seems to me that academic life will be most rewarding for those who consider it as a calling rather than as a profession. By entering academia, you will have responsibility for the intellectual treasures of the ages, and by teaching and researching, you will have a chance to increase them and to relay them to successive generations. It can become an almost sacred endeavor in a predominantly secular age. It can be pretty rewarding in the sense that you will see students benefit from your classes and advice, and the process of creation of knowledge is an exhilarating experience in itself. At its best, it can be extremely satisfying, and each day will be different, bringing its new challenges and rewards with plenty of opportunities for international contact in fascinating places. This is not a monotonous world by any means.[18]

Of course, there are many who make a businesslike decision to go to graduate school, obtain the credentials to teach, and pursue a satisfying career in academia. I do not know how many such people there are, but I tend to think that they are in the minority. Even for those who have not experienced their profession as a calling, it can still be very satisfying and exciting to engage in an intellectual endeavor, to seek answers to previously unanswered questions, and to have people hold you in respect for your knowledge. Moreover, it is not the case that a thoughtful life can be lived only within the confines of academia. One can earn a medical degree, for example, to pursue a career in medical ethics. Law, too, may allow one to practice on the edge of theory. Regardless of one's occupation, one can join literary clubs or just read extensively at home. There is no limit on a contemplative life if that is what one prefers.

In addition, let's not forget that people might well choose to go to graduate school as a career choice without making a commitment to stay in academia permanently. Some might obtain a Ph.D. in chemistry and thereafter work in the research department of a pharmaceutical company, or they might well be undecided and want to test the territory before deciding which career choice feels right for them.

Aside from financial considerations, then, why isn't academia the perfect career for everyone?

John Goldsmith: Good question! The truth of the matter is that there are other down sides as well. First of all, as John mentioned, in many academic fields there are not a lot of jobs. When there is a job in your chosen field, the job may not be in a geographical region in which you would like to live. If you're married and your spouse has a job in an area that she does not want to leave, you may have an impossibly difficult task finding an adequate job within commuting distance—or you may face the possibility of commuting over long distances (as much as 3,000 miles, in some cases, not to mention the distances involved in intercontinental relationships).[19] Now, this is something I know more than a little about, and I'll say more about it in due time.

Moreover, the tenure factor is a double-edged sword. Many people do not get tenure. Imagine such a situation: after investing five years or more in graduate education, and then six additional years in teaching at a university, a person may find himself out of a job in a field where there are far more applicants than jobs. It's true that anyone in the business world can lose his job, too; but in academia, to make matters worse, one can fail to get tenure not because one has been doing a poor job, but simply because one has not been turning in a stellar enough performance. To be sure, there are options in and out of academia. There is life after a denial of tenure. But not getting tenure is a heavy blow.

We'll discuss this at length later, but I should point out now that one of the most striking characteristics of academia is the tenure system, according to which an assistant professor is judged during his sixth year of service. Each university sets its own standards, though virtually all appeal to some combination of research, teaching, and service. For many universities, only research really counts, and the candidate need only do an adequate job of teaching and service. At other universities, outstanding teaching and service may well balance a mediocre record of research. But despite differences in tenure standards across universities, the professor who is awarded tenure receives, in all cases, the same quite valuable reward: a job guaranteed virtually for life, or until retirement, though there is no mandatory retirement age. A professor with tenure may decide to look for a job elsewhere, but if another university chooses to offer him a job, it will unquestionably be a job with tenure, even if the tenure standards of the other university are clearly higher than those of the first. A university will not attempt to hire without tenure a professor who already has tenure at his home institution. In sum, the tenure decision looms large in the career of the academic.[20]

Academia also requires an inordinate amount of self-motivation. Or put it more negatively: there is remarkably little in the way of a support system for the aspiring academic. Graduate students may be able to provide greater or lesser degrees of solidarity and support for each other, but in my experience, junior academics—who face equally heavy challenges and burdens—by and large have to make it on their own, with little support and little feedback from their colleagues at any level. It can be just as lonely at the bottom as at the top.

John Komlos: Some people join academia to change the world, only to be disappointed by the many obstacles in their way when they are unable to institute even basic changes. Although obviously you will be able to make a contribution, you will also be joining a bureaucratic administrative structure, in which change usually take place only slowly and infrequently. So patience is definitely required.

Academia is also big business and unfortunately has become increasingly so in recent years.[21] That implies that even for nonprofit institutions, academic freedom is constrained by practical considerations of a financial sort and that even professors are expected to conform to the basic habits of a bureaucratic institution. That means, for instance, that you may not be able to teach any course you like without consideration of student enrollments. Grants play an important role in one's scholarly activities in any event, but if the administration comes to expect you to be able to attract large amounts of federal funds, particularly in the hard sciences, the pressure to succeed can introduce additional constraints and stresses on your professional as well as personal life.

Your research, too, might have to conform to collegial expectations, and there is more peer pressure to continue thinking in the intellectual paradigm in vogue than one might think. Freedom of thought, of course, remains the true ideal, though, in practice, there is also self-censorship, by which I mean that scholars choose to remain within established norms of thought, particularly if editors and funding agencies are circumspect about taking chances with new ideas.[22] So there is a certain amount of conformism as well.

In sum, contrary to stereotypes, we in academia are not independent, ivory-tower scholars, though we aspire to such status. We like freedom, but actually we are embedded in a rich and complex social, institutional, and cultural network that imposes expectations upon us, of which balancing the institutional budget is but one of the more venal examples. In fact, higher education has to face challenges similar to those in the private sector: it has to attract and cater to a clientele, engage in fund raising in a bigger way than the political parties, compete fiercely with rivals for excellent students, lobby legislators for support, engage in cost-cutting measures, maintain federal standards, and so on. Nonetheless, we do enjoy more autonomy, more freedom of thought, and more control over our lives than our business counterparts. But there are limits, though not clearly delineated.

Penny Gold: I'd like to pick up on the issue of "changing the world," as I do try to contribute to changing the world as I go about my work. Change can be fostered in several arenas. One is the classroom. To change the world, one has to understand how it works—why people think and behave the way they do and how one aspect of life is connected up with and has an impact on other aspects of life. In the classroom, I teach students skills that are useful for such analysis. The techniques we employ to figure out the workings of medieval society from a twelfth-century monastic charter of donation can also be used to understand elements of contemporary society. And from time to time, as the opportunity arises, we talk about such examples in class and what the implications for action might be.[23]

The second arena is cocurricular. The classroom is only a small portion of students' lives, though teachers may not often recognize that. Over the years, I've been the faculty advisor to two sorts of student groups—feminist and Jewish—and this has been another way to contribute to social change.

The institution itself is a third arena of change. It's not easy to change a bureaucracy, even one as small as my own college, but it's not impossible either. I've witnessed and/or participated in a number of changes during my years at Knox, including the institution of a parental leave policy, the formulation of a hiring and tenure policy that facilitates jointly held and/or part-time positions, the hiring of a significant number of minority faculty, and the extension of insurance and other benefits to domestic partners of either sex. And then there's the world outside of Knox—both the local community and beyond. A number of my colleagues have used their expertise and the prestige of an academic position to contribute to a wide variety of social and political projects, something the college encourages and sometimes even rewards.

John Komlos: I agree that one can participate in institutional change, particularly if there is already a considerable consensus that such change is required or that it is deemed desirable by the administration; then one can have a marginal input. But if I ask myself how differently this or that committee would have voted had I not been there, then I invariably come up with the answer that my institutional impact was of negligible importance. My caution above pertains to how successful one can be in changing engrained institutional habits, and in my opinion, it is thoroughly unhealthy to join academia with the primary motivation to want to change the world. Some ideas are very deeply entrenched, as one finds out once one begins to challenge some aspect of an academic consensus. It is possible to do so, but it is not as easy as one might think.

Penny Gold: I appreciate the academic freedom I have as a faculty member. This doesn't mean I always say publicly exactly what I think about every issue—but the restraint is from a strategic concern about effectiveness rather than from a fear of losing my job. I once saw an administrator (a man of great integrity) defend the college's position on a particular matter when I knew from private conversations that he was personally opposed to it. Administrators have to be part of the "team," and their disagreements can usually be aired only in private, amongst themselves, rather than in public. Faculty members have no such constraints, and independent thinking is generally cherished rather than hidden.[24]

John Goldsmith: One more point about the lifestyle of the academic. Academics tend to let their profession take over much of their private and personal lives, for work and hobby often merge. Weekends and evenings are very often taken over by work—reading journals and books and student papers, going to conferences, drafting papers, correcting page proofs. Whether this is good or bad depends on your own take on life—and those of your friends and family.

Penny Gold: This tendency for work to swallow up every waking hour is one of the real dangers of academic life. I lived my life that way in the early years of my career, desperately trying to be prepared enough to be in front of each class at the same time that I finished my dissertation and then my first book. My second year of teaching, I made myself take a woodworking class so that at least once a week I would spend a couple of hours doing something unrelated to my job. But virtually all other waking hours were spent working. My husband worked at the college also, so even our leisure hours were often spent in talking "shop." Then two things happened. We adopted a child, and suddenly I had other very gratifying—and time-consuming—activities in my life that had absolutely nothing to do with work. In those early years, rather than feeling conflicted between work and parenting, I felt grateful for having this wonderful reason to not be working every minute. The other thing that happened is that I read Abraham Joshua Heschel's book *The Sabbath* and found his argument for setting aside a weekly "palace of time" extremely compelling. I began to observe the Sabbath in a moderate way, giving myself permission to absent myself from work from Friday evening through Saturday. At first, this seemed crazy—how could I ever get done what I needed to get done without working on Saturday? But, in fact, I think I get more done because I can work the rest of the week, knowing that I will have a break. Quite liberating!

A generation ago, the pressures to work were the same, but some relief on at least the domestic side was possible—if you were male. Most professors were male (if female, they were generally single and/or childless), and they were mostly married, with wives who did not work outside the home when the children were young. These wives made possible the devotion of their husbands to their work, as they handled all the shopping, cooking, child care, doctor's appointments, and entertainment of colleagues and students. I know there must be a few cases out there today where the roles are flipped and the husband is "Mr. Mom," but they are few and far between. Even in the households where tasks are divided up 50–50 (as they have been in mine and in some others I know), there is an extra layer of responsibility that somehow gravitates to the female in the household. She's the one who seems to be responsible for keeping the system running, for knowing what nonroutine things have to be done when, for initiating the conversation about dividing up tasks, for anticipating when the schedule will need to change, and for locating the backup help when the system flounders due to illness, travel, or other nonroutine circumstances. When I have to go out of town for a couple of days, I leave a list for my husband of our child's upcoming doctor's appointments, band practices, and so on. If it's the woman who has the more flexible academic schedule and the man who's working a 9-to-5 job, the situation will likely be exacerbated. From time to time it surfaces that underneath it all, my husband still fantasizes occasionally about a life where I would do all this stuff, just as his upbringing prepared him for. Good thing we can laugh about it.

John Goldsmith: I've seen that in my family, too. I've had any number of long periods in which I had to act like a single dad, so I feel competent to take care of a broad range of responsibilities for the family—but under more normal circumstances, it's still a constant struggle (which I frequently lose) to take the housekeeping responsibilities as seriously as I ought to.

John Komlos: The fact remains that after adding up all the pluses and minuses, obtaining an advanced degree appears to be an attractive option for a very large share of college graduates. Of the approximately 1.1 million bachelor's degree recipients in 1992–93, an amazing 30 percent enrolled in an advanced program within four years of graduation.[25] Admittedly, of these, about a third exited without attaining a degree, a third completed, and a third were still enrolled, mostly in master's programs, in 1997, when the poll was taken (see table 5 in appendix 3). To be sure, the most popular are master's programs in education and business; nonetheless, I infer on the basis of these data that graduate school appeals to a significant pool of students.[26]

What sort of personality traits does a successful graduate student have?

John Komlos: Academic achievement comes in discrete units. You won't find it of much use to complete 95 percent of your doctoral thesis, almost publish an article, or be one vote short of obtaining tenure. This lumpy nature of academic projects and milestones means that perseverance—the stamina to complete goals—is extremely important for success. The Ph.D. thesis is obviously a good filtering device for the selection of individuals with this desirable trait.

Furthermore, a graduate student typically should want to make a contribution to the intellectual life of the community. He should be well above average in intelligence; have done extremely well as an undergraduate; be able to argue dissenting positions; be self-disciplined, self-motivated, and good at time management; be able both to enjoy the anticipated freedom and autonomy of academic life and to juggle several tasks simultaneously; not be easily intimidated by many hurdles; and not be particularly interested in pecuniary rewards. Patience and creativity are also important qualities to have, as is the willingness to persevere in solitude for uncertain rewards well into the future. If you have a fair number of these attributes, you should continue to read on. If you need lots of pats on the back, instant gratification, and immediate rewards for your accomplishments or if you are easily discouraged by adversity, an academic career will not be the right choice for you. Are you really still interested? Well, read on then!

2 | Entering Graduate School

What is graduate school really all about?

John Goldsmith: I would say that the most important fact to bear in mind is that, in general, the purposes of graduate school and of undergraduate studies could hardly be more different. A college education—in the United States, at least—is aimed at providing a general education, a liberal education, even if the choice of a major subject does allow some degree of specialization. In contrast, graduate education is aimed at creating a professional. When I use the term "professional," of course, I am not using it in the most familiar way. The term is generally used in relation to disciplines such as law, medicine, and business. The schools in these disciplines provide specific training along what are generally well established lines, bringing the student to the point where she may, in most of the cases, pass a standardized examination, such as the bar exam or the medical boards. The professional schools do not require students to write a dissertation or engage in individual research efforts—those hallmarks of graduate education in a research university.

Yet it is still true that graduate education is aimed at forming a particular type of professional: a professional researcher. There are some important things to say about this. The most significant of all is that this kind of intellectual formation has relatively little to do with passing on specific information. Oh, it is true that all educators make similar claims: they are not teaching specific things, but rather how to learn; still, this is nowhere as clear as in graduate school. Alas, the graduate research environment is not structured so as to be the training ground for the most extraordinary minds either. There are too few of them to justify (or help shape, for that matter) the enormous institutions that we are talking about. No, graduate education is about training graduate students to become researchers (and to some extent, teachers) in a research environment, within a specific intellectual tradition. Psychologists create new psychologists; linguists create new linguists; musicologists create new musicologists.

Penny Gold: Let me give an example of what we mean by "professional training." In my very first term of graduate school, I registered for a course called "Medieval Biography." I was happily anticipating learning about a variety of medieval people, their lives, and their thoughts. Instead, each student picked one medieval author and then tracked all existing manuscripts and published editions of this person's work. I chose Einhard, the ninth-century biographer of Charlemagne, and spent hours and hours in the stacks of the Stanford and Berkeley libraries, pulling down very dusty volumes that catalogued manuscript collections across Europe and using various bibliographical tools to find all existing editions. (Some of this would be easier now because of computers.) I found this enormously tedious and complained throughout the term. I wanted to be learning about Einhard and Charlemagne, not about his manuscripts! By the time I began my dissertation research a couple of years later, I finally appreciated the research skills I had developed in this course. Another example was a graduate colloquium in "Renaissance and Reformation History," in which the entire reading list was recent scholarship, with not one primary source text from the period itself.

This relates to the issue of what is being taught in graduate school. It is certainly true that the foundation of graduate training is training in a method of analysis, whether that be historical, linguistic, economic, or some other method. Yet there is also a great deal of specific information that must be learned, as one is expected to very rapidly become knowledgeable about "what is being done in the field"—hence, the focus on reading the scholarship of others in many graduate school courses. It is also such stuff (masses of it) that one is tested on in the oral or qualifying examinations that are the gateway to beginning one's own doctoral research. In fact, one of the challenges of life after graduate school is to keep on top of the ever-changing scholarship in one's field when one doesn't have the concentrated time to do this that one does in graduate school.

John Komlos: While undergraduate education concentrates, in the main, on learning a body of knowledge in a wide range of fields, graduate school is essentially about exploring the frontiers of knowledge in a particular field.[1] Hence, the latter is an extension of the former, but differs from it greatly.[2] Being on the frontiers of scholarship (like its geographic counterpart in early American history) is not always a comfortable experience. There are no guideposts to tell you which path to take.

Can you offer any advice for the person who is seriously thinking about entering graduate school?

John Komlos: Yes, indeed. A very good rule is that you should be excited about the field you choose. This is most important! Do you really want to find out how the economy or society works? Are you curious about Stone Age cultures? Are you really deeply interested in the questions economists or sociologists or anthropologists are asking and the answers they are supplying? If not, you should seriously question whether these are the right career paths for you.[3] By the time you contemplate entering graduate school, you should have your goals well sorted out. The American undergraduate education allows, even encourages, a great deal of searching by trial and error. Flexibility is its strength, but at the same time, it places an immense amount of responsibility on the individual student to build a program that makes sense in terms of her intellectual development. By the end of your undergraduate education, you should have a good idea of what you want out of life. Is academia attractive to you? If you are still unsure, you must talk to people whom you respect and whose judgment you trust as much as, or more than, your own.

Bear in mind also that genuine introspection helps a great deal. However, as long as you feel uncertain, you should delay making a commitment. Premature decisions often mean excessive risk taking, and the chances are high that you will not be making optimal use of your time or talents. The point is that graduate school is much too challenging an experience for you to go through if your interest in the subject is merely peripheral. Halfhearted commitments won't work out very well. You have to find the field of your choice stimulating in order to come out of the process unscathed. Otherwise, the chances are good that you will be frustrated and disappointed.

If you have not done well academically, it would be foolhardy to think seriously about continuing in graduate school. If you are making plans to enter a graduate program, you should prepare yourself well in advance in the basic prerequisites of the specialization you have chosen. If you want to be an economist, for example, make sure that you have the needed mathematical background. Obviously, the sooner you decide, the sooner you can start working on the subjects that will be important to you in graduate school. It would be very helpful if you spent some time working for a professor in the field you are considering. As an undergraduate research assistant, you can begin to learn what the field looks like from within.

John Goldsmith: I'd like to second that. Oddly enough, students who are considering entering an academic profession often have little idea of what they're getting into. In most cases, they are coming straight out of college, where they were able to take college-level courses in some areas and do some additional reading in other areas. They as likely as not had no real contact with faculty researchers and as likely as not did not attend a university with any significant number of researchers. In a few cases, they may even choose a graduate specialization entirely on the basis of reading, never having taken a single course in that area. This is true, for example, in my area, linguistics, where students often come from language or psychology backgrounds.

And yet, as John said, a most important precondition for a graduate education to work out well is that the student must love the discipline. How do you know if this describes you? Utterly reliable criteria are hard to establish, but I'd look for a deep and enduring interest in and fascination for the subject, the profession, and its literature. It is surprising how often this condition is not met! Students may (so to speak) wander into graduate school in a specific discipline, take a year or two of courses (or more), and not be at all sure of the correctness of their choice. Still, inertia, the time and money invested, and the fear of losing face all push the students on, often propelling them to the point of writing a dissertation, or even beyond.

Yet as the student moves further along in the education process, she will find that there is less and less personal support and that the hurdles rise higher and higher, with longer periods between moments of reward and relaxation. (This trend continues, of course, when the student moves into faculty status.) Without a strong emotional attachment to the field— simply feeling fascinated by what one is doing—this difficult task becomes no more than a long-term commitment to masochism. Loving the field means that the hard work is its own reward.

John Komlos: Moreover, I would suggest that the student seek advice, again and again.

Penny Gold: I'd like to interject here some advice about advice—*who and what to ask:*

- To professors who know your work well: Do you think graduate school, in this particular field, would be a good choice, given my level and kinds of talents? Do you think I would have a contribution to make?
- To professors in your field who have completed graduate school within the last five years or so: What are the current issues in the field? Where do you see the field going? What is graduate school like these days?
- To these and any other professors whom you admire or whom you might aspire to be like: Are you glad you became a professor? What are the best things about life in academia? What are the most difficult or troubling things?
- To graduates of your own college or university who are now in graduate school in a field close to yours or who have recently obtained jobs (your undergraduate teachers, the Career/Placement Center, and/or the alumni office should be able to give you names and addresses): How have you found the graduate school experience? Did you find that you were well prepared for the program you entered? Is there any advice you wish you'd had before entering graduate school?

John Komlos: As with any other important decision, you should continually question and rethink this one as well. After all, it will have an enormous (and generally irreversible) impact on the rest of your life. By making this choice, you have in many respects chosen a lifestyle. If you're entering graduate school, you are about to invest several years of intense effort, often resulting in a considerable financial burden. So it behooves you to take the decision very, very seriously. New information may become available that might be put into the decision-making equation. Did you make the right choice after all? Are you as prepared for graduate school as you had thought you were? Do you still find the field as exciting as before? Do you actually have the skills, intuition, and talent you thought you had?

If you can identify some marked deficiencies, how long would it take to overcome them? For example, how long will it take you to learn another language? Do you write well? Depending on the rigors of your education so far, you may still not have perfected the art of written communication, even in your native language. You can teach yourself, of course, but it is best done before you enter graduate school. Obviously, the sooner you sort out these issues the better.

You might also consider if your motivations are sound. What are the rewards in the field you are considering? What is the ratio of pecuniary to nonpecuniary rewards you can expect? Is that mix about right for you? Try to avoid establishing potentially conflicting goals, such as rising to the upper end of the academic salary range while teaching in the humanities. Original research requires much self-reliance, perseverance, and intelligence as well as creativity. You also need self-discipline to complete the monotonous tasks that inevitably accompany even the most exciting research project. Do you have enough of these qualities to succeed?

Self-questioning is, of course, an important quality to nurture in yourself, but it certainly requires practice to be effective. One cannot develop such critical skills overnight. Do you know yourself well enough? Are you practicing self-deception without even knowing it? Are you able to judge yourself without making excuses? Do you rationalize your mistakes, so you cannot learn from them? You can improve your forecasts about yourself by consciously updating your information set periodically. How have you erred in the past, and what can you learn from these errors about your true abilities and about your expectations? Are the goals you are about to set for yourself reasonable in light of your past performance? Are you getting closer to formulating a reasonable strategy for solving problems?

If, for example, you have a tendency to start projects without finishing them, it is much better to acknowledge this attribute than to make excuses about why this is the case and externalizing blame. Disregarding that trait in yourself is a big mistake, one that may cost you dearly later. How can you use that information to predict your ability to succeed in a Ph.D. program? First, take that information into account, and then work on improving your predictive ability by searching for answers as to why your actions fall into a particular pattern and just how these mistakes are changeable. Just what is it that makes it so difficult for you to complete a project? Once you are able to finish some tasks ahead of schedule, you can be more certain that, with some probability, you can actually complete a particular goal you set for yourself in the allotted time. In other words, you should not be making systematic errors about your abilities or about your performance.⁴ If your mistakes are systematic, the chances are you are disregarding some significant information available to you.

I'll make this point yet another way because I think it is crucial for success. I believe that mistakes are OK, in general. They simply cannot be avoided, and if you are not making enough mistakes, it might well mean that you are not challenging yourself sufficiently to find out where your limits are. The real problems arise if you do not learn from the mistakes already committed. That can happen for many reasons. You might tend to put the blame on others, or else you might be so used to making these mistakes that you fail to see the patterns in your own behavior. Your mistakes might also be self-reinforcing. Perhaps underneath it all, you really do not want to reach the goal you set for yourself. Perhaps you let others set your goal for you. Perhaps you are just plain afraid of success. Though the reasons may be many and complex, the consequence is simple: if you continue along that path, you can systematically get farther and farther away from where you want to be. So make an effort to recognize your mistakes; try to face them squarely and explore the systematic reasons for your doing them, including flaws in your own thinking and in the assumptions you are making reflexively without thinking them over, and make a conscious effort to avoid the same mistakes in the future. I know that it is easier said than done, but you will find that practice does help.

And another thing: do not forget that your personal life should be in congruity with your current aspirations. If you are married, it is imperative that your spouse/partner fully support your going to graduate school. Otherwise, you will have too many frictions with which to cope, in addition to the tribulations encountered in your daily work. Your career choice will also put requirements on your spouse/partner, inasmuch as your obligations will limit your social life, including your ability to maintain contact with relatives, clubs, organizations, or friends to the extent you did before. You should be prepared for these changes in your life.

In addition, you will probably feel a certain amount of financial insecurity unless you are independently wealthy or are married to an employed spouse. Because the financial constraints could affect your peace of mind—and, therefore, your performance in school—I advise graduate students to earn some money during summers. In some fields, such as law, this comes automatically, since internships are common, but in other fields, it is less easy to do so. I particularly recommend nontraditional kinds of employment. Open a business preparing tax returns, for example, if you have the aptitude for it. Buy a house and renovate it. You are smarter than average, so use some of your talents to make a little profit. If you can do so, you will not be completely at the mercy of the academic job market.[5]

John Goldsmith: I think people's social experience probably varies widely. Surely academics are about as social and hospitable as people in other walks of life! There are forces at work that encourage people who work in, say, linguistics to socialize with other linguists, and I think that these forces are much stronger for some reason early on in a person's career than they are subsequently.

How should one go about choosing a graduate school?

John Komlos: Of course, most people will apply to several universities, and it is important to do so in order to test the market. You may have certain notions about your qualifications, but how do they look on paper? How do they compare to those of others? How do others perceive them? There is no reason to assume that you will not be accepted into a particular program simply because you do not have excellent grades in the field. You might have other qualities that can compensate any deficiencies in your grade point average. Good GRE scores, for example, do help. Different departments weigh these various components of your record differently. In addition, departments vary on their standards for admission. Some are strict, feeling that by admitting a student, they make an implicit commitment to her that she has a fair chance of completing the program. Other equally good programs might take a more relaxed, laissez-faire attitude with respect to admissions, thinking that students have inside information on their abilities and should be given a chance to prove themselves, even if their record up to then was not impeccable. Students, they believe, will be weeded out in due course anyhow, by various filters the department has instituted, if they are not really qualified to do graduate work. These idiosyncratic philosophies will not be spelled out in black and white in the departmental manuals. So you should cast your application net widely. In addition to some safe bets, you should try some unlikely possibilities. More choices ought to be preferred to less. The good news is that practically everyone (87 percent, to be precise) who applies to an advanced-degree program gets at least one acceptance, and that means that you should have no problem getting into graduate school.[6] You just need to seek out the right program for your set of abilities.

John Goldsmith: In smaller departments, it is usual for virtually all of the faculty to read most of the application dossiers, and read them quite carefully. Speaking personally, I am completely sold on a candidate who writes a perceptive personal statement that shows thoughtfulness and real interest in the field. I rarely see more than one or two of those in an entire year's harvest of applications. I suspect that applicants think their dossiers are going to some distant admissions office, but that's just not true. It's your future teachers who are deciding if they'd like you to come. Let me repeat that: real intelligence can be read in a personal essay, and this can easily outweigh the matter of grades or exam scores.

Penny Gold: The personal essay is also a crucial part of any applications you make for national graduate fellowships (Mellon, National Science Foundation, Javits, etc.). If you have begun work on an honors thesis or senior thesis or have done some other substantial piece of research work, you will have an advantage in writing such an essay, as this work will undoubtedly help you formulate your ideas on the kind of research you want to pursue in graduate school, the kinds of questions you anticipate asking. The people reading your essay are looking at how you present yourself intellectually and will use this presentation itself as a sample of your intellectual interests, the extent of your understanding of the field you are asking to enter, and your ability to write persuasively. You should expect to go through multiple drafts of this essay and should be sure to ask for comments from a professor experienced in graduate school admissions.

John Komlos: The essay also gives you the opportunity to reveal some of your significant attributes that may otherwise not be obvious from your application or to explain some of your apparent deficiencies that may no longer be relevant. You need to be credible, of course.

Before you make up your mind which program to choose, do visit the campuses because you can find out much more in face-to-face conversations about the atmosphere of the department than you can in correspondence. Be sure to talk to currently enrolled students. Ask them about the faculty's commitment to the graduate program. How well is the program organized? Talk to the graduate advisor. Ask her what the ratio of graduating to entering students is.[7] Note that even in the best history departments only about half of the entering students leave with a Ph.D. in hand, and the average is closer to a quarter.[8] These ratios vary by field and over time. If a program is well above or much below the average for the discipline, you have reliable information on which to base your judgment of how risky it is to enter that program. Another factor to consider is the success of the graduate students in obtaining employment in their field after earning the doctorate. Such information can be immensely useful when it comes time for you to make up your mind. If you are unable to find this information, ask the department's graduate secretary for help. In any case, you should not accept an offer blindly.[9]

It is also useful to ascertain if the department is well represented in the various subspecialties in the field. If you plan to study the economics of the Third World, for example, you need to make sure that the department has sufficient depth in that area to support such a specialty. Are the faculty members well known in their field? Are they actively engaged in research? You should be able to form a preliminary opinion by seeking out publications of the professors in your field of potential interest. If you find recently published papers or books, you can infer that the person is actively engaged in research and has been keeping up with recent developments in the field, not just living off past achievements. Another crucial consideration is her track record with graduate students. If she is frequently out of the country, she might be difficult to work with. Is she likely to retire soon? If so, you could be left hanging in the middle of your dissertation. Has she been producing graduate students lately? If she has not, that is an indication that perhaps she really does not have the inclination to do so, might be difficult to get along with, has too high expectations, or does not have the ideas to attract young entrants into the field. In any case, you should take such information seriously. By the way, do not assume that every professor is committed to working with graduate students. Those who are not will give you signals to stay away, though they will usually not tell you so outright. You may be able to confirm the meaning of these signals by talking with advanced graduate students in the department.

In any event, it is extremely important that you find the right program for your aspirations because this decision will have a significant impact on your career, including your ability to find employment. You should realize that your abilities alone will generally not suffice to be successful either in the academic world or in any other profession. We'll come back to this theme again, but I should mention now that the academic culture in America is influenced by the immense size of the market. In such a large market, it is costlier to acquire and process inside information than in smaller ones (Belgium, for instance), where the community of scholars is relatively tightly knit. In large markets, people might use symbols, images, and rule-of-thumb devices as substitutes for genuine information to arrive at a decision. Hence, a department's reputation is important, and affiliation with a top department will pay dividends. You need to know, however, that even the best departments will not cover all aspects of a discipline and will not cover equally well those parts they do cover. You need to keep these nuances in mind before making a decision.

What role do you see the Internet playing in this process?

John Goldsmith: The World Wide Web—the HTML part of the global Internet—has changed our lives in the last few years, and information is at your fingertips in a way that would have been inconceivable not long ago. Every college and university has enormous amounts of published information, including application procedures, right on their home pages. These are easy to find with any search engine, using the name of the institution you are considering as the keyword. An academic department can make a good deal of information available to students who are thinking of applying. There will be hard and cold facts about the program, and there will be softer, more personal information that can be gleaned from a department's Web page, and many—perhaps most—active academics now maintain some sort of Web page of their own, which may provide lists of recent publications and research interests and often includes such useful things as recent course syllabi and even lecture slides. A few hours spent researching departments on the Web is the most valuable investment a person could make.

Should financial considerations play an important role in choosing a department?

John Komlos: No. By and large, for once, money—here, the level of debt—hardly matters. How much is job satisfaction for the rest of your life worth to you? Money should be much less important in choosing a department than the other factors we have mentioned, although your aspiration and innate talent do play a role in deciding how much weight to put on finances. However, it should be clear that a scholarship from an average or below-average university will not help you a lot in the long run if your chances of employment—and, therefore, your lifetime earnings—will be adversely affected by it. Other things equal, it is hardly worth it. Do not forget that most of the sacrifice you incur in the course of your graduate education has to do with the fact that you will be out of the labor force for an extended period. In addition to not earning a real income, you will not have on-the-job experience, which will make it more difficult for you to reenter the labor force, should you decide not to complete your graduate program. Because not completing a program can be quite an expensive venture, it is important that you think about your prospects before you begin.

John Goldsmith: I agree only up to a point. I don't think it is prudent for a graduate student to take on really serious debt, and certainly not the kind of debt that can grow from paying large tuition bills for several years. Full tuition at a private university is over $20,000 now, and borrowing to pay several years of tuition at that rate would lead a student to a level of debt that would be difficult to imagine paying off in a reasonable period. I can't see recommending that a student borrow more than $20,000—maximum—for tuition over a graduate career and a maximum of about that for living on. That would come to a total of $40,000—about a car and a half, by today's standards. That's my view.

Penny Gold: Another matter to investigate regarding grants and assistantships is the percentage of students in the program who are funded and whether that changes after the first year. Does this department admit a large group in the first year, funding only a few, with funding in subsequent years based on how well students do in the first year? This creates some hope of future funding, but also can create a sense of competition with one's peers; it's a much more congenial and cooperative environment if all admitted students are funded similarly. Also, if the department funds only a portion of admitted students, and you're not in that portion, it means you are set up as having to prove yourself. This is an added stress in what will usually be a difficult transition anyway.

John Komlos: Often some financial aid is tied to teaching assistantships. This is actually a less lucrative option than it appears at the beginning of graduate school because such responsibility puts additional burdens on an already busy schedule. In fact, in some institutions, the burdens of teaching assistantships are such that they leave little time for the completion of the program, and most students leave after four years without a degree in hand. Such an offer of a graduate fellowship is almost tantamount to entrapment, as the institution avails itself of cheap labor, while the prospective graduate students are not savvy enough to find out what the probability is of their obtaining a graduate degree. It is quite another thing if

The Inside Track
Financing Graduate Education
Tom Thuerer

Tom Thuerer is Dean of Students in the Humanities at the University of Chicago.

In my experience, many undergraduates decide to apply to graduate school because they've sat at the feet of wonderful professors who have taught them brilliantly and influenced them in profound ways and now they wish to emulate those professors and have careers like them. They see the rewards of an academic career—studying a subject they love and sharing knowledge with others. Yet often they don't realize that their professors are the winners in a long and competitive process in which many others have fallen by the wayside. When advising prospective graduate students, I try to encourage them, before they accept an offer of admission, and especially before they borrow heavily to attend a program, to keep this larger picture in mind, to see not only the rewards of graduate study, but also its rigors and risks. Only then, I believe, do they have a sound basis for deciding whether or not to attend graduate school and, if so, how to finance it.

A Ph.D. education can lead potentially to a rewarding career in teaching and scholarship, but it is nonetheless long, risky, and expensive. On average, graduate students in social sciences and humanities require six to ten years to complete their degrees, and attrition in programs can be high, often approaching 50 percent. Moreover, in many disciplines, these students will enter a job market that may be depressed and will be extremely competitive. Even for those fortunate enough to find full-time teaching positions, tenure is by no means guaranteed. Graduate education is also not cheap. In the first year alone, the combined cost of tuition and living expenses is around $18,000 for a state resident studying in a public university and as much as $40,000 for a student enrolled in a private university. To make sure they can afford the various costs of graduate school—room, food, books, and tuition as well as the countless hours of free time needed to pursue studies properly— prospective graduate students should explore the various forms of graduate aid and understand the relative value of each.

Graduate financial aid comes principally from three sources:

- fellowships (i.e., gift aid awarded either internally by individual graduate institutions or externally by private and federal agencies),
- teaching and research assistantships, and
- loans.

Of these forms of support, the most valuable are fellowships, because students who receive them need not perform a service in return for them and need not repay them at the end of the degree program. For students entering in the social sciences and humanities, by far the largest single source of fellowship support is that offered internally by individual institutions. Unlike undergraduate aid, which is need-based, graduate fellowship support is merit-based, and academic departments offer it to attract those students they judge to be most promising at the time of admission. Merit-based fellowships frequently are multiyear packages, typically three to five years in duration, and may include full tuition and, in some instances, substantial stipends sufficient to cover a student's living expenses in full. Since graduate programs structure their aid packages in many different ways, prospective students should consult with the individual programs in which they are interested to see how fellowships are administered and awarded.

Grants in aid in the social sciences and humanities are also available to entering graduate students through various private and federal agencies—for instance, the Andrew W. Mellon Fellowship program and the Jacob K. Javits Graduate Fellowship program—but such awards are few in number, and the competition for them is keen. In addition, a number of fellowships are earmarked for specific groups of students. Ford Foundation Fellowships, for example, are awarded to increase the presence of minority groups most underrepresented in the nation's Ph.D. population. National Science Foundation Graduate Fellowships are available not only to graduate students in math and science, but also to students in certain fields in the social sciences, linguistics, and the history and philosophy of science. Students with outstanding undergraduate records should check with their college fellowship advisor to find out if they qualify for these and other aid programs.

Another source of financial support is teaching and research assistantships. Before prospective students accept an offer that includes a teaching or research service component, they should be certain that the assistantship is designed to help them progress toward the degree. Sometimes universities subordinate student interests to competing institutional and faculty interests and consequently compromise the educational value of these apprenticeship arrangements. Graduate students can suffer in assistantships where they are put into the classroom without adequate preparation or expected to teach for extended periods of time without advancing their pedagogical development. Workloads should be reasonable, compensation should be fair, and apprenticeship activities, including workshops and teacher training seminars, should be structured to provide progressively more advanced levels of responsibility. When they are properly designed and administered, assistantships offer graduate students not only financial support, but also valuable opportunities to teach and conduct research at increasingly more advanced levels under close faculty mentorship.

Though fellowships and assistantships are the most frequent sources of financial aid, most students find they must take out loans at some point in their graduate careers. Before deciding to borrow, however, students need to plan over the full term of their studies. They must keep in mind that the financial strategy on which they're about to embark must carry them through a program that in all likelihood will require the better part of a decade to complete. Eager students too often consider only the short term, borrowing heavily in the first few years and hoping God will provide later on. Such students, if they manage to finish a program at all, often emerge from their graduate years sixty to ninety thousand dollars in debt, a level of indebtedness that, while acceptable for a graduating law or medical student, is of far more questionable wisdom for an aspiring professor of literature or philosophy. To know when and how much to borrow, students must look ahead and imagine their futures, with a careful eye to what they can reasonably pay off without undermining their financial prospects for many years to come.

Back when I first began counseling students about graduate school and how to finance it, I would do little more than recite various funding possibilities and offer a few pointers on applying for them. Over the years, however, I've come to realize that many, if not most, seriously underestimate the enormous investment of time and money that graduate school will require, and often, too, they misjudge the risks they'll run of finding success in their chosen academic field. Today I still review the various sources of financial aid, but I also ask these students if they're willing to borrow many thousands of dollars, often in addition to their undergraduate loans, to spend the next six or more years in Ph.D. programs where rates of completion are relatively low and employment prospects are far from assured. I also ask them to consider that academic jobs pay less than careers in other professions, so university professors inevitably take longer and must sacrifice more in order to pay off large debts. This is not to say, of course, that undergraduates should abandon their dreams of pursuing a career in teaching and scholarship or that many excellent opportunities are not available to Ph.D. graduates in the social sciences and humanities. Few careers can be as rewarding as a life in teaching and research, but those who emerge as winners from the long and arduous path to the Ph.D. all have this much in common: they know the risks and costs of graduate education and they do their planning accordingly.

you would be allowed to teach during summers, when the burdens are less and teaching might be a welcome diversion from studies and research. In any event, good programs limit teaching by graduate students because they are usually not yet ready to do a good job. However, teaching experience during your third or fourth year will become an important asset when you start looking for your first job, though such experience is probably more important at teaching institutions than at research universities. Hence, if you are considering the trade-off between going to an expensive program with an excellent reputation and a small financial aid package or to a less expensive, but less prominent, institution with a teaching assistantship, spending the extra money is probably well worth it. To be sure, one needs to weigh the choices in the context of the totality of one's abilities, aspirations, and financial circumstances.

Penny Gold: And of the possibility of a professional-level wage when one finishes the program, even if one doesn't find employment in academia. This prospect is much brighter for some fields (e.g., economics, computer science) than it is for others (history, English).

John Goldsmith: The importance of having teaching experience—such as can be gained through a teaching assistantship—may also vary from field to field. In the humanities, it is a serious deficiency for an applicant not to have experience teaching.

John Komlos: An additional caveat in this regard is that it is already useful to be thinking of your long-range aspirations. If you would like to teach at a small liberal arts college with a local (as opposed to a national) reputation, you should be aware of the fact that such an institution might not be very open to hire from the top departments in the country. They may assume that if you invested heavily in acquiring a degree from Columbia, say, you would probably not feel particularly comfortable teaching at a small school in southwestern Montana. Thus, a degree from a top university will open some doors, but you might be surprised to hear that, in fact, it will shut others. Hence, if you aspire to the middle range of the academic spectrum, then, indeed, you might not necessarily want to acquire an expensive degree.

John Goldsmith: On the other hand, there are many small colleges where faculty are expected to do (and publish) real research—only to do it at a considerably slower rate.

Penny Gold: As the small-college person here, let me emphasize a couple of things. When applying for a job at a primarily teaching institution, it is definitely the case that a candidate with teaching experience will have an advantage over a similarly qualified person without such experience. But not all teaching assistantships yield the kind of teaching that really counts. Being a T.A. in a course taught by another professor is a useful experience to have, but even more helpful is being in charge of your own course once or twice and developing the syllabus yourself. If this opportunity isn't available at your school, such experience can sometimes be gained by part-time adjunct appointments in neighboring institutions. The importance of "real" teaching experience also explains why candidates who have had one-year positions elsewhere will sometimes be favored in a search.

Second, the job market in some fields is so tight that many teaching institutions (whether liberal arts colleges or universities with primarily teaching missions) can compete for candidates from the top research universities. It's true that some won't consider such candidates, worried about a bad fit, but other schools are eager to enhance the profile of their faculty and are delighted with such candidates. Also, as John Goldsmith mentions, many teaching institutions still expect faculty to do research and so will look for candidates with the relevant training and potential.

How do you pick the right school?

John Komlos: Once you've decided to pursue a career requiring a graduate degree, the next step is to find the right program. The American system of education is highly stratified. There are a couple of dozen top universities that are certainly the best in the world, but then the quality gradient becomes increasingly steeper. You ought to know also that you are joining a department as much as (or more than) a university. Even schools that do not enjoy a reputation for excellence overall might have outstanding programs in certain fields. The University of Pittsburgh, for example, has one of the best philosophy departments in the country—a fact well known to philosophers. Because tuition rates are less at Pittsburgh than at the elite schools, you would get a real bargain if you studied philosophy there. Hence, it is worth your while to ferret out this kind of information. You need to keep in mind that the department you join will be considered indicative of your abilities. Thus, if you are an average student capable of hard work, you might gain by going to a top-ranked school.

Do not forget that judging your potential as a professional is time consuming for anyone charged with assessing your competence as a future teacher and researcher. Judgments are imperfect and outcomes uncertain. As a consequence, it does make some sense for future interviewers to take your academic affiliation into consideration in arriving at a decision. It is a sign of your aspirations, your willingness to compete. It can also be interpreted as indicative of what you think of yourself. If you applied to Yale, you must have thought you were bright enough to mingle with the best. These are the kinds of information revealed by your affiliation. The fact that you successfully completed the program will be seen as a sign that you had a realistic assessment of your own abilities. In addition, your formal education involves more than acquiring knowledge. It also involves forming a network of supporters who might well remain your friends for the rest of your life. Hence, it is to your advantage to go to a school whose faculty is well known around the country. Letters of recommendation, after all, are taken much more seriously from people with an established reputation. You may well consider it unfair that so much depends on the reputation of the graduate program and that you are not judged entirely on your personal attributes. However, do consider that many qualities that are crucial for your future performance are hidden and not at all easily and credibly ascertainable by a committee that meets you for a short period of time. That is why it is practically unavoidable for them to use external information as a proxy measure for those invisible qualities.

It is not sufficient that the program you ultimately choose be a good one: it is extremely important, in addition, that there be a reasonably good match between you and the program. After all, if you find out subsequently that you made a mistake, transferring into another graduate program is time consuming and might have a stigma attached to it unless you have a good explanation at the ready, such as "I went to work with Professor so-and-so, but, in the meanwhile, she went to work in the private sector."

John Goldsmith: We're going to talk about mentoring later on, but I want to mention some advice I was given when I was in college. One of my teachers—a professor in the economics department, in fact—was going to be on leave in my senior year, and he asked to speak to me just before he left, at the end of my junior year. He asked me what I was planning to do after college, and I had to admit that my view was pretty hazy at that point. He gave the following advice: if you do decide to go on to graduate school, you should think very seriously about precisely with whom you are going to study. In the end, I took that advice very seriously and made a list of the people who I knew were alive and kicking in academe at that point whose work had greatly impressed me. So seriously did I take that advice that I applied to only one graduate school, and I expected I would get a job (probably as a computer programmer) if I wasn't accepted into that graduate program. As it turned out, I was accepted.

Penny Gold: I received—and give—this same advice, though it makes me nervous to even think about someone applying to only one school! In my own case, I ignored the advice, choosing the school I did on the basis of the fellowship offered, the smallness of the program (and hence relative assurance of attention to students by faculty), and its attractive geographic location. It could have been a disaster, but as fortune would have it, a new professor joined the faculty at the same time I entered the graduate program—someone I knew nothing about when I applied—and he turned out to be a perfect advisor for me. Ahead of time, students can investigate the scholarly production of the faculty at various institutions and even correspond with faculty with whom they might want to work. Then when your final decision is looming, it's time for campus visits, giving special importance to the query John Komlos recommends you pose to current graduate students: how is it to work with Professor X? No matter how brilliant the work, if the person is mean-spirited and remote, it is better to find someone else.

John Komlos: Do not be surprised if you find a trade-off between nurturing and academic excellence within a department. The top graduate schools have many professors on their faculty who are among the top scholars in their field. They are well versed in intellectual dueling and can easily make a novice feel inadequate, even if unintentionally. Their degree is not in pedagogy, and many have long forgotten what it was like to be a graduate student. It would be a mistake to interpret their lack of respect for you as even vaguely implying that you are not cut out for academia. I would like to stress that if you need emotional or spiritual support from your professors, you had better go to a small program, even if it is a less prestigious one, because you could feel lost in a large and impersonal program.

Penny Gold: I don't think it's one or the other—some of the top schools (depending on field) have relatively small programs, and the inclination to be supportive of one's students can vary significantly from one professor to another, even within one graduate program.

John Goldsmith: This may also depend on the discipline because in my area—linguistics—most of the very nurturing departments are consistently ranked among the very best in national studies.

John Komlos: It is good you brought up departmental rankings because this is important information for potential applicants, and the cost of obtaining it is minimal. Most disciplines have a system of grading departments. Economists publish such ratings regularly, and this would be one piece of information worth considering. Note that this rating is usually in terms of research performance or in terms of esteem among colleagues and, as far as I know, not according to teaching performance or nurturing. That kind of information is available as a rule only on an informal basis.

At the same time, do not be misled into thinking that just because you are going into a top-rated program your career is assured. In some fields, even top departments graduate more students than can reasonably find jobs. You might obtain valuable credentials that could pay off in the future if you have the patience to wait until an opportunity arises, but it might not be immediately.

You should do a bit of market research. How does the market for graduates in your field look at the moment? How has it changed during the last few years? Valuable information on graduate programs is readily available from professional newsletters, from the *Chronicle of Higher Education,* and on the World Wide Web. All you have to do is to look for it. Browse the Internet, ask the graduate secretary, read handbooks, and talk to the graduate advisor until you have reliable evidence on the program. Most important for you to know is the share of entering students who complete the program and the kinds of positions they have received within the last few years. Such considerations could help you make an informed guess concerning what your prospects are likely to be in five or so years. You should absolutely not make up your mind without being confident about your future chances.

Another important factor to consider, besides the quality of the department, is its intellectual orientation. Within any discipline, there are competing schools of thought. In economics, for instance, there are departments that are more concerned with theoretical issues, others with quantitative or institutional ones. Some focus on Keynesian economics, while others refuse to take its concepts seriously. The economics department at the University of Massachussetts at Amherst has the largest contingent of radical economists in the country, for example. If you prefer a more traditional line of analysis, this would not be the right institution for you. Political and ideological dispositions also differ markedly. As a consequence, you need to research this issue in order to be sufficiently well informed about the various intellectual movements in the field before you can make the right choice for you. The time spent on these preliminaries is well worth the effort, inasmuch as you are more likely to be successful in a program if your worldview fits well into that of the department. Not only that, but you are, in effect, attaching yourself to a particular school of thought, which will surely affect the rest of your academic trajectory. It will determine—more or less—in which paradigm you will spend a good part of your academic career, insofar as it is extremely difficult to change orientation subsequently. Hence, the choice you make will become a watershed of major proportions in your life, and it is important that you give some thought to the matter.

To what extent should a student specialize during graduate school?

John Komlos: Whenever a venture is risky, it pays to diversify, and education is no exception: no need to put all your eggs into one basket. However, the degree to which one should diversify is not so easy to specify. Thus, it is often worthwhile to develop an interest, or even expertise, in more than one niche of your discipline, providing the "price" is reasonable. Suppose you are in labor economics; you might be able to supplement your program with some additional work in demography. You would immediately differentiate yourself from other labor economists and possibly make yourself more attractive to some departments than you would be otherwise. You might also become eligible for grants, fellowships, and postdoctoral programs for which you would not have qualified otherwise. It is exactly such peripheral interest in demography that won me a two-year postdoctoral position at the University of North Carolina that truly gave me a boost. Without teaching and administrative obligations, I could really concentrate my effort on research and lived for many years off of projects started in that short time span. Of course, such diversification may not pay off, but the chances are that it will help you to find a comfortable niche in the profession. I know for a fact that it did for me.

John Goldsmith: I agree that diversification is necessary. The student may also not find this being emphasized explicitly by anyone during her graduate experience, I might add. I can mention some examples. There are a number of fields (including linguistics) where knowledge of computer programming is not a must, but is highly desirable. By and large, the generation of people currently teaching came of age in an earlier era, and they may be—indeed, they *are*—less sensitive to these shifting priorities, and they will frequently not be the ones urging students to strengthen their skills in the computational area. The same point holds *mutatis mutandis* in other areas, where it might be a matter of truly mastering an additional foreign language or of learning statistics or something else.

Penny Gold: Having some coursework in one or two additional subfields within one's discipline can be especially valuable if you come to be considered for a job at an institution where the department is relatively small and people are expected to teach beyond their research field. The ad I answered when I applied for a job at Knox asked for someone who could teach medieval, ancient, and Latin American history. I begged off on Latin American, but I had taken a couple of courses in Greek and Roman history that enhanced my profile for this job. The history department at Knox has five full-time faculty; we could not mount an appropriately diverse curriculum if we hired someone who could teach only one field of history.

What happens to life—what most people would think of as life, in any event—while you're in graduate school?

John Komlos: I think that graduate school is generally a trying period in one's life even under the best of circumstances. One is usually financially insecure in a materialistic world and is often surrounded by relatives and acquaintances who are already earning a "real" income. In addition, one's social position is in limbo, with plenty of uncertainty about the future. The typical graduate student is far away from home and family, and if she is already married, particularly with children, the complexities of life and the conflicts and stresses that they create can easily multiply. Moreover, this time in one's development is often intellectually very unsettling. The search for intellectual moorings intensifies, and while that can be, and at times certainly will be, a scintillating experience, it is accompanied by sufficient soul-searching to be emotionally demanding. In addition, you will no longer be merely assimilating knowledge; instead, you will be traveling in uncharted territory. Research—knowledge creation—is full of disappointments and failures. Hence, these years are not likely to be emotionally comfortable, well-balanced, or easygoing ones. In order to come through such a stressful experience unscathed, it is extremely important that you possess an inner certitude that you have made the right choices, that you are pursuing your true calling. It must be practically the only thing you want to do in life because, for a while at least, it will become almost synonymous with your life. As a consequence, it will also increase the pressure on personal relationships and generate a feedback effect on your academic performance. In short, many sacrifices will need to be made for a successful entry into the profession.

This is making a graduate school career sound rather daunting!

John Komlos: Intentionally so. Most people do not just breeze through it. That is why I think it is absolutely essential for you to take your time in reaching a decision. It is not something to decide on a Sunday afternoon at the beach.

John Goldsmith: But I'd like to break in and say that there are other experiences, too. I remember the years of my graduate career as being in some ways quite magical. It is true, as John has said, that it's important to really love the discipline that one is in. But when that's true, one thing that happens during one's graduate career is that what once was distant and mysterious becomes quite tangible, and one gets to meet and see close up the people whose work is forming and shaping the discipline. Intellectually this may be the most intense period of one's life.

I was in graduate school in Cambridge, Massachusetts, in the early 1970s—I was at MIT then—and it was almost unheard of for students to live by themselves; students generally lived three to an apartment, and this was as much an economic necessity as anything else, though it also contributed to everybody's social life—I am tempted to say, their real life. Many people roomed with their classmates, while others shared apartments or houses with other young people who did many different things. I myself did both, at various times. I don't know how things are in Cambridge these days, but my impression has been for quite a while that living three or four to an apartment is much less common now.

John, I share your recollections about much of graduate school days: the scintillating experience, the soul-searching, and the frequent sense of being off-balance and frustrated. But I don't have a recollection of sacrifice. Now, it's true that I didn't have a family at the time, and that changes the circumstances quite considerably. We'll come back to this matter later on.

Penny Gold: I look back at those years in graduate school as the time in which, in many ways, I became the person I am today—not so much intellectually (as my undergraduate education was the major shaping force there, with graduate school the necessary intensification and refinement), but emotionally, personally, politically. It's when I grew up, really. I lived in a shared house rather than a dorm, I had my first car, I was financially independent for the first time in my life, and I was challenged and inspired by the antiwar and feminist movements. Several of the friends I made in those years, people both in and out of academia, are still among my closest friends today, thirty years later.

And a word about the importance of an inner certitude that one has made the right choice. I wasn't confident that eventual work as a teacher and scholar was the right thing for me until I was well into my dissertation work. But I was funded, I was living with great people and had a nice circle of friends, my teachers liked my work, and I was enjoying life, so there was no reason to stop along the way. It turned out that this has, indeed, been exactly the right choice of work for me, but I did not know that from the start.

John Komlos: It might help you make up your mind if you read about the life of some of the prominent members of the profession you are considering.[10] If you can afford it, I'd suggest that you take a year off to travel. Or take a job outside academia and see what that is like. Such experiences will help you immensely to mature, and that will enable you to make more realistic decisions later on—not ones based on an idealized view of the world. The money you'll save can provide you a nest egg for you to fall back on. You are young; it is worthwhile to take your time in making a decision that will have an impact on the rest of your life. It is better to be sure about your decision a year from now than to take excessive risks now. In other words, making an informed choice is not a free lunch—you have to work for it—and making a commitment only after diligent investigation of likely alternatives is a strategy that will pay dividends down the line.

Finally, with all its challenges notwithstanding, graduate school will most certainly also be a period of intellectual growth. So you should try to get yourself in that frame of mind as you are beginning your chosen program. Cultivate friendships, develop your judgment, open yourself to new ideas, experiment with new directions, get to know your department, and, above all, open yourself to the possibilities that present themselves. If you can allow yourself to do all that, you will benefit enormously. And do not forget that you are privileged to be able to participate in the best educational system in the world. To interact with the best collection of scholars should become an uplifting experience. So make the best of it!

**When should I ask myself: Is this career choice the right one for me?
How will I know? Who will tell me if it's not the right one for me?**

John Goldsmith: What a tough question! It's one for which there are few
simple answers. Here's one of them, though. Many graduate programs
have an examination early on, often at the end of the first year—our linguistics program has such an exam, which we call our M.A. exam. In a
typical year, one person out of perhaps seven or eight does not achieve the
score of "High Pass" that we require for continuing in the doctoral program. The students who don't get a High Pass have the right to appeal to
the department, and they almost always do. Every three or four years there
is a perfectly valid reason why the exam score does not accurately reflect
the student's abilities (the student was running a high fever, had a sick
child at home, etc.), but most of the time the exam measures what it's
supposed to measure. Let me restate this in a less impersonal fashion:
most of the time we know what we're doing when we grade the exams,
and we are, indeed, sending a message. I think that a below-average score
on such an exam should be taken seriously by a student as an indication
that an academic career in linguistics is very likely not a wise career choice.
In general, I think that you're kidding yourself if you tell yourself, "Next
year, I'll study harder. I just didn't work hard enough this past year."

If you're not in a program with such an exam, or you're not there yet,
I think that you could reasonably expect yourself to get an A (or A−) in
all of your courses in the subject that you are studying—whether you're
an undergraduate or a graduate student. If you don't get such A's on almost
all of your courses, you're probably not doing well enough.

Let's pass to the next category of student, a more advanced student.
Let's say you've done well enough on your exams and you're into the more
advanced stages of your studies, perhaps already working on a dissertation
topic. My opinion is that at this point the question is not whether you are
smart enough to have an academic career, but whether the right fit exists
between your personality and the academic career—and frankly that's why
we've written this book: to help you understand what the academic career
consists of and to help you see whether you go well with it. If you find
yourself excited at the thought of reading and writing conference papers,
that's a good sign of a good fit.

Perhaps it is worth making this point explicitly: there are lots of brilliant people who don't make very good academics. Some of them never
made it into academia, and others slide on through, with a not very successful academic career. On the other hand, there are lots of successful

academics who aren't all that bright (dare I say that? I guess I do), but who have done very good work in teaching, in research, or in both.

Penny Gold: Teachers have lots of experience giving critical comments on student work—we do it all the time in the form of comments made on papers and during conferences over first drafts. But to criticize one particular paper is very different from saying about a person as a whole: "I don't think you're qualified to go to graduate school (or to stay in graduate school)." It's much more fun to encourage students who have too humble an opinion of themselves! Since I teach only undergraduates, the only situation I deal with is that of students wanting to go on to graduate school. I try to be as frank as possible if I don't think the student is cut out for such a program, but it's very, very hard. I'd love to know what others say in these circumstances. If subject matter or language training is weak, that's an easy thing to say. But what if I just think the student's not sharp enough intellectually? I would not say that to anyone. If their grades include too many B's, I'll point that out as not a good sign. I may encourage the student to apply for a master's program rather than a doctoral program, to test the water. And if they still persist, I'll tell them that I'm including in my recommendation the comment that I am happy to recommend for a master's program, but am less certain about doctoral work. I may also try to talk to them about career alternatives, but this works better in the sophomore or junior year than in the fall of the senior year, which is usually when the problem is arising.

3 | The Mentor

You've mentioned mentors. What is the role of the mentor in graduate school?

John Goldsmith: No doubt about it: the single most important aspect of graduate education grows out of the relationship formed with a single professor, the mentor. Oddly, the term has no official status in academia. The mentor is in most cases the "research advisor" or "chair of the dissertation research committee." But, more than anything else, the mentor is the person after whom the graduate student forms themselves—in a profound sense. This may not be the official chair of the dissertation committee, but it usually is.

I've already suggested that although the undergraduate education is, roughly speaking, a matter of learning, one's graduate education is a matter of restructuring and rebuilding oneself, a process that can be accomplished only on the model of a successful teacher. This may ring some bells in your mind: it sounds in some respects like the relationship between a child and a parent, or like the relationship between a patient and a psychoanalyst, or even, in still other respects, like the relationship between an aspirant and a guru. I'm sure this is no accident, nor is it just a poetic way of speaking: all these relationships involve profound attempts to learn in a way that touches one's soul. Becoming a graduate student should mean becoming some mentor's student and simultaneously a student of a particular discipline.

More important, it means submitting oneself to the teacher and to the discipline, to make it part of oneself. This may sound mystical, and to some degree, it is, though most people don't stop and think about it along the way. But it is worth remarking on if only because it represents one of the most difficult stumbling blocks for would-be graduate students. The best students coming into graduate school are not only intelligent—they are also independent-minded, and that independence has been encouraged for years, inside school and out. Of these, the very best will very likely think that they know what they want out of school. Many of them may think (often rightly) that they are smarter, or at least quicker, than any of their teachers in college.

When they come to the point of having to submit themselves in the way I have suggested to both a specific discipline and a particular mentor, many students find themselves unable to do so. As I have said, the issue is rarely, if ever, posed overtly in the way I have just suggested. It may come out as a dissatisfaction on the student's part or an inability to work comfortably with any of the faculty members in the department. But graduate education requires, in a sense oddly akin to that of the student seeking oriental enlightenment, a submission of the ego to that of the mentor for a certain prescribed and circumscribed period. This student-mentor relationship is fundamental to becoming a successful researcher (perhaps much as it is important to have had a good parent to be a good parent). I'd go so far as to say that if a graduate student does not find this kind of relationship forming, they should seriously consider choosing a different advisor.

Central to the relationship is your common and joint research. In general, what is shared is the research interests of the professor; in a more unusual circumstance, the student may bring a special research interest and involve the professor in it, though even then it will be the mentor's overall perspective that governs the research as it develops. The student gets to see, for the first time, what it means for knowledge to arise out of confusion and ignorance. That, after all, is the meaning of research; it is the patient struggle to achieve comprehension where there was none before. The student (we may assume) up until then had learned things only in an individual way: reading books, trying to understand what other people had already figured out themselves and expressed in written form. The mentor shows, by doing, how one reaches beyond what is known to come up with an idea, formulate it, and test it. As this process becomes clearer to the aspiring graduate student, the student becomes capable of undertaking that effort himself, and the result, after four or five years, is a research project that forms the body of the doctoral dissertation. Again, this may sound somehow mystical or miraculous, but only because it is—and it is only as miraculous as so many other episodes in our lives. It is certainly no more miraculous than a baby learning a language!

John Komlos: Creating new ideas definitely has a miraculous aspect to it. Always. Cognitive scientists study how it comes about, and if I am not mistaken, they come up with concepts such as "representational redescription" to refer to one way it can come about. It is truly a wonderful, but challenging experience, and there is not a good way to teach it in a classroom setting. Rather, a sort of apprenticeship with a mentor should make it happen for you: learning by doing and by observing. And this is the reason why it is so important that you find a mentor motivated to help you.

Penny Gold: In my experience, the range of graduate student–to–dissertation advisor relationships is more varied. Now, I have to preface my comments with the acknowledgment that I have not myself been a graduate advisor. I am speaking from my own experience as a graduate student and from that of my friends and colleagues. I would like to underscore the distinction between a graduate advisor and a "mentor." All graduate students must have a dissertation advisor, but they may or may not find a mentor. The advisor has an official role that must be fulfilled, which centers on direction of the dissertation research. A mentor, on the other hand, may have little to do with one's dissertation, but is someone ahead of you in academia, usually in your general discipline, if not in your specific field, with whom you come to have a more informal personal relationship. The mentor is someone you can go to for advice on all sorts of issues in academic life (as troubling as difficulties you may be having with your advisor or as mundane as advice on what to wear for a job interview). Sometimes the advisor plays this role as well, sometimes another faculty member (perhaps even at a different institution), sometimes an advanced graduate student. You can even have more than one mentor, but you'll just have one advisor (unless incompatibility or the advisor's leaving the institution means you have to switch). So, in what follows, I am talking about the dissertation advisor, who may or may not be a mentor to you.

I'm uncomfortable with the language of submission that John Goldsmith has used, even while acknowledging that it describes what often takes place. There is an unavoidable dynamic of power in advisee-advisor relationships. The advisor determines whether your dissertation is accepted or not and either helps you actively in your search for a job or not. Your career is quite literally in the hands of your advisor. In fact, this is why it can be helpful to have another person in addition to your advisor in whom you can confide or of whom you can ask certain kinds of questions. But some advisors use their power only on your behalf, without making you feel like a peon in the process. The best advisors will treat you like a junior colleague—which you are, indeed, in the process of becoming. I was blessed in having such an advisor myself (it's interesting that we're all resorting to religious language here), and his respect and high expectations for me were perhaps as valuable a part of his advising as his specific guidance in medieval history.

Another way my experience was different was in how far my dissertation research was from my advisor's research. In some fields, you will of necessity be doing "joint" research with your advisor. This is particularly true in many of the sciences, where your own truly individually determined research may be postponed until you are head of your own lab, with your own students. But in other disciplines, the connection with your advisor's research may be minimal, depending on the structure of the field. In history, for example, there are many subfields, usually divided by geographical place and time. There may be only one or two professors in any given subfield (e.g., modern Chinese history or early modern European history), so if you restrict yourself to the methodology and subject matter of those few professors, you will be very limited indeed. Some professors will direct dissertations only on topics they know intimately themselves. This can provide very deep training for you as the student, but may make it difficult for you to find a topic you really love,[1] and it may also limit the extent of the contribution you could make to the field by going off in a new direction. Some professors are willing to direct dissertations that are further afield, and I'm grateful mine was one of these. His work on the history of medieval universities couldn't have been much further from my chosen subject of women in twelfth-century France. Despite the large gap, my advisor agreed to direct the dissertation, led me through much related material, and helped me to locate other people in the academy who could give me further advice on the specific topic. It is also possible to have a professor from another institution actually be a member of your dissertation committee, something to consider suggesting if your research interests are outside the specific expertise of the faculty at your own institution.

I think every graduate student–advisor relationship is unique, varying both by individual advisor and by individual student. The critical thing is to find someone with whom you can have a productive and at least moderately comfortable relationship.

John Goldsmith: I know that the term "mentoring" has been used a good deal to refer to a sort of symbolic older brother or older sister relationship, not so far from the kind of help one receives from more experienced members of the informal network of professional colleagues one tries to develop. But that's not how I have used the term.

How does one go about finding the right mentor, once in graduate school?

John Goldsmith: It seems to me that it is ultimately the graduate student's responsibility to find someone to work with. Yes, after taking courses with many professors in your department, the time will come, perhaps in the second or third year of graduate studies, to try to establish an individual working relationship with one of the professors. How should you choose which one? In some cases, there may be a specific professor with whom you came to that department to study, probably because he was an expert in the particular area you chose. If all other signs are positive, then the solution to your current problem is easy. You may change your mind, however—there may be other professors with whom you would rather work. You must consider not only how your research style and personality mesh with those of the mentor-to-be, but also how he has dealt with his other graduate students: is he capable, in the best of cases at least, of providing the kind of supportive and yet demanding relationship necessary during this period of two to four years of joint research? That pretty much sums it up, and obviously that's a very hard question to answer—but it's the one that the student must try to come to grips with.

There's a particularly tricky question that I've been asked, and that I've tried to avoid: should a student aim intentionally to work with the professor who has the highest professional profile? One of the ways I find to avoid that question is to point out that there are much better ways to pick one's advisor. But if I were really pinned down and forced to answer the question, I'd say yes—all other things being equal, pick someone with a high professional profile. At the very least, you'll get a glimpse from closer up of what that person is doing, and very likely your own work will become better known.

Penny Gold: There can be a complicated dynamic around the height of your advisor's reputation at the time you apply for jobs. Your dissertation advisor's letter will be the most important one in your dossier, and most advisors write not only glowing, but also detailed letters about the work of their students. But the most illustrious names in the profession sometimes think the weight of their name is enough and write only brief letters, which can undermine your chances in the most competitive searches. Less well known advisors, on the other hand, may make a special effort to write the kind of detailed letter search committees need to assess your scholarly potential. If you can, find out the placement track record of various faculty members.

Besides obligation and responsibility, there's another reason many professors will go to great lengths to see to it that their students are well placed—they are gratified by seeing their students do well! And for professors newer to the academy, their own reputations will be enhanced by the developing reputations of their students. So there is a bit of mutual benefit that helps relieve the power dynamic of having your future rest in the advisor's hands.

John Komlos: From the very moment you arrive on campus, you should keep in mind that you will ultimately need to find a dissertation advisor, who will become a kind of role model for you. You must try to ascertain what kind of reputation professors have for working with graduate students. You should talk to everyone: to teaching and research assistants and to students who are ahead of you in the program as well as to as many faculty members in the department as possible during their office hours to see how compatible their ideas and interests are with your way of thinking about problems. See if the professor seems to respond to you in a positive way. If he is difficult to reach or to talk to, if he is fidgety in your presence, if he keeps on looking at his watch while you talk to him, if he seems disinterested in the issues you raise, or if he is not concentrating on the discussion, then you probably do not have a good candidate for the position you seek to fill. If, however, he is curious about your intellectual development, if he is helpful in solving some problems you present to him, and if he seems to be interested in working with you—in other words, if he appears to be nurturing—then you might, indeed, just have the right mentor for you. Needless to say, it is also important that he work in an area of the discipline that is of interest to you, that he have already made some significant contributions to the field, and that he have a character you respect. Of course, in order for the relationship to work, the commitment must be mutual. After all, you will definitely need his support and guidance well beyond graduate school.

The significance of the mentor is accentuated by the fact that the frontiers of knowledge are not easily mastered without a detailed map.[2] Navigation on the frontier is an arduous task for the uninitiated because it is not well defined except in the mind of a handful of scholars, and danger lurks in unexpected places. The frontier is fuzzy, and not contiguous, with few people working in any part of it. Much of the most recent research in a particular niche of the discipline is still unpublished, given the substantial lag between results and their publication. Hence, unless someone is able and willing to point out to you meticulously the direction and significance of recent research, you might be taking your research in a completely wrong direction. Moreover, there are hidden connections between various results that have not yet been written about, but are already known to a select few in the profession. Only someone who has been following the field carefully for some time can inform you about these relationships, saving you time and effort and perhaps frustration or at least months of fumbling around. You might even be duplicating the research of others, without knowing about it. Hence, there is considerable need for the guidance of a mentor, and only he can provide it adequately. Thus, the choice of the mentor is as important as the initial decision to enter a particular graduate program.

John Goldsmith: This business of forming graduate students is an intense process for both the student and the teacher. This intensity has several side effects. First of all, it means that the teacher cannot be an adequate mentor to twenty-five different students at the same time. There is a quite small upper limit to the number of students whose research the professor can supervise at any given time—perhaps a half dozen or so, probably less. When we talk about the teaching responsibilities of the professor at the research institution, we must bear in mind that he is (in the way of things) engaged in mentoring several graduate students at any given time, a process that may be at times nearly as time consuming as raising a child.

We may put it another way. It is commonplace to divide professors' duties into teaching, research, and service. But from the above description of the development of the student-mentor relationship, we can see that it involves, in equal parts, research and teaching. Helping a student become an active researcher is simultaneously a matter of teaching and research; the research is a cooperative process, conducted jointly with the student qua apprentice. So when we consider how much work is expected of a professor at a research university, or how much is accomplished, on the teaching side of the equation we must be sure to include the number of students with whom the professor is actively involved in research. For many—perhaps for most—this relationship can bring the greatest joy of the job; it is also a heavy demand and commitment on the part of the professor. As a consequence, quite a few professors, particularly below the very top departments, may be reluctant to work extensively with graduate students.

An aside on distracted or unresponsive professors: one of the most important activities of the graduate student is writing papers, all through the graduate career. These evolve over a period of several years into dissertation chapters. It is a universal experience of students that some professors are very slack (the blunt word, I suppose, is irresponsible) about returning papers with comments in a timely fashion. How's a student to deal with cases like that? For one thing, recognize that putting such a professor on your dissertation committee (worse yet, choosing one as your dissertation advisor) is a self-destructive move, all other things being equal. In our department, we came up with an explicit guideline for how long it should take a professor to return a paper (or chapter or dissertation): take the number of pages, divide by 100, round up, and add 1. That's the number of weeks. So any paper under 100 pages should be returned in 2 weeks; a 305-page dissertation may take 5 weeks. (As I write these words, I see that that formula may seem rather generous for the professor, but bear in mind that he is likely to be multitasking, having several such lengthy assignments at any one time, above and beyond his teaching and research.)

John Komlos: One should not lose sight of the fact that the mentor will not be able to hold your hand constantly. The nurturing relationship should not become one of dependence. In any case, in many disciplines after the start of your dissertation research, you might have to fall back on your own strengths for at least part of the process. Of course, consultations with your mentor will still remain extremely valuable, but not always practical, if you are in the field or if he is on sabbatical.[3] This is different in the laboratory sciences, where frequent contact and consultation develop automatically, but you should be aware of the fact that this may not inevitably be the case. You should realize that the more famous scholars have many students working on dissertations at any one time. While some advisors are there when you need them, others will not make themselves available to you for longer than an hour a month. Hence, you should be careful to choose a mentor who meets your personal needs. If you do not think you can handle much adversity on your own, you would be better off choosing a less well known scholar as your dissertation advisor who has more time for you. I should also mention that your progress, and ultimate success, will be much enhanced if you are able to collect a support group around you to help you through the inevitably difficult days. Do not forget to look beyond your own department for some friends who might be interested in your work from an interdisciplinary perspective.

Penny Gold: Yes, there will usually be other professors who have an interest in some aspect of your work, and you should consult with them. And there are undoubtedly other students with whom you can talk, not only about the substance of your work, but also about the process of and roadblocks to getting the work done. Some departments set up formal mechanisms to get groups of students and sometimes professors together, where people can present work in progress. If none exists at your institution, you might see if you can set something up or, at the least, find frequent, informal ways of talking with other people. And once you're embarked on your research, this is a good time to begin making contact with scholars at other institutions who are doing work related to yours. Conferences are a good way to get initiated into these networks, but even "cold" e-mail messages to people you've not met will often be answered with collegial help.

John Goldsmith: And when the student has come to full intellectual maturity, then he must face the task of no longer looking to his mentor for the support and approval that were a necessary part of the apprentice stage. This, too, is a difficult transition, but one that must be undertaken primarily by the student alone.

In most cases, too, the mentoring commitment goes well beyond the matter of the direct relationship between the student and advisor and involves the latter's professional relationships as well. This is the case insofar as the mentor has the responsibility of presenting the student's work to the professional world and of judging that work as the student begins to make his way out of graduate school into the field as a whole. In only the rarest of cases will the advisor ever feel comfortable in saying something negative about his own student—if only as a matter of personal pride. And yet the mentor's responsibilities are, to some extent, split, involving responsibility to the student who may be looking for a first job and responsibility to the field (that is, to colleagues at another university who need honest and frank letters of appraisal). To balance these commitments is not always an easy task.

I should point out that while each of us is concentrating primarily on those areas of academia that we know about personally, the situation in the grant-sponsored laboratory sciences (physics, biology, chemistry, psychology, and several others) is quite different in a number of important respects. In that environment, a grad student is part of a team and forms a partnership in a sense with other graduate students, with postdoctoral fellows, and with the professor in charge of the lab. There will typically be more or less formal laboratory meetings at least once a week and informal interaction among all members of the team on a daily basis. Such laboratories, too, typically don't shut down for summer vacation.

John Komlos: After you've chosen your main advisor, the other readers of your dissertation should be decided upon jointly with him.[4] As with your main supervisor, your personality should be compatible with the other members of the committee so that you can feel comfortable with them. After you have organized your committee, you are ready to concentrate on your dissertation itself, probably the most challenging task during graduate school.

Have you been in the position of turning down a student who asks to work with you?

John Goldsmith: Yes. One consequence of the complexity and demands made by the student-mentor relationship is that it may not always be the right choice, from the professor's point of view, to agree to serve as advisor for a particular student. The point is delicate, and certainly arguable, but it seems to me that the considerations that we have touched upon suggest that the decision to take a particular student on as an apprentice in a research capacity is not mandated automatically by professional commitment.

On both the student's and the professor's side, this is not always an easy relationship to maintain. The intellectual closeness that must develop if the relationship is to be successful may founder on other rocky coasts. It may be as simple as incompatible personalities on the two sides of the desk. There is no guarantee that two people interested in the same subject who, by chance, end up at the same university will have compatible personalities.

4 | Writing a Dissertation

Let's talk about the dissertation.

John Goldsmith: To become a professor in one of the academic disciplines at a research or comprehensive university or at most four-year colleges, you will have to have obtained a Ph.D. There is remarkable agreement across the disciplines regarding the requirements for earning this degree. A bachelor's degree is usually (though not always) a prerequisite for enrollment in a Ph.D. program, and a master's degree will sometimes also be required. If the degree of master of arts (M.A.) or master of science (M.S. or M.Sc.) is not a prerequisite, its equivalent is likely to be: somewhere between a year and two years of obligatory graduate coursework, some mastery of a foreign language or perhaps a computer language instead, and possibly an extended research paper a bit longer than a semester's term paper. The Ph.D. itself will have several additional requirements: frequently an entrance examination, which must be passed before the student will be formally admitted to the doctoral program; perhaps an explicit requirement of some additional coursework (though that requirement is often not put on paper, since the other requirements could simply not be met without the student taking the necessary courses); the presentation of a research paper or two; the ability to read a second foreign language; oral or written exams to demonstrate full mastery of area of specialization; and then—and only then—the biggest requirement of all, the doctoral dissertation.

The dissertation is the stumbling block that causes so much panic and distress among graduate students, and many are the students who have completed All (requirements) But the Dissertation (ABD)[1] and find themselves incapable of completing that final step.

What is this dissertation, and why is it so difficult?

John Goldsmith: A doctoral dissertation is a book-length manuscript, typically about 200 pages, though rarely exceeding 500. In a few disciplines, such as mathematics, it may be much shorter, and in others, it may consist of a simple bundling of three or four research papers already published by the student in professional refereed journals. These exceptions aside, though, a dissertation typically begins with a statement of a particular, well-defined problem within the area and a review of how the problem has been treated in the literature. This prepares the ground for the statement of a new approach to the problem, followed by the development and exploration of this proposal over the course of two or more chapters.[2]

Before the dissertation itself is actually written, and usually before the bulk of research is accomplished, the student must set down in writing a proposal concerning what she intends to carry out during the research period and what she intends to accomplish in the dissertation. In most cases, this proposal may be submitted only after all the other requirements for the Ph.D. have been satisfied. The dissertation proposal is not another requirement like the others, however. When a department approves a dissertation proposal, it is, in effect, entering into an implicit contract with the student. It recognizes that the research project that the student proposes to undertake is clear and well defined enough to be evaluated when it is finished and that it addresses an issue of sufficient importance and scope to merit a Ph.D. If a student submits a dissertation that conforms to the guidelines laid down in the dissertation proposal, the department may refuse it only on the grounds that there is something wrong with the specific content—it cannot turn around and say that the question it addresses is not important enough or that another chapter needs to be added to cover another topic. In principle, at least, the submission and acceptance of a dissertation proposal render binding an agreement on scope of the dissertation.

Hasn't there been some discussion about eliminating the dissertation requirement from doctoral degrees?

John Goldsmith: Indeed. It continues to surprise me how often I encounter the suggestion that a dissertation is something of an archaism—just a rite of passage—a suggestion made even by people who should know better. Writing (and defending) a dissertation might be a rite of passage, but it is not merely that. Writing a dissertation, and carrying through the extended research that that requires, is a demanding task, and the person who accomplishes it has been changed by the undertaking. In our modern age, it is perhaps easy to lose sight of the fact that rites of passage in traditional cultures are just that: demanding exercises that leave one changed for having been through them. The student is not supposed to leave graduate school after five years with the same mind and habits that she had when she entered; she is supposed to be changed, and the final accomplishment consists of writing a thesis, an achievement that presupposes all the other requirements of the Ph.D. and that is the most demanding of all.

How does one choose a dissertation topic?

John Komlos: With considerable care. Never lose sight of the fact that the dissertation should be the crowning achievement of your graduate education and will influence the direction of your career for many years to come. It will take years to write[3] and might well require a couple more years of polishing to make it publishable. Inasmuch as you are locking yourself into a project that will occupy a big chunk of your life, this decision should not be made lightly.

Some advisors are willing to offer a choice of two or three dissertation topics. This can be of great advantage, inasmuch as she has a better overview of the field, knows the sources, and knows if the dissertation is doable within the allotted time frame, and, in effect, you receive a crucial implicit promise that you will be closely guided along the way. Of course, some professors are reluctant to suggest thesis topics, either out of a philosophical conviction that that is the student's job or out of a concern about the commitment and responsibility that go with such advice, but they may also simply want to limit their involvement with students. Be aware that a reserved disposition might well signal a reluctance to work with you closely, and it might be wise to look for alternatives.

It is much safer to defer to your mentor's suggestion of topics if offered. By doing so, you will give yourself additional time to develop the necessary skills for selecting a good research project, which are difficult to acquire. To be sure, there are those who argue for a sink-or-swim approach on the assumption that the student will learn these skills by being forced to choose a dissertation topic. This point of view is surely reasonable, but my own experience leads me to urge you to err on the side of caution if you have the opportunity unless you have reason to think that you have already mastered such skills: the risk of sinking is too great at this stage. As a third alternative, you may find the choice being made through give and take with your supervisor.

If you have good reason to be confident in doing research on the topic of your own choice or if close guidance feels too restrictive to you, then proceed, but at least be forewarned that you can easily lead yourself on a wild goose chase. In fact, many students do not finish their dissertation because their topic turns out to be much too difficult for reasons that were not immediately obvious to them. In any case, do make sure you have your mentor's full support before embarking on a project.

It is imperative that both you and your advisor be interested in your thesis topic. It is important that your mentor be interested in it because otherwise she might be much less motivated to help you, and it is crucial that you be excited about it because otherwise you will have enormous difficulties mustering the momentum to succeed in completing the project. Original research is challenging, and even frustrating at times, in the sense that hundreds of obstacles need to be overcome in the process. Unless you are truly fascinated by the topic and consider it intrinsically valuable and rewarding to work on it, you can easily slip into becoming an ABD instead of a Ph.D.!

Make sure that you do not start a dissertation on an unfamiliar topic. You should prepare some plans, even if tentative ones, well in advance and have a good overview of the topic before you commence active research. It will be extremely useful if you have already made preliminary excursions into various related issues during the course of your graduate study. Having written one or two seminar papers on some aspects of the topic, you will enter the dissertation stage already somewhat knowledgeable about the field. You will know most of the literature, some of the issues that have attracted attention lately, and the scholars who are writing in that field. This knowledge will help you to formulate issues and to write up the thesis proposal in a convincing manner. Moreover, you should by now have a sense of how interesting the topic actually is to you.

Once you have chosen your dissertation topic in collaboration with your advisor, you should seek her active guidance to the utmost degree possible. Every topic has imperceptible pitfalls, and your advisor can and should help you over them. Dissertation research is multifaceted; it proceeds in complex, and unexpected, ways, and the result is unpredictable. I have never done research that did not hold some surprises for me, and at times, I even disproved my initial hypothesis. The closer your topic is to the expertise of your mentor, the more direction you can count on, and the easier it should be for you to avoid making mistakes or getting stuck along the way. These issues are less pertinent in the laboratory sciences because there the graduate student usually works in a close-knit research team, directed and funded by the mentor's own research program. In such fields, there is more group interaction, and perhaps more cooperation and conformity in research design.

In any case, you will need to learn who the important scholars are in the field. Ask your advisor who is working in your area, check their respective home pages on the Internet, and look for their working papers. Consult also the programs of the meetings of professional organizations in your field for people interested in related topics. Dissertations in progress are sometimes announced in the newsletter of a discipline's main professional association, or there is a centralized dissertation registry. Though incomplete, they are certainly useful. Check also the University of Michigan microfilms of unpublished dissertations.[4]

Because in some departments and in some disciplines your access to your mentor might be limited, you may find it advisable to talk over your preliminary ideas with your peers and even show them your dissertation proposal before you give it to your mentor.

Your dissertation is your first real research project, and you are not expected to strike out on your own into completely uncharted territory. That would be premature. You should restrict the scope of your topic as far as you can. You will be expected to work within a paradigm; that is, you aren't required to resolve a major controversy between two competing schools of thought in the discipline, although you can explore a pertinent aspect of a controversy in a case study. Dissertations are similar to the "masterpieces" that medieval guilds required for full membership in a craft: you might think of yourself as a journeyman demonstrating her skills to the members of a profession. In other words, the dissertation need not be an earth-shattering contribution, but, however modest, it must be original and demonstrate both technique and an expertise in the field. In addition, it must demonstrate your skill in research and argument. Actually, one of the unstated purposes of the thesis requirement is to filter out people who will not be able to do original research in their subsequent career.

John Goldsmith: I think there is considerable variation here across disciplines and across universities and departments as well. I can give a lot of reasons why I think a student should take on a topic that fits in very directly with what her advisor wants to be working on, and you've mentioned most of them already. But I would also say that the stronger a student's intellectual abilities and strength of will are, the more she should take seriously the notion of setting off in a radically new direction intellectually. But I mean that only for students who are intellectually mature enough to provide arguments that are cogent within the old paradigm for why the new approach is superior. That's a very tall order.

And in the real world, the selection of a dissertation topic is often going to be a matter of negotiation in some respects between advisor and student. I don't think I've ever had a student come to me with a list of three or four possible topics to get my take on them, but that seems like a pretty good idea.

Penny Gold: Whether one takes a topic selected by an advisor or develops one's own, I would emphasize John Komlos's comment that one has to be excited about the topic. I think it is more likely that this will happen if the topic is developed by the student, coming from questions that you really want to pursue. What difference will it make to you if your question is answered? If the answer is "Not much, it's just a nifty puzzle," you might want to search further. The interest has to be deep enough to sustain you over years of difficult work. Your professional identity will also be shaped by association with this topic. Is this how you'd like to be known in the field, at least for the rather long first stage of it, until you do your next large project?

John Komlos: If I may turn for a moment to the more practical issue of financing the dissertation, I would like to note that if you do not already hold a fellowship, you should look at the many compilations of available fellowships in your library. Ask your mentor for possibilities, and consult the graduate or departmental secretary as well as the university's research office. You should also be aware of what grants other students ahead of you have received. Some national professional organizations have their own list of prospective funding agencies relevant to the discipline. In addition, the newsletters of many organizations advertise such opportunities.[5] You should plan ahead, start early, and write the most convincing proposal you can. It's a good idea to apply for all the grants for which you might conceivably qualify, since it is easier to turn down an award received than to wait a year for the next cycle of competition if you are underfunded. Some fellowships are not mutually exclusive, but allow you to hold other awards either simultaneously or consecutively. The goal, of course, is not to get rich, but to obtain enough support to complete the dissertation comfortably. Allot yourself enough time. Be generous in your estimates, since many have a tendency to be overly optimistic about the length of time required to complete a project. Do not forget that this is the first time you will be doing original research. You should anticipate unforeseen detours requiring additional time to bring the project to completion.

How long should all of this take?

John Goldsmith: It might seem foolhardy to make a general comment about how long it takes to earn a doctoral degree, since observation seems to indicate that it can take from three years to twenty years, but there are one or two important points that don't obviously emerge from such statistics. Perhaps the most important is that speed of completion of the doctoral degree is quite important. I have shared notes with many friends and colleagues, and there is quite generally a sense that the best students finish their degrees with alacrity. This doesn't mean that there aren't outstanding students who have taken rather longer than average to finish. Still, a person going into the job market would like to display characteristics that suggest she is as strong a candidate as possible. And why should the best candidates typically finish in a shorter period of time? One can think of many reasons, not the least being raw intelligence, whatever that means. It may also indicate self-discipline and better organizational principles at work, or a strict taskmaster for a dissertation advisor.

In linguistics, it seems to me that four and a half years is the average time actually spent on completing the doctoral program. Many students spend more time than that, of course, but, more frequently than not, part of the time spent in excess of five years is time spent doing other things, whether those things be child-raising, money-earning, excessive-course-taking, or simply futzing around. I don't put those activities on any sort of equal footing! But no statement about how long a doctorate takes can take individual variation into account regarding activities that are, strictly speaking, a distraction from the goal of completing the doctoral program.

In my experience, there is an enormous disparity in the amount of time students give themselves to accomplish various tasks (and remember, once we start talking doctoral dissertation, most of the schedule setting is ultimately the responsibility of the student and no one else). Some will give themselves three years to accomplish what others expect to complete in nine months. As advisor, I can encourage the slower ones to work faster, but there's a real limit to what anyone can do to pick up a student's pace.

Penny Gold: There's a complicated calculus to be figured here. A relatively circumscribed topic will greatly facilitate a timely completion of the dissertation, which will look good on your curriculum vitae as well as help cut back on the loans or financial sacrifices you may be making. As one professor at my graduate school had posted over his door, "A dissertation is not a book!" It is, rather, an exercise to train you in research and then to prove that you can do it. On the other hand, an ambitious topic—well executed, of course—will be impressive to prospective employers. And while a dissertation is not a book, in many fields it has to have the potential of becoming one, as you will be expected to turn your dissertation into a book (and maybe go on to a second project) before tenure; if the dissertation is narrow in scope, this subsequent goal will be difficult to achieve.

John Komlos: Here's something else that may seem obvious, but often isn't: the student should consult the dissertation office of her university for the approved format and citation style for the dissertation before writing one sentence of the thesis. Redoing the format can be extremely time consuming; it is so much easier to do it correctly the first time. You may be surprised that there is no flexibility in this regard whatsoever. If you know in advance that certain information is needed in the bibliography, you will not have to waste time subsequently looking up the citations again. An example of such information might be the need to cite the month of publication of journal articles in the references instead of (or in addition to) the issue number.

One of the most difficult challenges you will face is the temptation to work on ancillary issues during the course of your research. You must do your best to stick to the topic approved by your dissertation committee. However, any original research will bring to the surface dozens of peripheral issues that have not been explored in the past. You will have to consciously avoid being attracted by them. Just tell yourself that you will come back to those questions later, and, of course, these are potential dissertation topics you can suggest to your future students. Avoid at any cost falling into the trap of thinking that answering these questions is a precondition to completing the dissertation. More often than not this only appears to be the case and is a sign of your lack of research experience. Ask your mentor (and your support group) on how to bridge the gap created by the missing information, without your having to spend months to fill that lacuna. And most of all, try your best not to expand the focus of your thesis.

Penny Gold: I would distinguish being led astray by peripheral issues or the temptation to expand from the shifts or "traveling" that may well occur in your topic or questions as you work. In fact, I think it a good sign of engaged, productive research that one's focus changes as one works, in response to the things one is learning along the way.

John Komlos: I agree that one should not be too rigid about the conceptualization of the thesis, but the main challenge to its timely completion will be an inability to resist the temptation to expand its scope. I think it is worth emphasizing again that the dissertation is not expected to solve all outstanding problems relevant to its topic. That is neither reasonable nor expected of you. Rather, you are expected to demonstrate that you can overcome the obstacles associated with original research and produce a coherent piece of work. Your success will depend on your ability to bridge the chasms brought to the surface by your research. And you don't have to fudge! Be forthright: "Further research is needed on this issue; the possible effects on my results are as follows." Then spell out the possibilities and how these might provide a more nuanced view of your conclusions. After you have thought it through in this manner, you might realize that, regardless of the importance of the issue at hand, your results are not particularly sensitive to it. Suppose you do not know the size of a variable, but you do have some pretty good intuition about the minimum and maximum values it could take. Then use these values to ascertain the possible effects on your results.[6] Thus, the goal is not to write a perfect dissertation; such hardly exist. All dissertations have strengths and weaknesses, and yours need not be the exception; the profession will understand that. That is not the main issue. The most important factor is that it should be a genuine contribution to knowledge. The reason I emphasize this point is that in my experience a perfectionist attitude can be a major career-impeding factor.

I grant that the above example is a rather trivial one, and choices confronting you are likely to be more complex. Yet my main point is that you need to develop skills that will enable you to avoid boxing yourself in on particular issues. Argue by analogy, argue by order of magnitude, or suggest that your conclusions are tentative and are subject to revision with further research. There is nothing to be ashamed of in admitting the limitations of your work. On the contrary, it is wise to do so, since it is hardly your fault that insufficient research has been done in your field. By framing your problem, you have already set limits on the horizon of your exploration, but these limits might be restricted further in the course of the research. Unless you can jump over the psychological hurdles posed by such difficulties, or if you insist on writing the first perfect dissertation at your university, you will encounter real difficulties.

What if a student becomes discouraged with her dissertation topic? How should she cope with that?

John Komlos: It may sound like an exaggeration, but be prepared: no matter what topic you pick, at some point the chances are that you will wish you had chosen another one. The dissertation is, of course, original research, and all research is a creative process full of unavoidable contradictions, mistakes, and frustrations. You should realize that even the simplest topic will hold plenty of surprises. To pursue unusual ideas, to dissent, to contradict, or to imagine that you had been wrong requires a certain amount of courage. Moreover, there will be ebbs and flows, and times when you will be stuck. Do not despair! Think about another chapter, or write about another issue; try your hand at writing parts of the introduction. You will catch your second wind, and you will find that you have days when you accomplish more than you did in the previous month. If, however, you find yourself completely stuck for an extended period of time, consulting a mental health professional on campus might be useful. Most universities have excellent counselors who see many students coping with writer's block.

Self-doubt will undoubtedly strike during the weeks or months when the work is not proceeding as expected. As with writer's block, a good strategy is simply to start working on another aspect of the dissertation. Sooner or later, you will likely see how to overcome what previously appeared to be an insurmountable obstacle. One thing, however, should definitely be avoided. Once you have invested six months or more in your dissertation, do not abandon the topic if at all possible. Try to find ways to rescue it by redirecting its focus or by conceptualizing the problem differently; starting anew would be quite problematic at this stage.

Intelligence is an important prerequisite to successful research, but just as crucial, if not more so, are your working habits. This is the case because discoveries—flashes of creative insight—are as infrequent as they are rewarding. They are soon overshadowed by the tedium of working out the intricate details of those ideas in two dimensions (i.e., on paper). The excitement of waiting for the outcome of an experiment will be overtaken by the boring task of actually describing the kinds of equipment used. That is one of the reasons why the initial attraction to the topic and reliable work habits are extremely important; otherwise, the drudgery of such tasks can become overwhelming.

John Goldsmith: I don't think I've ever met anyone who didn't begin to hate his dissertation around the time it was being completed—a feeling that typically lasts a year or two after it has been submitted and accepted. This is such a widespread phenomenon that it would be wise to accept the notion that it will occur and to discount those effects as much as possible. And this feeling is likely to hit in the final, critical months before completion of the dissertation. Beware!

Penny Gold: There is a good side to this feeling of disgust with the project in the final stages—it can help motivate one to finish it up and get it out of one's life! I have now come to welcome the onset of this feeling, as it has become a sign to me that I am at the tail end of a project and that it's time to hurry up and get it done.

What happens after the dissertation is written?

John Komlos: Once the research is completed, written up, and approved by the committee informally, it still has to pass the final hurdle of a "dissertation defense." This is by and large pro forma; if the advisor (and the entire research committee) has agreed to set up a time and place for a dissertation defense, it is more or less agreed that there are no major objections to its acceptance. The defense consists of a statement by the candidate of the main findings of her research. At that point, all the members of the dissertation committee, and any other members of the department who wish to be present, will have the opportunity to ask questions of the student, at times to the point of challenging the student on her command of the scholarly literature or the complexities of the issues covered in the dissertation. While it is rare that a dissertation will be rejected at that stage, it is possible for a committee to require some additional work on it before it will be accepted. Typically, it is left to the advisor to determine informally that this additional work has been completed; it is most uncommon for a second dissertation defense to be held.

John Goldsmith: This is true, but those unforgettable defenses after which a dissertation is not accepted do, on occasion, happen, and they happen to people who don't expect it. So be prepared, and talk with your advisor and your committee members at length before the defense.

Some departments permit and even encourage students to attend defenses; that is the case in my department. The students who have attended a half dozen defenses before their own have learned important lessons, and they bring a bit of moral support to their fellow students who are on the spot that day. I suspect there are few departments that do this, but I think it is an excellent tradition, and I encourage others to join us in it.

5 | Landing an Academic Job

Is there anything I should be doing while I'm writing my dissertation to prepare for entering the academic job market?

John Komlos: As your dissertation nears completion, you should think about ways to disseminate that information and increase your visibility both on campus and beyond. That will ease your transition into the actual job-search phase. You should seek out every possible opportunity to talk about your research formally even before completing your thesis. You will benefit from presenting preliminary ideas and findings to a wider audience. The scholarly world thrives on the exchange of ideas, and the sooner you begin to practice making effective presentations, the better. The feedback that you receive from your audience is always helpful in letting you know how others see the problems you discuss.

You could talk about your dissertation while you are still in the field doing research away from your institution. Locals sometimes have a different perspective on the issues you raise and are also going to have more firsthand knowledge of the sources than you, and possibly your mentor. You can certainly profit from that, but be aware of the fact that research styles can vary considerably from country to country. Your approach might not be appreciated abroad as much as you would like, but you need to keep in mind the audience you are writing for: in the first instance, your dissertation committee.

In addition, you should start attending conferences—if you haven't already—in order to mingle with like-minded people, and especially to meet other people working in areas close to yours, both graduate students and faculty. You can exchange views on your progress so far and learn more about the research currently being done in your discipline. Such exposure helps to socialize you into the profession. You should propose to make a presentation at a smaller conference first because these are more informal and friendlier than larger meetings. Large meetings tend to be hectic because people are trying to talk to many people very briefly. You can start the ball rolling by asking your mentor to help you prepare a proposal to submit to the appropriate committee of the organization.

Penny Gold: And keep an eye out in the professional newsletter in your field (either in print or in electronic form) for announcements of conferences that may be of interest. (You should subscribe to one or two journals in your field or develop the habit of checking them on a regular basis at the library.) The call for papers will tell you how long the proposal should be (usually one or two pages suffice) and to whom it should be sent.

John Komlos: In addition, it would be extremely useful if you could start publishing while still in graduate school. There is no better way to impress upon the future readers of your curriculum vitae that you are serious about embarking on a life of scholarship than to show written evidence to that effect. Obviously, a chapter of your dissertation is a likely candidate to consider for early publication, but an article can be even shorter than that. For example, *Economics Letters* is a journal dedicated to short publications (four to six pages in length) that enables new results to be communicated quickly to the profession. Submitting an article at this point is desirable because it begins to get you thinking less about your research itself and more about disseminating it. If you succeed, it should help to build your self-confidence and will signal to the profession that you are not only well trained and intelligent, but also likely to be a productive scholar. With such a feather in your cap, your chances of landing a good job improve substantially.

Penny Gold: In some fields, competition is so strong that some publication is virtually required for success in the job market.

John Komlos: Another way to enhance your visibility is to review books in your field. Most of the main journals do not allow unsolicited book reviews, but you can still let them know of your willingness to be of service. They will keep a record of your expertise on file and will almost certainly contact you eventually. However, some of the lesser known journals have more difficulty finding reviewers and might be more open to specific suggestions. Write to the book-review editors, informing them of your research[1] and suggesting a book just published in your field that you would be willing to write about. This will give you valuable experience and allow the profession a glimpse of your own work.

Think of other ways of informing the profession of your "coming of age." Many dissertations qualify for consideration or nomination for a prize, for example. Ask your advisor, and also ask your librarian for compilations of such information. Many professional organizations have dissertation sessions at annual meetings where the results of your thesis can be presented. Try your best to get on one of those sessions (your mentor might have to recommend you). Once your thesis is completed, send copies to major figures in the field, soliciting comments for revision prior to publication. The point is that you ought not to keep your work a secret. Information on your thesis is not transmitted instantaneously, and there is no stigma attached to trying to help the process along, as long as you do not overdo it (say, by pestering people).

Penny Gold: I agree that sending one's work to scholars beyond one's dissertation committee is a very useful step. But if the purpose is simply to inform others of one's work, I would send something smaller, and published. I'd send the dissertation (unless it's very short, as it will be in some disciplines) to only a very few people, probably just one or two, whom you have reason to think would be able to give you helpful suggestions for revision. It's a lot to ask of someone. I've found people to be very generous with their time—people prominent in the field whom I did not know personally—but there was always a good reason to send it to just this person (another scholar's recommendation, the closeness of their published work to my area of exploration).

John Komlos: Gee, I was more frivolous about sending my dissertation around. I must have sent a couple of dozen copies to scholars in the field. As I recall, I had some nice feedback, too. I did not regret the expense at all. Nowadays it is much simpler, of course, to use the Internet. As an aside, I might mention that I now have a distribution list of more than a thousand economic historians to whom I send information on my publications and those of graduate students working with me.

How should I prepare for presenting a paper at a professional conference?

John Komlos: Oral presentations have some things in common whether made in the context of an invited lecture, or a job talk, or a meeting of a professional organization. It can be a version of a completed chapter of your dissertation or part of your larger research project, but it must be self-contained; that is, you should coherently explore a specific question and provide some results with a plausible conclusion, even if still somewhat tentative. The results need not be earth-shattering. However, there should be some effort to clearly pose a question, develop an idea or a thesis, or resolve a controversy, while holding the audience's attention.

John Goldsmith: I have a talk with all graduate students who work with me before their first conference presentation in which I try to make them confront their worst enemy. They are always surprised to find out that everyone who's about to go public and make a presentation is challenged by a nasty voice inside their head that whispers, "Is that all you have to say? That's so obvious. People are going to think you are downright stupid if you stand up and read all of these obvious conclusions." This critical voice goes on to say that the program committee that accepted this paper obviously misunderstood the abstract and must have mistaken it for a paper with real substance.

I haven't yet met a student who hasn't admitted that that's exactly what is going round inside their head. They're stunned to find that they're not the only ones who have heard this nasty little voice in their heads! And the consequence of all this is that—in order to placate that voice—the student eliminates the material that is well worked out and well understood, only to focus on the part of the problem that they're currently struggling with, the part that they don't understand very well. Obviously, this is a recipe for disaster. You must take very seriously the idea that you should present only material that you understand very, very well. I don't mean you can't drop a speculative note at the end, but that's after all the work has been done; it's the dessert. If you talk well and cogently about even an old topic, chances are you will have something new to add; if you talk about something you don't understand yet, be prepared to feel frustrated and disappointed when your presentation is over because you will not have done your best to communicate something to your audience.

John Komlos: I urge you never to give a talk cold! Before you make a formal presentation, it is all but mandatory that you first give the talk to your peers and mentor as a test run in order to get some useful feedback. After making note of their suggestions, you should continue to practice your delivery, at home, with friends, on the airplane, or in your hotel room—that is to say, wherever possible, until you have perfected it. This training will be helpful to you later, when it comes time to give a campus talk as part of the interview process. Initially, you might even think about memorizing your talk if it improves your self-confidence or if you feel that it will improve your talk substantially. In other words, do whatever you need to do to fine tune your delivery.

John Goldsmith: I've been giving talks for twenty-five years, but if I have a very formal presentation to give, or a very limited amount of time, I still give my talk aloud, in my office with the door shut—and I may do it twenty times. It's important for inexperienced speakers to grasp the simple fact that public speaking is work and that it requires effort and preparation, and hours of it. I wish I could say this loud and long: good public presentation of difficult material requires as much training and preparation as professional athletics. It is an egregious faux pas not to prepare an oral presentation and not to spend all the time that it requires.

When preparing an important presentation, an absolute minimum is to have the text all written out ahead of time and, while preparing, to note in the margins where you are at one minute, two minutes, and so on, right up to twenty minutes, or fifty minutes, or however long the talk is. I think it is an inexcusable lapse to find oneself at the end of the allotted time of a formal presentation with something important still left to say.

While I'm on the subject, I'll mention one other point. Contrary to popular belief, speaking fast is not always a bad thing and, in and of itself, does *not* lead to being difficult to understand. What is much more important is pausing. Right. Pausing. Giving the audience a moment to process the sounds, process the thoughts—and perceive, from the pause, the importance of that last phrase. Repeat, when necessary—or when simply appropriate. But plan, prepare, and practice. And then practice some more.

John Komlos: I couldn't agree more. Performance counts a lot. There is no valid excuse for bungling. If the presentation means something to you (possibly leading to a job, after all), you should work on your delivery. And as John mentions, do not fear silence. It can be a powerful tool for communication. Unfortunately, graduate school does not actively teach public speaking except by example. There are few oral examinations and very few opportunities for improving one's ability to think out loud. So the responsibility to improve your oral communication skills rests with you.[2]

You should not rely exclusively on your mentor to pat you on the back, even if you have written a good dissertation. You need to seek confidence-building experiences elsewhere. You should actively seek out opportunities to talk about your research at workshops in other departments on campus, at other universities, wherever possible. With some successful talks behind you, your self-confidence will increase, and experience will translate into more coherent talks and, very important, the ability to field questions.

Conference papers are short—usually fifteen to twenty minutes. Make absolutely sure you stay within the limit if you do not want to alienate your fellow panelists and risk annoying your audience. Do not forget that even the most complicated ideas can be simplified for presentation, and your paper is no exception. A lecture need not go into great detail. That can be found in the written version for those interested.

The large national professional organizations usually have annual meetings, which provide great opportunities for advanced graduate students to present their work. In addition, these organizations often have regional affiliates that hold their own meetings. While a presentation at a regional meeting might provide only limited exposure, nonetheless, it does provide valuable experience and is more easily accessible. You should try to get on a panel at one of their meetings even before you have finished your dissertation. Ask your advisor if a completed chapter or seminar paper is suitable for presentation. Write to the organization in order to find out who is in charge of next year's program. Inquire about deadlines. Make sure that you plan well in advance because the lead time is always substantial. Proposals for a December meeting are usually due the previous February. Thus, you need to start to make plans a year in advance to get on a program. Make your case by sending the organizers a synopsis of your proposed presentation. Many organizations encourage graduate student participation.

Of course, the degree to which this is the case varies. For example, it is generally easier to obtain a slot on the program of the annual meeting of a regional association than on that of a national one. If your topic is interdisciplinary, you might try an organization in one of the sister disciplines. You should also find out which associations are particularly receptive to younger scholars. For example, if your topic has a historical component, you might try the Social Science History Association,[3] which welcomes younger scholars.[4] In other words, if you keep on trying, you should be successful in finding a venue for a presentation, and it is important that you do so. Your job talk, and hence your job chances, will be much improved if you have availed yourself of every opportunity to make presentations and lecture at professional meetings.

John Goldsmith: In my field, there are a number of regional meetings that have a higher professional profile than the national one. There is a certain homogenizing factor at the national meeting that is typically not present at the smaller meetings, which, in turn, can make the smaller meetings more theoretically high-powered. But I don't imagine that all fields are like that.

John Komlos: Do bear in mind that you can improve your chances of getting on a program of some professional organizations if you organize a complete panel consisting of a chairperson, three papers, and one or two discussants. Organizers generally prefer to receive such a proposal because that saves them the trouble of putting together the session themselves, a fairly time-consuming task. So if you know of others working in the same field, you might attempt to organize a panel on a theme. This is more time consuming than you might think. You have to contact potential presenters, obtain commitments, make sure they send you their proposals, and find commentators and a chair for the session (who might be one of the discussants). Note that even after you have a commitment, presenters might change their mind. So you might have to scramble to find a replacement. In addition, the panel might not be accepted, so your efforts might be in vain, except for the experience, which will be useful later. Initially, it might be best to get on a panel organized by your mentor or a colleague you've met at a previous meeting of the association.

The effort of organizing a panel or finding a suitable panel for your paper is well worth it, however. In addition to improving your self-confidence and enabling you to make contacts, presenting a paper gives you the opportunity to disseminate your ideas. Of course, it also looks good on your resume. Just as important, it will also improve your thesis by providing you new ideas and new perspectives on ideas you already have. I have never ever given a talk without benefiting from it in some way.

Penny Gold: I would underline the "making contacts" aspect of organizing a panel. In the early years of your career, this is a great way to move into (while sometimes also helping in the creation of) a network of people in your field. Besides the sheer pleasure of interaction with people working on subjects related to your own work (especially helpful later if you are teaching in an institution with no one else doing work close to yours), you will be getting to know people who may be in a position to help you—by reading your work in draft, giving you tips on places at which you're interviewing, writing letters of recommendation, and so on.

Should I go to conferences even if I am not going for a job interview or to give a talk?

John Komlos: Absolutely. Going to conferences is a good idea, even if you are not yet ready to make a presentation yourself, because it will afford you an opportunity to exchange ideas and to try out ideas on others. It is also a way to publicize your impending entry into the life of the organization. This is part of the process of your professionalization. You will meet scholars who were mere names to you until then. You will exchange information with graduate students from other universities and, through them, learn more about what others are doing in the field. You will sharpen your understanding of the convictions held by others on important unresolved questions in the discipline and develop ideas on the likely directions new research will take. In which direction should your research go when your dissertation is complete and you are no longer so closely attached to your mentor? Participation at a conference will also offer you an early look at how your work will be received by others.

In addition, you will learn about the rules and techniques of a formal presentation. You will see firsthand how others perform in stressful situations and what the unwritten etiquette of intellectual jousting at such meetings is. You will make acquaintances, and friends, some of whom might become important contacts eventually. You might obtain invitations to make presentations at workshops around the country. You can talk to publishers about your work in order to ascertain how receptive they appear to your research, even in a preliminary fashion. You can talk to journal editors to learn what they are looking for in a submission. You will have a chance to observe what awaits you when you go to a meeting as a full-fledged job seeker.

Do not be overwhelmed by the fact that you might not know anyone; after all, they all started out the same way.[5] In all the confusion, some people might appear rude in not following the rules of polite interaction: they might interrupt a conversation, or they might see someone across the floor, leave you in midsentence, and rush to shake hands with that person. It does take a bit of getting used to, but after several such meetings, you, too, will be accustomed to the different norms and be more comfortable in saying hello to people you met last time.

Penny Gold: A few more words on speaking with publishers' representatives. Editors are always on the lookout for promising manuscripts. The people at those publishers' booths are not just cashiers, but often the acquisition editors for your field, looking to talk with people about what they're working on. You can approach them cold at the conference, but more effective is to send letters a couple of months ahead of time to ten or twelve publishers who publish heavily in your field. Give a description of your work, say that you'll be at the upcoming meeting, and ask if they would be interested in speaking with you about your manuscript.[6]

How does the specific process of searching for a job begin?

John Goldsmith: In a sense, the process starts long before the student focuses on getting a job, since the job search involves the dissertation topic and conference presentations. But in a practical sense, the job search begins with the decision, made in consultation with the mentor, that the dissertation completion and defense are imminent and that it's time to send out letters of application to universities that have announced job openings. The job search also typically involves going to the profession's large annual national meeting, such as that of the Modern Language Association or the Linguistic Society of America.[7]

   A colleague of mine has pointed out to me a difference of strategy employed by graduate students finishing up. He distinguishes between a strategy of waiting until the dissertation is complete and then applying at once for all jobs that one conceivably qualifies for, on the one hand, and a strategy of applying for only the most attractive jobs over a period of several years, beginning perhaps even before one is quite ready, on the other. (Real people probably fall somewhere between the ends of this continuum.) His view, and mine, is that the second strategy is most likely to lead to disastrous results.

Penny Gold: Moreover, even if you succeed in landing a job that way, it's self-defeating to take one before you have the end of the dissertation somewhere in view (even if it's a long view). But there is also the annoying fact of needing to have some money to live on, and your fellowships and assistantships may give out before the dissertation is done. If you are within range of finishing the dissertation, taking a job might actually speed up the completion rather than slow it down, unlikely as that may seem at the time. This is because keeping your job beyond the first or second year will probably depend on completion of the degree, and there's nothing like a fixed deadline and the threat of loss of livelihood to give one motivation to finish!

John Komlos: The job market starts with advertisements appearing in early autumn, most frequently in the newsletters of professional organizations, some of them on the Web and continually updated. The *Chronicle of Higher Education* also lists job openings throughout the year in all disciplines, including some administrative openings for which you might qualify. In addition, you can write to or call colleges in your vicinity or in a location for which you have some preference.

How should you read the job advertisements?

John Goldsmith: Early and often. In many disciplines, most job announcements are well advertised with fliers that have been mailed to graduate departments throughout the country. But it's your life, after all: make the extra effort to look for other job opportunities. Foreign job openings will typically not be advertised through fliers.

John Komlos: Often the standard procedure is to have a dossier at your university's employment office, and you can request that your credentials be sent out to potential employers. This file is created as a general-purpose application dossier in order to save time and effort, but it does not suffice by itself. This dossier consists of a transcript, three letters of recommendation, and a resume, which includes an abstract of your dissertation, all written on standard forms provided for that purpose. Establishing such a file saves your advisor from having to send recommendation letters himself to each of the jobs you are applying for. Instead, he has to write only once, and the employment office does the rest of the work. However, such recommendations tend to be a bit too generic, and hence less effective, because they are not tailored to the specific needs of a particular opening. Thus, in cases where the match between your qualifications and the stated needs of the department in the job advertisement are not obvious, you should ask your mentor to write a more personal letter on your behalf. The other two recommendations would come from the other readers of your dissertation unless you had worked more closely with some other members of the faculty—as a teaching assistant, for example. The better known the professor is who recommends you, the more effective the letter is likely to be in getting you an interview, but the precondition is that he must be acquainted with your work to some extent or with another aspect of your graduate school performance. A generic letter of superlatives from even the best-known scholar is not likely to be of much help in obtaining you an interview. Of course, after the interview, the effect of the recommendation letters wears off very quickly. Thereafter, you will have to stand on your own merits.

You need to send a letter of application to the chair of the search committee, stating your interest in the announced opening and letting him know that your personal file is on its way. It is crucial that your cover letter be tailored to the specific application in order to emphasize that you are particularly qualified for the job, and you had better give it some serious thought. Highlight those aspects of your experience and achievements that make you especially suitable for the position, but that might not be immediately obvious from your dossier. You should again summarize your dissertation in a short paragraph, even though that is already included in your dossier. But, more important, do include some supplementary material that could support your application, such as teaching evaluations or publications. If you feel it might be appropriate, do send the introduction to your dissertation, or include a statement about your philosophy of education. Moreover, try to find some connection to members of the faculty. That implies that you should familiarize yourself with the department to some extent, at least through its Web site. Your mentor might even contact persons he knows in that department by phone or e-mail to stress the degree to which your qualifications meet the job description. You, however, should not call; instead, wait for them to contact you first.

Penny Gold: You may include more than three letters in your dossier, but don't overdo it, as each letter requires more time from the person reading the file. If you've taught a course at a neighboring college or university and someone from there can attest to your excellence as a teacher, have him write a letter. If not a letter, at least mention in your application the name of an individual who could be called. And if you've left your graduate institution and have been teaching elsewhere full-time (either in a temporary position or in one you would like to leave), be sure to have a letter from either the chair of that department or someone else in a good position to know how you've done there. Experience in teaching can be helpful to your candidacy elsewhere—and all the more so if someone can speak in detail about how you've done.

John Komlos: If I may interject a not-so-obvious caveat in this context: the person who is writing the letter on your behalf should be at an institution of approximately equal rank (or better) to the institution to which you are applying. Otherwise, in my experience, recommendations do not help, and can even detract from the strength of your application.

Penny Gold: If your job search lasts longer than one year, as it well might, you should be sure to keep your letters (and other parts of the dossier) updated. In particular, if you have finished your dissertation since the letters were written, you should ask all your recommenders to write a new letter for the file. Even if you get a job in your first year, you may still have your eye out for a better job, and your dossier can be used for a year or two beyond completion of the dissertation. Even if not much has changed, you should ask at least your advisor to redo the letter with a new date. Current letters will be more helpful to you than ones more than a year old.

On what to include with your application: I would advise a bit more caution in how much you send. A typical history search at my institution generates one to two hundred applications, and searches in English and philosophy can generate twice that many. This is a lot of paper to manage. If each candidate's material can all be put in one manila file folder, the secretary maintaining the files will thank you, as will the faculty, who have to carry armloads of files around for weeks, never mind reading them. Of course, if the job ad asks for samples of your work (as will certainly be done for a position in studio art or creative writing), then send them. But, otherwise, I advise waiting or sending something slim (e.g., an article reprint, a sample syllabus). If you survive the first cut, you will probably be asked for more material, and certainly will if you receive an invitation to campus, at which point you'll need to provide your whole dissertation, or however much is written.

John Komlos: I would be less concerned about overwhelming the departmental secretary with written material. Sure, it is a cumbersome task to choose a handful of candidates from a field of hundreds, but that is exactly why the applicant needs to use every bit of information to make the case that he is the best for the job. If you learn that a member of the search committee is in Iberian history and you have a publication in Portuguese, by all means do send it along.

Penny Gold: I would also add a caution about sending teaching evaluations: I am usually more impressed with a letter from someone at the institution where you've taught than with the teaching evaluations. If the teaching evaluations are qualitative (pages of student comments), one doesn't know if you are submitting all the comments or only the nice ones. Quantitative evaluations are more reliable in this regard, but without comparative data about what the average scores are at an institution (which some evaluations provide), they don't tell too much. I can't remember such enclosed evaluations ever being mentioned as a strong factor one way or another in any of the Knox College searches I've been on, even though we are concerned with candidates' preparation for teaching.

I would stress even further the importance of your own cover letter. Look at samples from peers who have recently been successful in the job market. Yes, each letter should be tailored to the particular institution, but you should first write a "stock" letter, which you then adapt for each separate job. Like the personal essay you wrote for admission to graduate school, it's this letter that is going to be the main distinguishing feature of your application, as there will be many other candidates who come from graduate schools similar to yours and who have stellar letters from professors of good reputation. And many candidates are doing fascinating work. Your letter will be scrutinized for what it can tell the committee about you, and certainly the articulateness and style of the letter itself will be judged, as the letter is its own kind of "writing sample." I take quite a few notes on each file I read, but what it comes down to is "Is this a person I'm eager to talk to?" It's your own voice that will convince me of this or not. Of course, you should have your advisor and perhaps another faculty member critique your basic letter before it goes out anywhere.

Because the letters in your file are of great importance to your success in the job market, you might consider asking one of your professors or a colleague at another institution to request a copy of your file and "vet" it for you. Your options are limited if someone has written a less than glowing letter, but if your reader tells you of a significant problem, you can ask to have that letter removed from your file and then find someone else to write for you.

John Komlos: Not all letters in the dossier are confidential. I think that professors have an option to make their letter available to the student who requested it, but, in general, I would be a bit more cautious about advising one to obtain confidential information through a third party. It really is at odds with the delicate relationship that should exist between mentor and student, and if found out, it can be a great detriment to further cooperation. I think that the student should be able to get a sense of what his advisor, mentor, and other professors in the department think of his abilities and prospects directly from his interactions with them.

Penny Gold: If there are things you do not want your recommenders to mention, let them know before they write the letter. For example, I would advise you to exclude personal data (marital status, children) from your own curriculum vitae, and if you go this route, you should also ask your recommenders to refrain from mentioning such. You might also ask them to refrain from mentioning physical characteristics (still sometimes mentioned for women) or any disabilities. Some characteristics will likely become known at some later point if you receive an interview, but there's no need to risk possible hesitancy from a prospective employer concerning issues you know to be irrelevant to your job qualifications. You should also sit down with your advisor and check that he has full information about your experience and accomplishments. Of course, he'll talk about your dissertation and your performance among your peers. But perhaps you've had informal teaching experiences he's not aware of, or even some significant community service work that you'd like him to mention. And if you are a member of an underrepresented minority, it would be helpful for him to mention that as well, as many institutions are working to bring more diversity to their faculties. Some minority candidates may prefer that such identifying information not be included in the dossier, and that is certainly a reasonable approach. If this is the case for you, you should mention your preference to your recommenders.

Why avoid giving out information about marital status and children? Because in my experience, such information can come up for comment in a way that detracts from a candidate's appeal, especially if the candidate is female. Remember that when the search committee is narrowing the field to ten or so candidates for conference interviews, there are many more than this number who are qualified. So various factors that may seem to interfere with the perfect suitability of a candidate are likely to arise at this time in the consideration, and even more so when the list is reduced to the three people who will be invited to campus, when the institution is investing a significant amount of money and time in each person brought. The main criterion is, of course, the academic excellence of the candidates.

But it is hard to prevent people from asking questions like these: How likely is this person to come here if we offer them the job? How well will this person fit into our kind of institution? These questions take some specific forms: Will someone who has lived their whole life in California really move to the Midwest, or stay here if they come? Will someone who has received their entire education in large universities adapt well to a small liberal arts college? Will someone who is married be willing to come here if there's no appropriate work for their spouse locally? Some of these questions you have no control over (geography, type of institution attended). But I recommend saving the personal data for a later point in the process, after an offer has been extended.

There's also a gender differential here. For male candidates, the marital status information seems not to impact, one way or another.[8] But I have often heard the concern raised for female candidates. Perhaps it is difficult for my male colleagues, particularly those of a somewhat older generation, to imagine that a man would actually be willing to move for the sake of his wife's job, even though we have examples at Knox where that has, indeed, been the case. Not surprising, since it would have been unheard of in their own generation, when wives routinely moved for husbands, but not vice versa. Depending on the location of the hiring institution, women may be in a no-win situation with regard to marital status; being single can also be held against you because of a concern—in a small town or city environment—that you will have an unsatisfactory social life and so be on the lookout to move. When I applied for my current job in 1975, I did not include on my c.v. the fact that I was married. The department assumed I was single, which I found out when we were having lunch and one of my future colleagues warned me that the social scene might be limiting for me in a city this small. I said that wouldn't be a problem, since I was married. That information set off questions about my husband, which I did my best to answer in a reassuring way. My husband was also a graduate student at the time, though not yet on the job market; I think it likely they saw this as a risk. I'm glad they hired me anyway! It's very common that once you apply for a job, you will start imagining scenarios of what life would be like if you get that job. What you may not realize is that a parallel imagining is often proceeding at the other end. I would recommend to both sides that these projections be held in check.

There is one major exception to early avoidance of information about marital status. If you and your spouse or partner are in closely related fields and you are willing to consider sharing one position, then it is in your best interest to present this as a proposal from the very beginning. Taking a passive approach (e.g., applying as separate candidates, hoping that you'll both reach the final cut and can talk about possible arrangements at that point) is unrealistic. So how to do this? You should each write separate application letters, as you are two separate people, but cross-reference each other's letter, explaining that you would like to be considered together for one shared position, and send the letters together in one envelope. My institution now has several shared appointments, and while it certainly is a financial sacrifice for the couple (the main down side), they are both able to do the work they love, in the same location, and it gives them the bonus of extra time for other activities (family life, research/writing, even leisure).

John Goldsmith: Going back to the issue of letters of recommendation, some professors—and I am one of them—prefer not to use the standard dossier. Linguistics is small enough that it is customary to get letters that have been personalized at least a little bit for each institution to which the letter is being sent. I am likely to want to add something about a student's work that is specifically aimed at people that I know at a given institution, and, of course, my letter will change over the course of months (or years) as the student in question completes more work or reaches other goals. I would add that in my experience—in my field—the substance of the applicant's letter is very important. This is an open opportunity to shine and to give some information about your interest, experience, and plans. Letters of recommendation vary a great deal. I'm sure I've read many, many hundreds of these letters, and I continue to be struck by how much work goes into their writing by some of the busiest people in my profession. At some level, the detail of the letter is intended to give the impression that the candidate's papers have been so important to the letter writer (ever since the candidate was a lowly first-year graduate student) that he remembers each and every one of them. And this can be very effective! Of course, there's an irony involved because it does, indeed, happen that the letter from the advisor is head and shoulders above the letter written by the candidate as far as intellectual rigor and punch are concerned.

Let's not overlook the importance of a good c.v.—a good curriculum vita (or vitae). This is a short document that gathers together the essentials of your academic career, from your education (college and beyond) through your employment, your conference presentations, your publications, your grants and scholarships (if you have received any), and, in many cases, the names of scholars who may be contacted for written evaluations.

Putting together a good c.v. is not an easy task, though having the right stuff to report in it is even harder! I can offer just two pieces of advice: get hold of at least a half dozen examples (it's not too hard to find them on the Web these days, and you can ask people for copies, explaining your reason) to look at before you put yours together, and then show it to people (especially faculty members) when you've put together a draft. Find out if you've left anything out, or put in too much. If you have some experience with drafting a resume, do bear in mind that the task here is similar, but by no means the same. A c.v. tends to have less text and explanation, and it may be longer (many suggest that a resume be no longer than two pages, or even one, while there is no limitation on how long a c.v. may be). Do be sure to highlight the most important items by placing them strategically.

John Komlos: Your c.v. must be accurate and complete: there is absolutely no room for mistakes or a hiatus in your career without an explanation. Your c.v. should be clearly formulated, concise, and coherent and have an esthetic appeal. It should highlight all your achievements and contain a short paragraph on your dissertation. Members of the search committee usually do not have more than twenty seconds for the initial screening of a c.v., so you do not have much time to introduce yourself, explain what your research is all about, and impress the reader that you are the one the department is looking for. There is no room for error: misspellings, contradictions, grammatical mistakes, awkward phrases, and chronological gaps can cause your c.v. to land in the wrong pile very quickly. In addition to the obvious information, the c.v. might also include forthcoming publications (i.e., those already accepted); papers currently being refereed; papers completed, but not yet submitted to a journal; and research projects under way. Note also that the c.v. needs to be attractive.

Penny Gold: A word on chronological gaps, which can occur for a variety of reasons, some of them potentially unappealing to some employers. Age discrimination is illegal, but that doesn't mean that people don't experience it. When people are hiring at a junior level, they usually have an image in their mind of someone "junior," and a person of their own age or older may create, for some, an uncomfortable (even if illegal) dissonance. If, for example, you're a woman who didn't begin graduate school until age forty, after you had raised a few children, how should you deal with that gap on your c.v.? Since it's typical to put dates of degrees on your c.v., if you've received your B.A. twenty years ago, people will know you've been doing something else, so you may as well make a brief note of it. Some people try to prevent age discrimination by putting no dates at all on their educational career, but that only tips people off that you're trying to disguise your age. No need to hide anything if some years out of academia were in some other line of work, though some professions are more appealing than others (law, for example, as opposed to elementary education or secretarial work). Perhaps the most awkward gaps—or the ones about which people will have the most curiosity—are ones that come after your dissertation has been completed. I think it's always better to let people know what you've been doing than to give them a gap that may fill up with their uncontrollable imaginings.

John Komlos: Because of the keen competition for positions, a little extra help from your mentor can be extremely useful. Some advisors are actually willing to go to great lengths to "create a market" for their students, that is, to enhance their prospects. Others are less inclined to do so for philosophical or practical reasons. Some mentors are willing, on their own initiative, to send out a mass mailing to their friends announcing your impending entry into the job market. Such extra efforts are extremely important because they provide a kind of "guarantee" backed by your advisor's reputation. In effect, he is saying that he is willing to put his friendships and reputation on the line on your behalf, promising that you will not disappoint them. While you may not know if your mentor is willing to undertake such an effort before you start to work with him, such factors will obviously have influenced the success he has had in placing his students, and this is information you should have very soon after you enter the program. Professors interested in maintaining a steady stream of graduate students have an incentive to find employment for them because that is one way to convince future generations of students to work with them. Your mentor might also ask colleagues to write on your behalf to persons they know at the institutions to which you are applying.

Some programs, such as the economics department at the University of Chicago, rate the students entering the job market in order to make it easier for prospective employees to sort out the applicants' qualifications. The ratings, along with a brief description of the dissertation topics, are mailed out to major departments. The top handful of departments will absolutely not even interview students unless they are ranked at the very top of a graduating cohort.

Penny Gold: My own opinion is that this practice is unfair to the graduate students and not always helpful to the hiring departments, whose judgments on merit may not match those of the graduate department. But given that it sometimes happens, I would advise you to still apply for jobs in which you are interested, even if you have not been rated at the top of your cohort. There's no harm in giving the hiring department an opportunity to make an independent judgment. A similar thing can happen in a less formal way—and you will not necessarily be aware of it. In their individual letters of recommendations, professors may compare you to other students they know are applying for the same job. (This would rarely happen in a standard letter written for your dossier, but could happen in an individualized letter sent in for a particular job.) But in my experience, this is fairly rare. Most professors do their best to write good letters for each of their students, and the search committee is then left to weigh the particular adjectives and verbs used.

John Komlos: Given the amount of information that must be processed in an extremely short amount of time, hiring committees automatically rely in the first instance on the judgment of the home institution as a kind of upper bound on your abilities. They realize that if the department errs, it will do so on the positive side. If your advisor did not think highly of you, the department will not either, and the hiring committee will consider that ranking in its own evaluation. It is convenient information.

Of course, selection of candidates is a complex and uncertain process, at times perhaps even chaotic. Dissertations have to be read (or at least looked at), letters of recommendation evaluated, and interviews completed before one has a basic impression of the candidate. Even with such a carefully orchestrated process, the possibility of misjudgment remains. Letters of recommendation are often full of superlatives. Even for average students, they are sometimes quite laudatory: "Ms. Palmer is among the best two or three graduate students with whom I have had the pleasure to work since I came to the University." What that sentence really means is not at all obvious because the author failed to note how many students he had in all. If he had only two or three students in total, the recommendation is not as laudatory as it sounds. Yet the statement is not false, though it is difficult to interpret. So search committees have learned to read between the lines and with some skepticism. If there are any reservations on the part of the mentor, they are generally couched in such oblique language that they will be apparent only to the trained eye. I exaggerate, perhaps, so that you can understand clearly how difficult the search committee's task is of choosing a short list of the most suitable candidates for a position. Insofar as it is an extremely time-consuming task to evaluate applications, special efforts of your advisor or department can help you to gain the benefit of the doubt.

How high should one set one's aspirations?

John Komlos: I'd like to emphasize that it's important to ascertain if your mentor's assessment of your work coincides with your own. He must be an enthusiastic supporter, for otherwise your chances of landing a decent job are minimal. Others will think that if your mentor, who knows your scholarly qualifications best at this time, does not support you enthusiastically, then what sense does it make for them to invest the time and energy to obtain an independent judgment of your potential? It is much more cost effective to rely on your mentor's opinion in the first instance. Hence, I would argue that your mentor's candid view of you should be considered as the upper bound of your current (as opposed to your future) aspirations.

Both the advisor and the student are obviously in a delicate position, and it is very important to listen carefully to what the mentor is actually saying—and implying. What he is *not* saying can be just as important. The mentor may be trying to communicate his assessment indirectly without hurting anyone's feelings, and being blunt is not considered good form in our culture. Picking up on this is difficult for those who have devoted years of effort to honing their logical faculties on clearly expressed propositions. It might not be easy for you to ascertain exactly how your mentor rates your abilities unless you are an exceptional student. Most professors (myself included) are not forthright enough to tell you if you are a B— scholar in their estimation, even though this would be an extremely important piece of information for you to possess. Instead, they will resort to subtle ways of suggesting to you that you need to lower your sights, perhaps by slight modulations in their responses to your queries. You should listen carefully: the subtext might really be that he does not think you have the necessary attributes to get that particular job. He is embarrassed to tell you outright and would be also embarrassed to recommend you to his colleagues there. Within the realm of polite conversation, it remains for him only to intimate his evaluation of you, which gets him off the hook momentarily. You should be aware that there are usually multiple interpretations of your achievements. If you are open to subtle clues, you might be able to avoid applying for positions that are out of your reach.

Penny Gold: One way you might solicit a clear sense of your advisor's estimate of you would be to go in with a list of current job openings in the field and ask for advice on which of these he thinks you would have a chance at. The concrete scenario of specific institutions may more readily solicit a realistic assessment of what he sees as your potential than a more general inquiry.

What happens after I've sent out my application letters?

John Komlos: Once the application letters have been sent out, the ball is no longer in the applicant's court. In many fields, the standard practice is for the chair of the search committee to contact by phone those candidates who made the first cut and ask them to meet with the committee at the annual meeting of the professional organization. You should keep a schedule to make sure you are not going to have conflicts or interviews too close to one another. Initial impressions are important at this stage; hence, you need to avoid the embarrassment of being late to an interview at all costs. Self-confidence and an air of competence are crucial throughout the remainder of the process. If at all possible, you should avoid back-to-back interviews because you may appreciate being able to relax and think a bit about what just transpired before you proceed to the next one. Because the meetings can be spread out over several hotels that are not always conveniently located, you should give yourself a minimum of half an hour between interviews if you want to be on the safe side.

John Goldsmith: In my field, interviewing at the national meeting is by no means a requirement for the candidate hoping to make the "short list" (that is, the list of those to be invited to the campus for a real interview). When we're doing the interviewing at the meeting, we're pleased to be able to meet candidates there because we can eliminate people who looked good on paper, but clearly don't fit with what we're seeking, and also because we can look at a wider range of candidates and perhaps boost someone up to the "must invite" category who looked only modestly interesting from the written materials we had received. But when we know we have an outstanding candidate, we know it whether we have met them at the Linguistic Society meeting or not.

Penny Gold: On the other hand, the candidate cannot count on this if a conference interview is offered. Should you go to the conference (which means a sizable expenditure of money) if you have only one or two interviews? I would say yes, or you risk being eliminated from the search entirely. An exception may be made if you're abroad, and sometimes an employer will be willing to meet briefly with you on campus if you are close by the institution. But that is rare because it is rightly seen as giving unfair advantage in comparison with candidates interviewed serially in the neutral setting of the conference.

As John Goldsmith says, the conference interviews can significantly alter the search committee's assessment of individual candidates, either in your favor or against you. In fact, I always find this humbling, as it shows the extent to which one cannot fully rely on paper credentials to know what a candidate will be like in person.

How is it decided who will be chosen for an interview?

John Komlos: Selecting a list of people to interview at the conference is a challenging task for a committee. We are fortunate to have an oversupply of very smart people, and usually the committee has plenty of comparably good candidates to choose from. In such cases, the reputation of the school and that of the mentor matter a lot. In addition, the committee often looks for small differences, such as taste in research: What kinds of issues do you find attractive? Will you be a good citizen in the department? Your social skills also matter. In a pool of equally qualified candidates, the impact of slight differences is likely to be magnified. This is true at all scales of the academic hierarchy, although stellar performers will be at a disadvantage at a below-average department. This is the case because equals generally attract equals. Colleagues very often do not want to be outperformed.

John Goldsmith: The task of reading job ads has some subtleties that may deserve some consideration. Job ads tend to be short, communicate relatively little information, and, in many cases, are worded sloppily or written by people who will play only a minor role in the final job selection. A job ad may specify some subareas as "desirable," but it's impossible to divine from outside just what that means. It may mean that a few members of the faculty would really like someone with that specialization, but the rest of the faculty really don't care, or it may be a strong preference. You really can't tell. If you think you have a good chance even though your field is not the one that is apparently desirable, it would be prudent to apply.

Our department is going through the process of searching for a junior appointment right now, so a number of points are very much on my mind. I might mention how I read the applications that come in. I use my computer and make a chart for each application and letter of reference that arrive on my desk, and after I've seen all the material for a given candidate, I make an initial division into three categories: the truly outstanding, the ones not worth rereading, and everyone else. I think of these as categories A, C, and B, respectively. When I'm done, I reread all of the dossiers briefly, just to remind myself why I had categorized them into these three rough categories as I had. The sad fact of the matter is, then, that it's only those in the top category, category A, that make my first cut. Now, I'm not the only one involved; all the members of the search committee are ranking the candidates, and some of my category B names are going to be top candidates for someone else, and that's fine with me. But if someone else pushes a name that is on my category C list, I'll argue against it, giving reasons why I think that person is not worth our consideration.

I find I put around 10 percent of the applicants into category A. I'm actually trying all the time to make it smaller than that, but I keep finding people doing amazing work about whom I'd like to hear more. But if we have 100 candidates, that means there are about 10 people I'd like to interview, and perhaps have come visit us. Unfortunately, our dean has given us far too little money to bring in 10 visitors; we can realistically aim for only 3 or 4. So other factors will come into play in eventually settling on a short list. It's difficult to know ahead of time what those factors will be. But every applicant should know that even the details count in cases like these.

Penny Gold: It's true that the job ad is only an imperfect reflection of a complicated mix of departmental desires, so you shouldn't cross off a job from your application list just because the description doesn't fit you perfectly. On the other hand, you should take into account the specifics of the ad in your cover letter. Let's say the ad solicits applicants in modern European history, with preference given to candidates who can also teach African history. If you have some background in the secondary field, describe its extent. If you have no background, but would be willing to learn enough to teach it (with some credibility, given, for example, your work in British imperial policy), then say that. If you don't mention the second-

ary fields at all, it will be assumed that you have neither background nor
interest in that area. It is still well worth applying for the job, as the ad
language indicates that the main concern is modern European history, and
if no outstanding candidates appear with African history, someone else
will be hired. And if your main field is African history and your secondary
field is modern European? I'd say it's worth applying for the job, but keep
your hopes of an interview low.

There are nonadvertised factors that will inevitably come into play
when the search committee faces the daunting task of narrowing the field.
Your methodology, for example, may be either a good mesh (a behavioral
psychologist in a department that favors such an approach) or a useful
supplement (a diplomatic historian in a department otherwise filled with
social and intellectual historians). You may come from a school where
people on the committee have personal—and hence emotional—ties. Or
there may be so many people already in the department from your school
that this is a negative factor. Since there are so many factors out of your
control, all the more reason to take great care with the part of the process
that is in your control—that is, your presentation of yourself in your cover
letter.

What happens if I do get an interview?

John Goldsmith: Let's consider first an interview at a professional meeting,
such as that of the Modern Language Association. Here you may be meeting one person or a committee of several people, who have just a brief
period of time to speak with you, and possibly answer questions that you
may have.

What is an interview about? Many things, and all at the same time.
The first is to get a sense of your personality: as the expression goes, they
want to see if you have two heads or just one, like everybody else. About
this, there's nothing you can do: you've come too far now to do anything
about your personality other than wear it for all to see. But you will surely
do your best to be charming, in your own particular and unique fashion.

Beyond personality, there are specific things that the interviewer will
be looking for. The job will most likely have a number of specific qualifications attached to it, and the interviewer will want to have some sense
that you fit that description. If an English Department feels the need for
someone who does nineteenth-century English novels, then you should

know something about *Jane Eyre*. Much of that will be on your c.v., but you can't assume that your interviewer knows what is there. It will be your job to acquaint the interviewer with your background.

Behind this transmission of simple information is a more important tacit message, though. When a department is hiring a professor, it is looking for someone who can work autonomously and responsibly to carry out the functions that the department needs carried out: typically, preparing, organizing, and teaching certain courses; advising students; and—last on the list—interacting with other faculty members of the department.

This is a point that is often completely missed by graduate students preparing for their first job, for quite understandable reasons. They may expect the major requirement to be a fit between their research interests and those of the department they are about to join. This is important, no doubt about it—but only in an indirect way, most of the time.

In an interview situation, the message the candidate should attempt to get across is that he is capable of getting the job done without supervision and without extra input from the other members of the department. If a music department is hiring someone to teach music theory, for example, it wants to be convinced, first and foremost, that the candidate has mainstream music theory under his belt and that he will be able to provide the appropriate kind of training to its students with no questions asked. It's all well and good that the candidate has revolutionary new ideas that will change the course of history; what the department needs to have taught are well-established courses, and it's that basic competence that the hiring department will want to be assured of. The revolutionary ideas will certainly be important for establishing a publication record, and when longer on-site interviews come, these ideas will come more into focus. But the first impression must be one of general competence, plain and simple.

Penny Gold: My experience with interviewing is a little different. We spend about half the interview talking about research and about half on teaching. In fact, I think we're likely to spend more time on research in the conference interview, knowing that this may be the easiest thing for graduate students to talk about, and to spend more time on the teaching aspect once a candidate comes in for a campus interview. We typically begin each section with a general question and then follow up in a variety of directions. You should certainly be prepared to answer queries like these: "Tell us about your research." "What contribution is your research making to the field?" "What other research topics might you pursue?" "What do you most look forward to teaching?" "How might you structure an introductory course in the field?" "What are your primary goals in an introductory course?"

John Komlos: Needless to say, this is a critical moment in your career. Let's say that you have been contacted by one of the universities to which you've applied, to schedule an interview with you at the national meeting.

The higher your department and mentor have ranked you, the earlier you are likely to be contacted by search committees. Most of the preliminary arrangements will be made about a month in advance, but in a few cases, I have seen them being made at the last minute as well—this largely depends on the speed with which a search committee moves through the files and makes its decisions. You should sound professional and straightforward on the phone (your answering machine message, too!). No inflated claims or jokes are expected.

By the way, the expenses of this preliminary interview are borne by you. An unexpected major problem you may face is finding out the room number in the hotel where the interview is going to take place. While organizations have registers where this information could, in principle, be found, professors do not always take the trouble of registering. The hotels do not give out the room numbers of their guests, so you will have to call well in advance in order to find out where the interview will take place. Do not leave this to the last minute! You must avoid being late for the interview or arriving in an anxious state because of the problems you have encountered in locating the room. Hotels have a limited number of phones, and they are often overburdened with hundreds of applicants seeking to contact their respective search committees. Some of the in-house phones can be out of order, in which case you might need change or a credit card to use pay phones. So do give yourself plenty of time because all sorts of things can go wrong. For instance, I remember one interviewer gave me the wrong name of the hotel where she was staying, and I had to scramble to find out where she actually was staying. Or there might be more than one search committee from a given university, and that might confuse matters. So the search for the venue might take longer than you expect. The price for appearing late is too high to take chances, and you will not be relaxed if you are rushing.[9]

Some graduate students entering the job market from top departments would like others to believe that they are really outstanding scholars by exhibiting a level of self-confidence that often comes off as arrogance. They think this is a reasonable strategy in a competitive market, where interviewers might use candidates' assessments of themselves as an indicator of their potential contribution to the profession (in the same way that some people use price as an indicator of the quality of a product). I do not know whether such a strategy does, in fact, pay off. Perhaps it does in the short run. Yet I personally would not recommend it.

Penny Gold: My main advice to people going off for any sort of interview is to *be yourself*. It's counterproductive to try to shape what you say and how you present yourself to what you think the other people might want to hear. For one thing, you can't know what they want to hear, and you may badly misjudge them. But even if you have somehow figured out how to "please," such efforts are usually transparent. Teachers have a good deal of experience with being played up to by students, and it's not any more pleasant in job candidates. Also, the line between careful shaping of self-presentation and misrepresentation or lying is quite fine, and you don't want to get tied up trying to make yourself look consistent so you're not "found out." This doesn't mean you need to volunteer information that you're pretty sure the committee would interpret negatively. (For example, as an East Coast person who's never been west of the Hudson, don't say to an institution in Iowa, "I really can't imagine myself living in the Midwest.") Tact is a good quality to foster. Now, how to follow my advice to "be yourself" if you're generally a tactless person? This is a challenge you'll need to work on long before your first job interview.

John Komlos: However, you also need to think about yourself from the point of view of the interviewer. If you know you have certain undesirable habits, you might want to think about them consciously. For example, if you tend to give short answers to questions, you might want to practice how to expand upon them because they might not be effective. Suppose you are asked if you would like to live in Iowa. An affirmative answer will not be terribly helpful unless you can say something about driving through once, or visiting Des Moines, or hearing stories from relatives about it. And that may not come to you automatically.

Penny Gold: The same advice I gave above—"be yourself"—applies to the issue of what to wear to the interview. Wear something that you're comfortable with as being "you"; otherwise, your physical discomfort in the costume will probably be projected. And at this all-important, most nerve-wracking of occasions, your goal is to be calm, collected, and articulate! You also want your interviewers to be focusing on what you're saying, not on what you're wearing, so don't wear something so attention-getting that it is a distraction to the conversation. This is a lot easier for men than for women, as there is a basic "uniform" for men that will pass for almost all occasions: a sports jacket, tie, and most any kind of pants other than jeans. A suit is not necessary. If you're very uncomfortable in a tie, even this could be modified (maybe a shirt and vest instead, or a jacket and sweater). For women, there's no uniform, and since women are more likely to be judged on their clothing (no difference from the nonacademic world here), there's greater risk in what you do wear. Besides the general advice of wearing something that is "you" and in which you are comfortable, here are some things to avoid: Don't bother with a "power suit," as though you were interviewing for a *Fortune* 500 firm. Don't wear a low-cut top or a very short skirt—you want the interviewers looking at your face, not your cleavage or your legs. Be sure you're as comfortable sitting in the outfit as standing. Do take a couple of outfits to a friendly female professor who is experienced with job searches and ask her opinion. If you go to your national meeting once or twice before interviewing, note what people are wearing. At some meetings (like the Modern Language Association), high fashion is in mode, while at others conservative garb predominates. And if you find yourself spending as much time thinking about your clothing as about how you'll answer questions about your dissertation, rest assured that you have lots of company. When women can stop worrying about what they wear, we'll really have equity in the academy.

John Komlos: People attribute all sorts of personality characteristics to one's clothing, and while there is a certain uniformity of expectations for men, they do vary some by institution. I find, for example, that hats can be quite a problem, especially during winters. I was taken out to a restaurant for dinner for an interview, and I wore a beret I bought in the Pyrenees, and the minute I met my interviewer in front of the hotel, I inferred from his look that this was one job I was not going to get. Perhaps he thought I was too much of an intellectual for his campus, or that I was too much of an individualist, or that I was a radical of some sort. I do not know what he thought, but I do know that all I wanted to do was to avoid getting a cold. I succeeded in that, but did not get a job offer. My Russian hat was in the cleaners. Perhaps that would have worked better.

Penny Gold: One other warning about subterranean aspects of the interview. It may be that among the people who are interviewing you there are deep personal or political divides. If you feel hostility during the interview, it may be because of this rather than because of anything you have said.

It may be that some questions are asked in an effort to see whose "side" you would be on if you joined the department. If you see this in the making, all you can do is go forward with your best combination of straightforwardness and tact.

What should be avoided during an interview?

John Komlos: No committee in the real world—as opposed to the ideal one, the one in which none of us lives—can be run completely democratically. The chair of the search committee, as well as the membership of the committee itself, is usually determined by the chair of the department and has not been decided by departmental vote. Wherever there is a group of people, there is a hierarchy, and it is unavoidable on the search committee. Some people may be put on the committee because they are easily influenced by others. The distribution of influence within the committee will not be known to you; hence, the only reasonable approach for you to take is to be open to signals to that effect, while being as cautious as possible.

Initially, it is prudent not to commit yourself to extreme positions. You need to be diplomatic, without making too many assumptions about what is expected of you. Keep an open mind about the wording of the advertisement, and try to have the committee members interpret it for you. Try to ascertain what characteristics are really sought by the department. Do not think that what ought to be actually is. In our academic culture, political convictions, for instance, ought not be one of the open grounds on which hiring decisions are made. But there is no reason to think that the committee you are actually facing will live up to that ideal perfectly. People might well be "snookered" (eliminated) on the basis of their ideological position as well as on some personal attribute or eccentricity that theoretically ought not have been taken into consideration. My beret anecdote above is one such example. With so many equally good applicants, it is much easier to exclude than to include someone. Try your best to avoid giving anyone an issue that can be used as an ostensible reason to eliminate you from competition. The real reason why someone might want to do so might be entirely different from the one asserted. Yet, in the absence of a valid alternative, people resort to the use of any possible publicly acceptable reason to argue against you.

The committee members are interested not only in your scholarly attributes. They will judge you as a potential colleague and teacher as well, and this aspect is usually as important as your intelligence and accomplishments. Thus, your self-confidence and ability to express yourself clearly are also crucial factors. Your potential colleagues would like to have some idea of how pleasant (or confrontational) you will be in department meetings and how effective a teacher you will be. These issues will surface again and again if and when you obtain an on-campus interview as well as much later when you are considered for promotion. Remember that you are not making a firm commitment to anything during the initial conversation. The interviewers just want to probe your mind a bit in order to get a sense of how you think on your feet about certain issues. How responsive are you to questions? How open are you to criticism and suggestions? Do you have any unusual desires, hidden agendas, extreme political positions? Someone might ask you, for instance, if you are willing to teach at night, not necessarily because there is a real need for it, but because he might want to see how flexible you are. Thus, even if this might not be most desirable as far you are concerned, unless you come across as someone who is genuinely willing to do so without reservations, you are diminishing your chances. I have seen people be eliminated on similarly trivial points, inasmuch as people can use such responses as a proxy for more fundamental attributes in your personality. A response such as "I have not thought about that" might unnecessarily leave some people wondering how much time you will need to think about minor decisions before you can make up your mind. Note that an affirmative, even enthusiastic, answer does not mean that you will be asked to teach at night once you actually obtain the job. In addition, you can always change your mind. So your response at that point ought to be considered not as a firm commitment, but rather as a test of your flexibility or interest in the job.

Even though it is hard under such circumstances, try to relax as much as possible. Keep in mind that this interview is preliminary; hence, your responses should also be preliminary. A too enthusiastic response, such as "Yes, I'd love to teach at night," perhaps sounds insincere, even if it were true, since most people's preferences are different (but even that exaggerated answer might be rescued by adding quickly: "I am a night person anyway"). Note, however, that from that answer the interviewers have learned a lot about your personality, which is what they really had in mind.

Invariably, you will be asked about your dissertation. You should anticipate such questions by preparing a three-minute summary in advance. You can expect plenty of discussion, and experience in fielding questions will come in handy at that point. The interviewing committee members might be reluctant to ask personal questions (many of which are inappropriate, or even illegal), but they would like to know if you have any outstanding commitments that would make it difficult for you to accept the job if it were offered. You might hint that you are flexible as to your place of residence or that your spouse's profession gives him sufficient flexibility in employment to allow him to relocate.

Penny Gold: I wish interviewing committees were more reluctant to ask personal questions! Even if inappropriate or illegal, they will sometimes come up, and then you are in the awkward situation of figuring out what to say. "That question is illegal and I won't answer it" will probably not go over very well. Information about marital status and spouse employment situation or moveability is relevant only after an offer is made, even though an employer is understandably curious about these things earlier on. But, given that the questions may come up, how should you reply? I wish I had a good answer. I would urge that you not take Ms. Mentor's advice, which is to lie and say your husband is a free-lance writer.[10] Besides being unethical, it's silly, since if you get the job, the truth will come out, and your colleagues will only have learned that they shouldn't trust you. If asked if you're married, I'd suggest you give a brief yes or no, and not go further unless they ask another question. If you've said yes and they ask follow-up questions, I'd keep your responses short and stress flexibility, as John Komlos recommends. You might ask, "Would this make a difference to you?"

John Komlos: I would be concerned that a *terse* answer might be misinterpreted, however. A quick "Yes, I am" might well be interpreted as also implying "So, and what of it?" I see no harm in being a bit more forthcoming, though I do agree in principle that only one's academic credentials should count. However, in the real world, committees do make judgments based on any number of personal issues, and the fit has to be reasonable from their point of view.

Your research area will certainly be a significant factor in your candidacy. Scholars are always looking for colleagues to whom they can talk about their work because that helps them in their own research. If you have similar interests, you are likely to be plugged into the same scholarly network, and your work may jointly increase the department's visibility in that niche of the discipline. You may also be able to serve as second reader on dissertation committees chaired by the more senior colleague. So, by bringing you on board, the department would be getting not only, say, a labor economist, but also someone whose presence would contribute to building a program in that field. Note that your diversification in your

studies could very well start paying dividends now. There might be someone on the committee, for example, who is interested in demography, so
it could help you immensely if you have developed that subspecialty in
addition to your work in labor economics. At the same time, you need to
be careful how you stress this skill. If you ask innocuously, "May I teach a
course in demography?" it might be taken as your really saying, "I am not
that interested in teaching labor economics; I am really a demographer."
It might also give the impression, even if false, that the future course of
your research will take a detour from mainstream labor economics toward demography. In addition, such a question could be interpreted as
offering competition to the senior scholar in that field, who might want
to continue to teach the introductory course, having invested considerable energy into developing it, and would like you to take a back seat
for awhile. Caution is required to gain maximum advantage from your
diversification.

Penny Gold: Toward the end of the interview, you may be asked if you
have any questions for the committee. One question might be "How
much choice do people have to teach what they want and to develop new
courses?" Some departments have very fixed curricula, and you will be told
exactly what you have to teach, while others have a great deal of flexibility.
This is a legitimate question and will also tell you what you may like to
know about how far afield you will be expected—or allowed—to go in
your teaching.

John Komlos: I agree that it is important to have some questions for the
interviewers. Otherwise, they might think that you lack interest in their
department. Yet I would be more cautious about asking outright about
flexibility because if there is not much of it, then the committee just
might interpret your legitimate and perhaps innocent question as implying that you are *looking* for flexibility and, therefore, that there might
be a mismatch between your expectations and what is possible in the department. A question such as "What other needs might the department
have?" or "What other courses would you like me to teach?" might be
more neutral.

John Goldsmith: Among the most important words of advice that I can give
to someone who has applied to a particular university is to develop a real
interest in what they do there. Suppose you're a graduate student in lin-

guistics, and there's an opening at the University of Oregon, and you've been invited to an interview at the Linguistic Society meeting. Fire up your computer, get on the Web, and, first off, learn the names of everyone in the department, and find out what they do. In the best case, you'll already know many of the professors there by reputation and will have read papers by some of them. Take time to study these people and their work. If you can make some connections between your work or interests and those of professors or students at the University of Oregon during your interview, then do so. It will help you immensely. There's nothing phony about this; quite the contrary. You're taking your job seriously. It astonishes me how few students actually do this. If you can say something intelligent (sympathetic or critical—it doesn't much matter) about one of their publications to everyone you meet—well, I've never seen it happen, but it would make a very good impression, to say the least!

Let's talk a little about teaching experience as well. Most search committees will care very much about undergraduate teaching. My feeling is that interviewers looking to fill any job at a four-year college or at virtually any large public university will place an extremely high value on undergraduate teaching. You can expect to have some leading questions thrown at you about this subject. It is your job to see this as an opening to express interest in undergraduate teaching (and I would hope that this interest is genuine). I would advise you to discuss this topic during the interview in as much detail as the interviewer seems to want. The student obviously knows less about teaching than he does about his research topic, but the interviewer wants to know about teaching: so talk about teaching. I remember one professional meeting where a student of mine had an interview with the committee from a large state university. The next morning one of the interviewers (whom I knew personally) came up to me and said that she regretted that Candidate X had so little to say about teaching introductory linguistics. Now I knew for a fact that the student had in her briefcase some very nice handouts she had prepared for an undergraduate course she was teaching that semester, but apparently she never took them out. In the end, she hadn't put her best foot forward, and she didn't make the next cut.

Until recently, it was generally assumed that a candidate's teaching would be adequate, particularly if he had given an effective job talk. However, it has been increasingly recognized that this has not always led to the expected results in teaching quality, and universities are becoming much more conscious of the need to advise and train graduate students to become effective active teachers.[11]

After an initial interview at a conference, should I contact the faculty members who interviewed me there?

John Goldsmith: I don't think there's a single answer to this question. Some might feel that a thank-you note is simple courtesy, and it certainly couldn't hurt. If that's your feeling, then send one, and forget it. On the other hand, if some real professional issue was joined in the conversation and you either have written something on the subject or know of a reference that the interviewer didn't know, but seemed interested in, then by all means continue the conversation with some e-mail or send a copy of the paper. But do realize that this is a miserable time of year for professors as far as demands on their time are concerned, so don't expect anything back in return.

What's the next step in the process?

John Komlos: The search committee will meet within a week or two after the initial interviews are completed in order to shorten the list to a handful of candidates, usually three, who will be invited to campus for a more thorough discussion. If you do not hear from a university within three weeks of your initial interview, you can be pretty certain that you did not make the next cut. Unfortunately—and I say unfortunately because I do find it uncollegial—the department is not likely to notify you officially for months to come of a negative result. You just have to infer it.

Penny Gold: This is painful for the candidates, but there's a good reason for it from the institutional point of view. It can happen that none of the first three candidates brought to campus works out, either because they do poorly at the on-campus interview or because they are offered the job, but decline it. The department will then need to go back to the conference interview pool and, even though weeks have passed, may prefer you not know that you weren't among the first three choices. I prefer candidness on both sides of the job search and think it best if the department sends out letters to those interviewed at the conference, indicating that they have not made the initial cut for campus visits, but that the search is still open and their file will be kept active until the search is concluded. Whether this is done may depend more on the level of organization of the search committee chair and the depth of secretarial help than on a conscious decision to keep candidates in the dark.

John Goldsmith: Perhaps now with e-mail being essentially free and universal, departments will find a way to send a brief acknowledgment by e-mail every two months or so regarding where the process stands, but as Penny explained, it's generally not possible for a department to announce where it is (or who's been cut from the list) until the whole procedure is over, and that means much later into the hiring procedure than most would imagine.

John Komlos: I fear that the normal practice has slipped into laxity about informing those that have not been selected. Candidates will infer the result much before they see it in writing. I have heard of some applicants not being notified at all, and I have even seen searches discontinued without notifying applicants. It seems to me that in a field of sixty applicants, forty could be easily informed within a week of the first committee meeting that they have not made the first cut in the selection process. This is one aspect of academia that seems like it could use improvement.

What if I do not make the next cut?

John Komlos: Do not despair, and there is no need to call the chair of the department. There will certainly be other opportunities. The fact that you did not interest that search committee need not have had anything to do with any of your attributes or qualifications. Search committees have all sorts of unexpressed objectives. The department might have given the particular committee the charge to look for a labor economist, but the committee chair is intent on finding a person who specializes in Third World labor markets because she was unable to get authorization to hire a development economist, her first choice. Seeing that this valuable colleague was disappointed, the chair of the department put her in charge of the committee in order to placate her. She does not have the authorization to advertise for a labor economist of the Third World because the department did not approve that, but she now has a chance, nonetheless, to obtain a result satisfactory to her. There would have been no way for you to know that some of the questions directed at you were aimed at ascertaining your willingness to develop your specialty in the direction of developmental economics. But rethinking the interview might help you to pick up such intimations next time.

Another factor outside of your control is that people are usually attracted to like-minded people. Academics can be envious of, and may not want to have, colleagues who might outperform them. So if, for example, you are interviewing with a department for which scholarly excellence is not at the top of the agenda, giving interviewers the impression of being on the fast lane to the Ivy League will not necessarily impress them. On the contrary, it could work against you. They have made the legitimate decision to be educators rather than creators of knowledge, and they perform an extremely important function as interpreters of the humanities or of the natural or social sciences at regional campuses of state universities or at liberal arts colleges. Perhaps this is your goal as well. You might not want to do much writing or research after you have completed your dissertation. That is all right, too. You should let the search committee know that you are interested primarily in teaching and not in publishing. Stress teaching even more than your preferences might otherwise warrant in order to appeal to your interviewers. While you are not likely to be very happy being in a place where your aspirations differ considerably from those of the rest of your colleagues, your goals might well change over time, and even a temporary job enables you to keep a foot in the academic world until you can find an institution more to your tastes.

Ideally, there should be a match between your goals and those of the department in which you are interviewing. Necessity may force second-best options on you as well as on a department. Do not assume by any means that the department will obviously choose someone with your aspirations. Its sights might be set higher or lower than yours, and it is possible to be overqualified for a position as well as to be underqualified.

Penny Gold: I would warn here against making assumptions about the relative importance of scholarship at various institutions. Beyond the top-ranking universities, where you can be sure that expectations about publishing are very high, it can be hard to tell. Many teaching institutions, even those with heavy teaching loads, want to have active scholars on the faculty. This is another question you can ask when it's your turn: what are the expectations for tenure with regard to publication?

John Komlos: Yes, you should certainly seek information about this. And, of course, it is not only what you are being told that matters. It is also important for you to find out eventually (and cautiously) what decisions they have actually made recently.

John Goldsmith: This is a good place to mention one general law about academic departments: somehow departments almost always succeed in reproducing themselves. When seeking new members, they find people who fit their mold and will continue their traditions. You may think I mean this in a purely intellectual sense, and that certainly is true, but I mean it in other ways as well. Style, personality, and theoretical outlook all tend to be reproduced. At some level, the job candidate is going to be tested for how well he will replicate what is already there. The job candidate typically doesn't know too much about these more subtle aspects of the personality profile of the department as a whole, and there's little that one can do to appear to fit in better or worse, though here I'd repeat what I said earlier: research the department you are visiting, and actively use your knowledge of what goes on there.

John Komlos: I agree, but I'd go further. I'd say that *universities* tend to reproduce themselves. One might think that a department is small enough to be able to change rapidly, but things are more complex. Departmental standards and culture are kept in equilibrium by dozens of interlocking factors and are influenced by social interactions within the university as a whole. They are part of the politics of the institution, and people have accommodated themselves to them. The ethos is maintained partly through encouraging conformity and partly by filtering out those who would not fit into it. The faculty have made investments of time and effort based on the assumption that things will remain as they are; hence, change is not in their interest.

Penny Gold: I do think this can be different at a smaller institution. In a department of five or six, one can experience a sea change with two or three closely spaced retirements. You may turn out to be part of the wedge of a new guard.

John Komlos: I alluded earlier to the division of the intellectual community along various ideological dimensions, political as well as intellectual. If you believe strongly that the free market is a highly efficient institution of economic organization, it hardly pays for you to apply to departments that prefer to accentuate market imperfections and failures. If you are on the left of the political spectrum, you may not become a prime candidate in a conservative department, or vice versa.

There are numerous other reasons why you might not have advanced beyond the first interview. There might have been an "inside" candidate for whom the committee already had a preference. To be sure, the search committee is obligated to bring at least a couple of credible candidates to campus because otherwise the competition would not appear acceptable to the dean. However, it is just possible that you will not be invited because you would pose too much competition. So there is no need to despair; the job market is large and rather well functioning. The chances are excellent that you will find a niche for yourself in due course. It might not be immediately, however. Hence, you need patience, a realistic assessment of your own talents and aspirations, and a little knowledge of how this market functions.

In short, you should not automatically think it was your own fault that you failed to advance in the competition, but because you will not be privy to the real reason for this result, you may want to discuss the interview with your mentor in order to have another perspective on it. There is no need to spend excessive time speculating, however, because ultimately you will not be able to second-guess the decision. Yet it might still be possible for you to learn something from rethinking the conversation you had. While I strongly urge you not to blame yourself for not advancing in a competition, it is true that the more frequently you fail to advance, the more important it will be for you to seek the cause of that failure.

Note that while you should apply for every job that you can imagine yourself accepting, you should also keep in mind that an application is costly in both time and effort: it might take as long as a day per application. Thus, it pays to do some research about the departments you are considering even before you apply in order to find out if there might be a suitable match between you and the department.

What about the candidates who advance to the next stage?
What can they expect?

John Komlos: They will receive an invitation to visit the campus, either from the chair of the search committee or from the chair of the department. That will come within a couple of weeks of the initial interview, and the visit will be at the university's expense. The second interview is usually a full-day affair, though under special circumstances it can stretch into a second day. You will be asked to give a lecture on the topic of your choice, and it should be about the most significant aspects of your dissertation. The talk should not be about your next project or your most recent paper, even if it has been quite some time since you finished your dissertation and it feels like old hat to you—unless, of course, you are already an established scholar. Do not discuss extensively how you came to choose your topic or gossip about your dissertation committee. Leave such chit-chat for dinner conversation. I have seen job talks fail needlessly on such grounds. Even though it was clear that the person was well qualified for the job, he simply did not appear to know what a formal job talk should be.

The talk ought not be preliminary, a mere overview, or primarily biographical or anecdotal. It is also important not to overwhelm your audience. Instead, do give an overarching conception of your thesis. In the introduction, you should present the state of the debate relevant to the topic and give a short overview of your thesis. Then proceed quickly on to your approach to the issues, the data, or the methodology, and finally to your conclusion. In contrast to written work, you should repeat yourself occasionally in order to remind listeners of your main ideas, keeping in mind that to be effective the outline of the presentation should be simple enough to maintain the interest of your listeners. You have gone over your topic repeatedly, and as a consequence, ideas might appear clearer to you than to those who hear it for the first time. The effective use of visual aids will help the audience absorb your ideas and make your presentation more lively.

Don't worry if you think your thesis topic will be somewhat esoteric for your audience. People will be interested in seeing if you can generate enthusiasm even for a topic completely unfamiliar to them. Your performance as an effective communicator can be gauged regardless of the topic, and that is one of your qualities the department will be assessing, inter alia, as a measure of your ability to teach.

Nervousness makes a negative impression: it is not necessarily interpreted as a sign of inexperience, but more likely will be taken as an indicator that you will not be an effective communicator in class, which can easily eliminate you from further consideration. If you have a persistent problem with nervousness when you give talks, you might consider contacting a counselor to explore ways you can overcome it.

Don't lose sight of the fact that the most important aspect of your visit will be this lecture. Most of the members of the faculty will not take the time to read your manuscript and will make up their mind mostly, if not entirely, on the basis of your lecture and the impression you make during your interaction with them.

There is no reason in the world why your lecture should not be impeccable. You have been working on the topic for a couple of years; you should know more about it than anyone else. Your major task is to summarize the salient features of the dissertation in a short talk. Ask yourself what is essential to your thesis. What issues have you raised? How did you frame your question and why? What is novel about your approach? Why should people pay attention to it? Be concise, and leave the nuances for the question-and-answer segment. It is important that you appear self-confident, but not arrogant. Again, your audience will want to ascertain what kind of a colleague and teacher you will be.

Penny Gold: My recommendation about the subject for your job candidate talk is a little different. If you're still writing your dissertation or have only recently finished it, speaking about some aspect of it is certainly the best choice. But if you're a year or two beyond the dissertation and have been working on something else, go ahead and talk about that. What is most important is that the talk give your audience a good representation of the kind of research you do, how convincing an argument you can make, how well you can explain the significance of your work, and how engaged in it you appear to be. Choose a talk that gives a good picture of what currently defines your research approach and agenda.

John Komlos: However, your talk should present a coherent whole. It should pose a problem or a hypothesis, explain your approach and methodology, and have a significant conclusion. If you cannot make such a presentation with confidence, you might just as well not show up. In my view, research-in-progress reports do not generally meet this criterion and are less effective than research that is completed and digested and that has been tested in other settings.

John Goldsmith: I've recently seen a couple of job talks that failed for a reason I would not have expected: they aimed too low. These two candidates were quite different: different in years in the field, in stature, and in sheer intelligence, to mention just a few traits. Yet both undermined their candidacies by giving talks that were perceived as fluff rather than substance.

I'd also like to mention something very unusual that occurred to me at one interview and that has been reported to me two or three times since. While a graduate student, I was invited to a Canadian university for an interview, and I was told that I would just be interviewed, that no talk was expected. When I got there, I was informed that it would be very convenient for me to make a little presentation at a department get-together. So I had to prepare something on the spot. I'll never know whether this was a diabolical strategy on their part or a hopeless lack of organization, but I pass it on for what it's worth. Always expect to be required to give a talk, and prepare for it.

   Candidates are also sometimes asked to teach a class—with faculty sitting in. I can't imagine having a candidate do this without forewarning, though.

Penny Gold: You should always ask ahead what the department's expectations are for the talk, and, most especially, who the audience will be. Will you be speaking to professors and graduate students in the hiring department, or will the audience be a more general one, with people from a variety of fields, including undergraduates? If the latter, you have a large challenge. You will want to impress the hiring faculty with your control over the intricacies of your research field, and yet you'll want to speak simply enough that an undergraduate can understand you. In some fields, this is easier than in others. If faced with a choice, I'd say aim high rather than low. But it doesn't hurt to throw in a brief definition or explanatory phrase here and there. Some of the faculty may even appreciate it.

   John Komlos has mentioned that your delivery style is being judged as much as your substance. If you have not been asked to teach a class, this is the only chance the department has to gauge what kind of teacher you might be. For this reason, the question-and-answer session also takes on special salience. A lively question-and-answer session can do wonders to make up for a somewhat tedious lecture, and a demonstrated inability to interact agreeably and productively with questioners will bring even an excellent talk down several notches. At the heart of teaching is dialog, so all your interactions with people—at your talk and elsewhere—will be used as a litmus test of your teaching potential.

John Komlos: That is why you should seek out opportunities to develop your extemporaneous speaking skills before you enter the job market. Now you want to impress your audience and demonstrate that you will be a good lecturer and, by implication, a good teacher. Hence, your presentation should not be taken verbatim from your written text because effective oral communication differs significantly from its written counterpart. You can effectively present a much more nuanced view in writing than you can orally. Inasmuch as you would have worked on the topic of your presentation for an extended period of time, you ought to be able to talk about it with authority and without resort to a script. Some notes or a brief outline to which you might refer on occasion are, however, perfectly acceptable. A winning presentation is short—and never, never extends past the allotted time. Attention spans are limited, and forty minutes should suffice in most cases. You have a chance to impress your audience with your ability to synthesize material, but if you get bogged down in detail, you will not be successful. Leave ancillary issues to the question-and-answer period. Simplify. Leave complicated data or information for footnotes in the written version. Summarize occasionally so that your audience does not lose sight of your main argument and so that it can follow your logical progression of ideas. Repeat yourself if necessary. The presentation of numeric information is best left to a visual medium, such as an overhead projector.[12]

During the discussion, you will probably encounter some unfriendly sounding counterarguments. Make sure you keep your composure. You know the material better than anyone else in that room, so you have reason to be self-confident. It is much better to respond even to critical questions diplomatically by saying something like "That sounds like a good idea; I'll have to think about it more" than to appear recalcitrant. Such a response is more likely to disarm your critic than giving a patently antagonistic answer or talking around the issue raised. Alternatively, if it is appropriate, you might point out that you, in fact, explore that issue more extensively in the written version, available from you upon request. You might also be asked about your next project, not because anyone will hold you to it, but because people might want to assess your research direction.

John Goldsmith: The perceptive candidate should feel, in preparing this talk, a conflict between wanting to appear to be up to the minute in his own work and wanting to communicate maximally with the entire audience. Here a graduate student's training in his home department is likely to be misleading. There are many views that can be presumed in conversation with one's teachers and fellow students that are not shared across the profession. The successful candidate will have taken some steps to figure out what views fall into that category and will not assume them in the job talk. If there is a new vocabulary in the field in which you work, be sure to have at your fingertips an equivalent phrase from a more traditional vocabulary, and be sure to use both in your talk.

John Komlos: Moreover, do your best to answer every question, without being evasive, if at all possible. There is no shame in saying, "You know, I thought about that, but I cannot answer the question at this point. It will require further work. However, I did think about a related issue, because. . . ." That is much better than responding with a terse "I don't know" or trying to pretend that you actually do know the answer. Your audience will surely know you are bluffing. More important, you should be generous whenever appropriate: "Thanks for bringing this issue to my attention" should be seen as a conciliatory response. Do not humiliate members of the audience by responding to a dull question from a junior scholar with "I thought I had already spoken about that issue." People who paid attention will know that and will appreciate your not embarrassing one of their colleagues. Do not point out inconsistencies in the questions being asked. Be polite to a fault. Though the degree to which scholarly bluntness is accepted varies considerably from campus to campus, you should assume that diplomatic answers are expected of you until you are convinced of the contrary.

John Goldsmith: It's important to practice the talk before your campus visit. Most graduate departments now have established semiformal venues for students to prepare their presentations. In our department, there are talks most Wednesday afternoons at four o'clock, and if a student is going for an interview, he will usually go through a dry run at one of these sessions.

It goes without saying that you will be nervous. Nobody will hold that against you. As a general rule, I'd encourage young candidates to err, if necessary, on the side of conservatism in such traditional matters as attire, even though most academics don't dress up on a daily basis. In this day and age, relatively few male academics go so far as to wear a tie during their normal workweek, and jeans are normal at many universities. But I think it is a mistake for a job candidate to opt for comfortable casual wear; by and large, it is the professional image that you want to project, not the casual one. Incidentally, though I myself am not particularly conscious of styles of attire—I need someone else's judgment as to whether a pair of pants goes with a particular sports jacket—I have been surprised by the sloppy dress of a couple of candidates. Obviously, this isn't going to be a make-or-break factor for any candidate, but why not put your best foot forward? This matter is undoubtedly a good deal more complex for women.[13]

Penny Gold: I can almost always spot a job candidate on campus because they're so much more dressed up than everyone else! My advice for dressing for the conference interview still holds, with this additional provision: whatever you wear for the on-campus interview has got to be comfortable for the whole day. I don't mean wear sweats and a T-shirt; rather, wear something that looks moderately professional, but in which you feel you can be yourself rather than someone acting like a professional. My department once had a candidate on campus on a very hot day in June. She was wearing a jacket and was obviously uncomfortably hot as we walked around on a tour of the campus. I finally suggested that she take off her jacket. She replied, "But my advisor said that I should be sure to wear a jacket for my interview!" So use common sense as well as your advisor's advice. This candidate was a lot more comfortable once the jacket was off, and she got the job offer, too.

John Komlos: Needless to say, all sorts of unexpected things might happen, but it is not possible to prepare for them in advance. I remember, for instance, that at the beginning of one of my job talks the lights simply went out, and there were no windows in the room in which I was going to speak! A dim hallway was found where we at least could see one another, and I gave my talk without the use of the overhead projector on which I was planning to rely extensively. I did not let that bother me, and I did receive an offer. No wonder—the unanticipated turn of events turned my normal talk into an extraordinary performance.[14]

Both before and after your talk, you will meet with quite a few people for about half an hour at a time and be invited to breakfast, lunch, or dinner with some members of the faculty and perhaps students. You might have to tune your social skills for the occasion if it does not come automatically to you, but be prepared.[15] Topics of conversation will vary enormously. One question often asked is where else you are interviewing. I do not know of a good answer, particularly if you do not have many other interviews lined up. Whatever you say might sound negative. Of course, if you have lots of other interviews, revealing this might sound like bragging, or it could have a bandwagon effect: they should want you because everyone else is about to give you an offer. However, whenever I was asked this question, I always interpreted it as a sign of intellectual laziness on the asker's part and was too inhibited to provide an adequate response.[16]

Penny Gold: I'd rely here on my baseline advice to be straightforward, but brief whenever awkward subjects come up. If the question is asked while you're on campus, I don't see that you have anything to lose with a forthright answer. Either answer can be taken in either a positive or a negative way: no other interviews means either relief (we don't need to worry about any competing offers) or concern (have we misjudged your merit?) and the reverse for a long list of interviews. However, in my experience, this question is more likely to be asked once an offer is made and the department then needs this information in order to be able to give you a realistic time-table for your response to the offer. More often I've seen candidates bring up the matter themselves while they are on campus. I see no benefit in doing so.

John Komlos: You may be given your approximate salary by the chair of the department before the interview is concluded. Do not make any commitments at this point. Just nod. You do not yet have any leverage, but you might a little later on. Needless to say, you should conduct your-self throughout the process with the same caution as during your first interview.

Be aware that decision-making power is seldom distributed evenly within a department, and those exercising the most influence do not nec-essarily want to be threatened by upstarts. Hence, it would be useful for you to signal that you are a team player and it is the farthest thing from your mind to question the political status quo. The department just might let even a good scholar go elsewhere if you seem to think too highly of yourself.

John Goldsmith: Here's another sensitive area that anyone can stumble into. Just how to deal with it is a very tough question, though. Not all that infrequently, the department that is hiring feels like there has been far too much dissension and bitter division within. Any prospective new faculty member may be viewed from this admittedly skewed perspective: whose side will he take, they may wonder in the worst of cases. In the case of a more senior hire, some of the people may specifically be looking for some-one who will bring some strength or force of character to the situation and to be a leader more than a conciliator.

After I return home from my interview, should I do anything?

John Goldsmith: Here you're more likely to come away with some oppor-tunities for follow-up contacts. If you've got a paper that you mentioned in a conversation with someone, send them a copy; if an important paper, or one that you especially like, came up in a conversation, send that ref-erence by e-mail, or maybe even send a copy. Act a bit like the faculty member you hope soon to be. These are all very optional things to do, but why not (as I've said before) put your best foot forward?

Let's talk about the bad news first. What if I end the season with no job offers?

John Komlos: If you happen not to have received an offer at this stage, you should not despair. You have gained valuable experience about the process of job seeking that should be useful later. For some jobs, there really *was* an inside favorite, someone whom the committee knew and was from the start predisposed to hire. So those who were not chosen should not take it personally. In fact, it is important that you not feel rejected. Though you did not win this contest, there will be others. And remember that if you were one of three people on the short list, then two-thirds of that list could not possibly win. So maintain your self-confidence!

You no doubt have the solid foundations of a good education, but you are not alone. A strength of the American university system is its tendency to overproduce. There is an excess supply of excellent academics. However, the other side of the coin is that regrettably everyone is not guaranteed a position, which leads to the keen competition for good jobs, and the selection from the best applicants might well depend on fortune.

But do not give up yet. There are still local "aftermarkets" to consider. These include smaller colleges and universities, which tend to find faculty after the national market is over. In addition, many non-tenure-track jobs open up at the last minute because fellowships are announced in the spring and faculty members can notify their chairs only at this late date that they will not be teaching next year. This forces chairs to scramble to find credible temporary replacements, lasting from one semester to as long as two years. Although these are usually dead-end jobs, they can, nonetheless, have many advantages. You have a greater chance to find one of these positions if you are willing, and your family circumstances allow you, to become an itinerant academic. Such a job will give you valuable teaching experience and an opportunity to join the academic world, even if on disadvantageous initial terms. On a more positive note, you will develop courses that you can use later on in your career, and even a temporary job can turn into a regular tenure-stream position. In that case, you could become an "inside" candidate and enjoy comparative advantages, inasmuch as you would already be known to the department, and you will also make friends whom you can ask to provide you letters of recommendations later on. Most important, you are most likely going to be treated as a guest: you will not be asked to serve on committees or even to go to departmental meetings. This is an enormous advantage, for it leaves you much more time for scholarship than if you had a tenure-track position.

Plus you retain a foothold in the academic world and have more time to wait until a full-fledged job opens up in your field.

Penny Gold: My first job was just such a one-year position. One of my teachers consoled me with the advice that it could be a good thing to begin one place and then move on, as you can make all the mistakes of a new professor in your first institution and then not have to live with them. This cheered me up, and it also contained a good deal of truth.

John Komlos: However, just as in the case of a full-time job, such a visiting position will tag you with a particular market value. This will be taken as your revealed value, much as for a baseball player who signs a contract for a particular price. Just as your school affiliation is used by many as an indication of your scholarly potential, the affiliation with an employer is used by the market as a determinant—and at this stage of your career, as an important one—of your "value," that is to say, your potential. It is a signal that almost always overrides the ranking of your graduate department. After this initial determination, it will not be possible for you to move up easily in the hierarchy of academic institutions. Upward mobility is exponentially more difficult the further you would like to move from your current position. This, by the way, is the case once your dissertation is completed, whether you have a temporary or a tenure-track position. Consequently, it might make sense for you to sit out a year rather than accept a position that you think might make it much more difficult for you to achieve your market value next year.[17] In other words, the letterhead from where you are applying matters a fair bit.

Penny Gold: Perhaps this is how the handful of most highly ranked institutions would view you later on. But given how tight the job market is in many fields, it is very common for people to have had one or two temporary jobs before landing a tenure-track one. In my experience, these candidates are still judged more on the reputation of their graduate institution than of their place of employment. I think that a one-year job at a high-ranking place will help you, but that a similar job at a low-ranking place will not hurt you.

John Komlos: I think it is more than a handful of institutions that use your current affiliation to judge your overall quality. I am not saying that it is impossible to get a tenure-track job once one has accepted a visiting appointment, but I do think that the members of the search committee will be asking themselves all sorts of questions about how you landed in the position in which you find yourself. And if you are asked for an interview, you will need to have an explanation.

John Goldsmith: My advisor once said to me, when I had been rejected in a job search, "That's a chapter out of their biography—not yours." Meaning, in essence, that he was sure I had done my best in the task of presenting who I was and that, after that, it is a function of the complex psychology and sociology of the department doing the searching how the hiring decision will be made. It may be of some consolation to point out that there are many, many jobs filled with people who don't seem to be the best all-round candidate among those who applied. We've touched on a number of the reasons why this might be the case.

Penny Gold: I would just reinforce that it's very difficult to second-guess the choice of any one department. People are looking not just for a beginning assistant professor, but also for a potential colleague-for-life, since institutional relationships may last longer than many marriages.

How long should I keep my hopes up?

John Komlos: I would consider two cycles to be appropriate, provided you really put your best foot forward. I mean by that that your dissertation was in hand and you applied to a wide array of institutions and did not limit yourself geographically or any other way. You really have to apply everywhere because you have so little credible information about your abilities relative to other applicants. If you were unsuccessful in the first year in both the national and the local markets, it would be too radical to withdraw from academia immediately, unless—of course—you were unsure about the degree of your commitment in the first place. Perhaps you have skills that you can market successfully in the business world.[18] Or you can find a job in government or in academic administration. Do give it a try, and see how it feels. But it would be completely understandable to try to obtain an academic job again the following year. After all, you have already invested a number of years, and you should not give up on your goal without a good try. Do keep in close touch with your mentor, and discuss your options and likely prospects. What can be learned from your lack of success, and how different might your experience be next year?

Perhaps your lack of success the first time around was caused by the idiosyncrasies of the job market that particular year. Perhaps you did not pursue certain segments of the market with sufficient vigor. You will be more informed and have more experience under your belt. During the second cycle, try not to let the fact that you were not successful the first time around affect you. Tell yourself that you were just testing the waters. If you begin to think of yourself as a failure, others will also, and it will be even more difficult for you to succeed the second time around. You might tell yourself that you had not completed enough of your dissertation to be taken seriously the previous year. Perhaps at this point your mentor can find you a post as a teaching assistant, or perhaps you qualify for a grant or postdoctoral scholarship. And, most important of all, do retain a positive attitude. Your self-confidence will be contagious. After all, you have more information available to you about yourself than does anyone else.

Penny Gold: It's difficult to tell someone else, I think, how long to persist in looking. I don't know that I would have had the stamina to last through more than three hiring seasons myself. But one of my colleagues at Knox had been on the job market seven years previously (employed all along the way in temporary jobs and not wanting to imagine another kind of profession for herself) before the tenure-track job at Knox came through for her. From my perspective, it is difficult to imagine how she could not have been hired earlier, as her credentials were stellar and she's a nice person to boot. But she's in a very competitive field, and an oversupplied subfield within that field. We at Knox are lucky she persevered.

The longer the string of temporary jobs you've had, the more a committee looks askance at your application, wondering why you haven't already found a tenure-track job. But if you're still committed to academic life, and you've been continuing to mature as a professional in these years, increasing your network of contacts through conferencing and publishing, and you can attribute your difficulty in obtaining a job to market conditions rather than some essential aspects of your own person and qualifications, then perhaps it's worth continuing to look.

John Komlos: I have a friend who undertook job hunting as a traveling salesman sells encyclopedias: during the late season, he literally went door to door (in an area where he wanted to live) and said, "Here I am. Do you need a mathematician?" He found both of his jobs this way, and the second match was sufficiently satisfactory for both sides that it turned out to be a permanent arrangement! The timing obviously has to be right, and I grant that this is an idiosyncratic way of seeking employment, but it shows that with a little improvisation you can turn the market in your favor.

For example, you might want to contact again those local institutions to which you might have sent applications earlier in the season. Your c.v. might already be on file, but a renewed expression of interest can be helpful. Given all their other responsibilities, chairs want to minimize effort, and if they know that you are still available, they are much more likely to give you the job than to contact the dozen other applicants on file with them, whose availability is unknown. Hence, a phone call to the chair of a local college periodically, beginning in March, can be quite useful.

Another possibility with many more advantages than temporary employment is a postdoctoral position. There are a large number of such programs available in all disciplines, and in some sense, they are preferable to a full-time job, even at a slightly lower income. They are valuable because they afford you one or two years to concentrate on research without any teaching obligations or administrative duties. You will be able to get an immense amount of work done compared to full-time employees with teaching obligations, office hours, course preparations, committee meetings, departmental meetings, and so forth. As a consequence, your publication record will increase substantially. In addition, obtaining such a fellowship will increase your market value, inasmuch as you will have proven to potential employers that you were successful in winning at a national competition. In the sciences, postdocs are much more prevalent than in the social sciences and humanities. While a mere 4 percent of the economics Ph.D. recipients in 1998 went on to postdoctoral positions, the share in physics was 48 percent.

Penny Gold: Of course, one needs to apply for postdocs long before the job-hiring season; that is, one is usually writing grant proposals at the same time one is writing job letters. If you get both a postdoc and a job, one or the other will usually let you postpone for a year.

John Goldsmith: In some disciplines, especially the laboratory sciences with their heavy support by research grants, the postdoc phase of an academic's development is thoroughly obligatory: one goes to work as a postdoc in someone's lab after receiving the Ph.D.—no ifs, ands, or buts. In other areas, such as the social sciences or the humanities, this is by no means a certain thing (though it is quite common in fields like psychology). Be that as it may, it is very much worth checking out in your own discipline. And bear in mind that many postdocs can be obtained even when one has landed a regular job; it's possible to take off one's third or fourth year in a tenure-track appointment and hold a postdoc appointment somewhere else, using the time to strengthen one's research and publication record. (I did that, spending a productive year as a Mellon fellow at Harvard during what would have been my fourth year at Indiana.)

John Komlos: Yes, the postdoc is a marvelous institution. It can be very helpful in providing a good start to a tenure dossier.

In any event, the major factor in succeeding in obtaining a job is your own belief in yourself! If you continue to maintain your confidence and persevere, you will be successful, provided, of course, that your goals are matched reasonably to your aptitudes. It is, therefore, important to keep on updating your own information about yourself in order to make sure you are not aiming too high, or too low. To have a valid evaluation of yourself, you need to remain observant, keep an open mind, and discuss your future with people who know you, and whom you trust.

John Goldsmith: Let me mention a story that a colleague of mine related. There are occasions when a department, for one reason or another, is deadlocked, and no decision is made—and hence no offers made. On one occasion, one of the candidates who had been interviewed learned of this unhappy state of affairs, got back in touch with the chair of the search committee, and said, "I think you've made a serious mistake. How can I convince you to reconsider my candidacy?" The upshot was that he was brought back for a second interview and was offered the job.

Penny Gold: You might also want to use the occasion of a rejection to get some substantive feedback. If you've gone through the campus interview and have felt a good rapport with the chair of the search committee, you can consider asking the chair for feedback on how you did on the interview. There's nothing to lose in asking, and you may gain some helpful constructive criticism—or reassurance about elements that were beyond your control.

And the good news: what if I receive an offer?

John Goldsmith: First of all, congratulations are in order! This is the moment you've been waiting for. This may be one of the defining moments of your life, and it's one you've been working toward for many years.

John Komlos: The offer is usually made by phone within two to four weeks of your campus interview by the chair of the department.[19] He will reiterate in more detail than earlier the conditions of your employment, such as your salary, benefits, how many courses you will teach, tenure-stream status, sabbatical policy, parental leaves, and so on.[20] All of these conditions vary enormously from institution to institution. You need to know that the verbal offer needs to be put into writing before it has much legal validity, and a letter from the dean or provost is usually preferred to one from the chair. Mix-ups have been known to happen at this stage, when the chair thought that more money was available for salary than was actually the case, but this happens rarely. A letter from the chair usually does suffice.

John Goldsmith: I'm sorry to say that, in my experience, there are more cases of foul-ups here than one would expect—cases where verbal offers did not materialize as written offers, though most of these cases involve more senior appointments, an area we will turn to in a later chapter. So bear in mind that while a verbal offer is almost certainly real, don't sell the farm until you see it in writing on letterhead stationery.

But there are some possible hitches to consider before going any further. In a surprising number of cases, the candidate is subject to some unusual questions just *before* the actual offer comes, and we should talk about what to do if this happens.

Consider this scenario. It's four weeks after your visit to Indiana University, let's say, and you know they have interviewed two other candidates for the same position. One morning the telephone rings, and it's the department chair calling. He seemed very enthusiastic about your candidacy, and you had the strong feeling that he backed you all the way. But, then again, he hadn't seen the other candidates when you met him on your trip. And he has news for you: the department is undecided. You're the leading candidate, but he needs to know if you'll accept the job before the department can settle on you. He asks you, point blank, if you'll accept. What should you say?

Well, under the circumstances, what can you say? Your first inclination is to say, "Of course! You want me? Great! I'm yours!" But your second reaction, a split second later, is likely to be, "Wait a minute—what kind of a question is that? What do you mean 'if'? Are you offering me the position, or what?" But you shouldn't say either of those things. Still, of the two reactions, it's the second that is more reasonable. The department has no business asking you whether you'll accept until it makes a legitimate offer. And so you have no choice but to politely and graciously offer a platitudinous response—something along the lines of "You know how impressed I was during my visit last month. I can't imagine a department I would rather be a member of." Or "Your department is exactly the kind of department I would like to join, and if I were made the kind of offer we discussed last month, I could hardly imagine not accepting it."

Your job is, indeed, to make those in the department feel loved and cherished, just as they should be trying to make you feel valued. But despite the fact that this kind of odd questioning from the would-be future employer happens surprisingly often, please bear in mind that it is not appropriate for anyone to ask you if you'd accept something until it is actually offered.

But finally the real thing, an offer, has come. It will almost certainly come by telephone. In this business, good news comes by telephone, and bad news comes in the mail. The chair calls you up and offers you a job. Do you accept? Answer: not right off, no. The negotiation has only just begun.

John Komlos: You will have about two weeks to make up your mind. If you need more time, in case you are waiting for other offers, you should say so after the two weeks have elapsed, not before. An extension is usually granted.

Penny Gold: On the other hand, if you know that it will take more than two weeks to hear from another school where you've had or are scheduled to have an on-campus interview, I would suggest you say something like "I'm waiting for other offers and may need more than two weeks. But I will call the other institutions where I've interviewed and ask if they can speed up their process." It will not hurt your standing at the place where you have an offer for them to know that other offers may be pending, and it will help them to know in advance if it is likely you'll need more than the two weeks to make your decision.

John Komlos: However, the point is to make sure you do not mislead your prospective chair. If you don't know (and how can you, really?) what the other department will do, being initially noncommittal will gain you some time to evaluate your options and to make a firmer judgment of what you would like to do. It might be to your disadvantage if you reveal immediately that you are waiting for another offer and it does not materialize.

It is important for you to realize that once you have the verbal offer in hand, you are in a position to bargain, even if this is your first appointment and your leverage is limited. You have gone through a grueling competition, and the chances are you deserved to come out the winner. Departments do not want to miss their chosen candidate for a small amount of extra money. They do not want to call another department meeting or hold another round of balloting. It is much simpler for the chair to make a quick deal with you now directly. If, for example, you would like a year off to do some postdoctoral work, most departments will have no problem giving you a year's leave of absence without pay. Your starting to teach a year later even provides some advantages for the dean because your salary for that year then comes under a different line in his budget, and the dean then has more flexibility in its use.

It is important that you not conflate negotiation with demands. You should not have any demands at the starting level. But the art of negotiating is really finding out what the possibilities are: what is within reach, and what is not. In the course of the discussion, many issues at least become defined or information revealed that can be useful subsequently. In any case, do ask for a slightly higher salary than you have been offered, or for a supplementary allowance (for a computer, for example), or for both. Note that once you have agreed to the offer, you have locked yourself into a salary for a long time to come. That has become your "market value." Substantial increases in your salary will not be forthcoming until you are able to generate outside offers, once you become better known. Until then, you will have to rely on tiny annual, automatic cost-of-living adjustments and even smaller merit pay increases. In other words, you have a little bargaining power now. Make use of it to your best advantage, without going overboard. A request of a salary one to two thousand dollars higher than the one being offered will not be held against you. The chair will try to accommodate you to the extent possible, but he has to convince the dean that your request is reasonable. At the same time, chairs are aware that faculty compare salaries, and people would be unhappy if your salary as a beginner were too close to others with more seniority in the department (though salary disparities of this sort can arise, especially in state universities). The chair does have some leeway, but not much. In any event, do not accept the offer immediately. There would be no benefit in doing so. Wait and think about it during time allotted to you. Talk it over with others before you commit yourself permanently.

Penny Gold: It can help if you have some basis for asking for a higher salary, other than just knowing you might be able to get another thousand or two dollars. As you read job ads all year, keep track of what the beginning salaries are at other institutions, and if your offer seems low in comparison, tell the chair that. If you are currently in a job where you're earning more than what's being offered, you should ask that the institution at least match that salary (or what you could anticipate earning in the following year in your current position). And, of course, if you have another offer that is more money, that is another good reason for the institution to increase its offer.

John Goldsmith: There are many sides to an offer; there are many things that can be offered. Let's consider an abbreviated list:

1. salary
2. moving expenses
3. a job for a spouse
4. tuition for children's schooling
5. help in buying or renting a home
6. size or type of office
7. an office computer and/or other computer resources
8. summer financial support
9. time off for research during the first year or two
10. laboratory space, in some disciplines
11. rank—assistant, associate, or full professor (not likely to be an issue now, but don't lose sight of this for the future)
12. years to go until consideration for tenure (often negotiable if you've had previous years of teaching experience)
13. money to buy books for the library or your office
14. travel funds
15. research assistant expenses
16. copying funds
17. teaching load
18. course schedule, courses to be taught, and number of preparations
19. secretarial assistance
20. starting date
21. sabbatical leave
22. benefits

Yes, there are that many, and more. And remember the following rule: you can negotiate about anything until you have accepted the offer. Then your chance to negotiate quickly fades into a distant memory.

And don't forget another rule, while we're on the subject: you are likely to feel guilty about asking for things for yourself. Don't. Remember that when you get these things, you are not taking things away from anyone else; you are strengthening the department that you are joining. You may be negotiating now with your chair-to-be, or (less likely) with the dean above the chair. The chair may or may not be a skilled administrator and may or may not be a people-person.

I think that opinions are mixed with regard to one more rule that I'd like to offer. We will come back to it in the context of other negotiations that you will have over the course of your academic career. It is a very tough one to learn, and most academics never learn it—indeed, many challenge its very propriety here! Here it is: if you conclude a negotiation and you receive everything you asked for, then you undersold your position.

At first blush, this may sound like a very strange maxim. It seems to be saying that if you get what you asked for, you did something wrong. But it is to be taken in a more nuanced fashion. The principle does entail the view that you should not expect to get everything you ask for, and it also implies that if the university does not give you everything you ask for, this doesn't mean that it doesn't think highly of you. In fact, you will have gotten a good reality check—you'll have learned a lesson—on how the university distributes its resources. Some, but only some, go to "outside hires" like you—people joining the university from outside.

That same rule also entails the view that you should ask for what you'd like and you should give the appearance of being flexible. If some conditions that you are aiming for are not really flexible, then specify that in the course of the negotiation. But this maxim should not be taken as *carte blanche* to ask for unreasonable things: you won't get them, and you'll look like (indeed, will be acting like) a prima donna, and no one likes that. I just mean to drive home the point that there is a considerable margin for negotiation in an area where the candidate's requests are entirely reasonable. I hope it's clear that I don't mean for anyone to ask for all of the things I listed above. Some things would be thoroughly unreasonable— say, a personal secretary for an assistant professor, or a salary that is truly out of line for the professor, in view of what others in the field and the department are receiving.

Under certain conditions, ones that it will be difficult for the candidate to identify, resources that the successful candidate negotiates for and receives will be resources no longer available to colleagues within the department. To the extent that this is true, I, for one, would be much more circumspect in pushing hard for such requests. Unfortunately, it is not at all easy for the candidate to obtain information about whether this is true or not. One way to try to find out is just to ask, once one is in the thick of the negotiation. A candidate can ask the chair with whom he is negotiating whether a salary increment he is requesting will have a negative impact on the money available for others in the department next year.

Penny Gold: I would stress the importance of doing some sounding out to help you decide what the range of reasonable requests might be. No point in wasting time asking for things that are automatically provided (perhaps travel funds and copying funds) or for things that are fixed and nonnegotiable (perhaps sabbatical leave, teaching load, and benefits). If the negotiations are with the department chair, this will be your first sustained interaction on a somewhat sensitive issue, and the "prima donna" risk factor might be high. You're in an easier-to-manage situation if the negotiation is with the dean because you can then use the department chair as your resource for information about what kinds of things are negotiable at this particular institution. Talking with friends who have recently gotten jobs will also provide some helpful comparisons.

If you've been offered a shared appointment with your spouse/partner, this is an important time to clarify the institution's understanding of how the appointment will work. Splitting the teaching load is relatively easy to figure out, but what about committee work and other nonteaching duties? Will you each have a full vote in the department? Are expectations for research the same as if you were full-time, lower (because you're only half-time), or higher (because you have more time free from teaching)? Will you each have an office? How will sabbaticals be handled? Will you be evaluated separately, or is the tenure of one conditional on the tenurability of both? (You should push for separate evaluation.) If the institution has a written policy on shared appointments, study it carefully before accepting the job. This is the best time to negotiate any areas in which you would like the policy altered. (See appendix 2 for a sample policy from Grinnell College.)[21] The more information you have from others who have shared a appointment, the better position you'll be in to know what you should ask for at this crucial negotiating point.

John Goldsmith: Of all the areas of negotiation, the hardest by far is the issue of employment for a spouse—what's come to be known as "the two-body problem" (with apologies to the physicists). In some cases, this involves a spouse who is also seeking an academic position, while in others, it means assisting a spouse to find a nonacademic professional position either at the university in question or in the area. A few enlightened universities have taken serious steps toward establishing a realistic policy in this area. One large midwestern state university has a special fund set up for this purpose and tries to broker a spousal academic job by breaking the cost of the second job into three equal pieces: one-third is covered by the department making the original offer, one-third by the department that would become the home of the spouse, and one-third by the general fund. But few universities have established any such plans.[22] I know of one chair who has promised himself to get a headhunter hired the next time he has to negotiate with a hot prospect whose spouse is dissatisfied with the move. And I know of a case where a university has offered full tuition in professional school, for example, for a spouse desiring to enter one, but the appointment in that case involved a senior position.

Penny Gold: Institutions located in major urban areas with many colleges, universities, and professional opportunities may be less likely to offer substantial help to a partner, figuring that you'll be able to find something on your own. But institutions in smaller towns and cities can't make that assumption and may be willing to do a fair amount to help you. For this situation, partners come in two kinds: nonacademic and academic. The first are a bit easier. It may be that when you describe your partner's job (say, upper management in a large company), it's clear there is nothing in that field available in, say, the small southern town in which the college is located. End of negotiation. But usually there's more of a chance, and the department chair should be willing to help you identify contacts in the area for your partner's field. Academic partners are harder because, in addition to identifying contacts at nearby institutions, what you will most likely be hoping for is some kind of position for your partner at the same institution. Unless your partner is in the same discipline as you (but a different enough field that you could not apply for a shared position), you'll most likely need to talk with the dean about possibilities for your partner rather than with the department chair. It may be that your partner can teach courses for which adjuncts are frequently hired (e.g., English composition, introductory languages). Such opportunities are something, but they are usually without security and poorly paid (as little as two or three thousand dollars per course). But sometimes your partner matches well enough a need of the institution that a regular appointment will be crafted for him. It might well be part-time and non-tenure-track, but it could be salaried at a regular assistant professor rate. My own institution has made enough such appointments in the last several years that a policy has been developed for them.

John Goldsmith: There are two other areas to think about relating to offers. First, what do you do when you've been made an offer by one university (let's say it's Harvard, where assistant professors can count on not getting tenure) that is not your top choice among the places that you are interviewing? You must get back to the chair of the other school—let's say it's the University of Chicago—immediately and explain the situation. Tell him that you would prefer to accept an offer from the University of Chicago, but that you have only two weeks to respond to Harvard. Chicago will tell you where you stand in its process, and if you're the top candidate, there's a very good chance that it will speed up the process to meet your deadline. Certainly, the chair will give you very strong indications that you're the top candidate if you are, and he should also tell you if you're not.

If this goes down to the wire, it's usually possible for Harvard to wait a little bit longer than it would prefer to. If you need an extra week, Harvard is not likely to take back its offer because of that. After all, Harvard really does want you.

This brings up a much trickier subject on which nobody has good advice. Suppose you've accepted a position at, say, Iowa State University, when out of the blue, for some reason, comes an offer from Stanford University. This happens more often than one might expect. It can happen if Stanford simply couldn't get its act together to make an offer early enough in the year to beat out an offer made by Iowa State, which wanted a reply within two or three weeks. Iowa State may have thought that it had been smart to grab a candidate early in the season, but what if Stanford comes along and makes an offer to a candidate who has already signed on at Iowa State? My personal feeling is that, after due meditation, the candidate should go with his heart and risk leaving Iowa State in the lurch. After all, how much will he enjoy being a professor there if he knows he would really rather have gone to Stanford? And there's an enormous difference between the relative losses. The folks at Iowa State will have to scramble to make a quick (and probably temporary) hire and have their courses covered next year, and that's a pain in the neck for them; for the candidate in question, it's a big part of his career that's on the line. But the issue is not at all clear, in my view. It's easy to feel that one has made a commitment to Iowa State by accepting its early offer, and that's true; backing out of the commitment is not something that should be done at all lightly, by any means. But it's also important to bear in mind the enormous difference between the impact on the candidate and the impact on the university and to make a decision based on all the factors.[23] (If academics had sign-on bonuses like star athletes, the bonuses would have to be returned, of course, but there are none; the differences between these two professions are worth meditating on.) Each person will have to make his own judgments as to what factors can legitimately play a role, too. Does your desire to be on the West Coast count as legitimate? My personal inclination is to say, "No, it doesn't"—but I'd reverse that decision if your spouse has a job in the same city and no significant chance of obtaining a job in the other city, the one that's not on the West Coast.

What about a job outside of academia?

John Komlos: You might have gone to graduate school with the legitimate goal of not staying in academia. There are plenty of opportunities in government as well as in the private sector. In the latter, you will also have a much higher salary, though less job security and less vacation. There are many, many other factors to consider, of which we have discussed a few.

John Goldsmith: I have talked with a lot of people about the shift from academia to industry; my friend Ami Kronfeld has shared some of his observations. I have worked with quite a large number of linguists now who are working in industry and have gotten more than a foot inside that door myself. These are people using the knowledge that academics teach and develop every bit as much and as often as academics do, and I'll say a bit more about that in a moment. I also have friends who, after earning their Ph.D.s, have become lawyers or business consultants or have worked for companies like Educational Testing Services that routinely hire Ph.D.s with good academic records for their academically honed skills.

From my point of view, the bottom line on this subject is that these other professional tracks seem to me to be, on the whole, quite as satisfying as academia. The fundamental issue is finding the right fit between the person and the career. It would take another book to line up and compare all of the strengths and weaknesses of these paths; our goal here is to focus just on academia, which is, after all, the one that we know the best.

But as long as we're on the topic, I'll say a few words about something that has happened in linguistics, something that is making a nonacademic career a truly viable alternative for Ph.D.s in linguistics. I'll call it industrial linguistics (as far as I know, I'm coining the term here). The rapid integration of computers into the daily life of the average person has rapidly increased the importance of developing software that can process, use, and even understand human languages. This means that advanced training in linguistics is quite suddenly in demand in the world of software, both in established companies and in start-ups. Our graduate students read the job postings: in the field of linguistics, there is an e-mail-based service called Linguist to which most linguists subscribe, and job opportunities are posted almost daily to people in our field. It's not hard to see that a very healthy proportion of the jobs coming on-line are a part of industrial linguistics: using linguistics to develop software for natural language analysis, generation, translation, and so on. This is a very exciting development, and I would encourage any graduate student to consider a job in this area just as seriously as a job in academia. I'll say it again: each person must determine what kind of career satisfies his needs best and brings the fewest impediments to the style of life, values, and personal development he desires.

The Inside Track
Leaving Academia for the Corporate World
Ami Kronfeld

> *After receiving a Ph.D. in philosophy from Berkeley, Ami Kronfeld taught at Cornell for two years and re-enrolled as a graduate student in a master's program in computer science. After that, he worked at SRI International in Menlo Park, California; at a start-up company in Berkeley, California; and at Microsoft Research. He is now an independent consultant.*

I am often asked why I left academia. There were many reasons. One of them was the academic job market. Both my wife and I were academics (she still is), and when both of us began looking for jobs, it quickly became obvious that we would be very lucky to get university positions within the same *state,* let alone the same city or county. Such prospects were quite depressing.

But not all my reasons for leaving academia were related to a tight job market. I enjoyed teaching quite a bit, but I sure did not like grading papers. I liked my area of specialty (logic and the philosophy of language) very much, but I did not have much interest in other, fairly central areas of my discipline. Moreover, although I was fascinated by the conceptual complexity and abstraction of the philosophical problems

I was working on, I also craved involvement in something tangibly useful, something that writing an esoteric academic paper definitely is not. In short, although I liked my academic field and by all indications was pretty good at it, it was far from a perfect fit for me.

But above all, in retrospect, it seems to me that my decision to leave academia had to do with the simple fact that I *changed my mind*. Of course, the process was hardly as easy or as painless as it might seem, given this description. The "changing of mind" part was not even entirely conscious.

For those of you contemplating a move out of academia, I would advise you, first and foremost, to give yourself some time to find out what you might want and *like* to do outside academia. If my own experience is any indication, the view of the nonacademic world from within academia is rather narrow. As I was to find out later, there were lots of interesting possibilities outside academia I was not even remotely aware of.

The good news is that you already have considerable skills that are very much in demand. The bad news is that, like many academics (including myself at the time), you are in all likelihood vastly underestimating what you can offer a potential employer outside academia. My own biggest problem initially was the little voice inside my head asserting that the one and only thing I knew how to do was write academic papers in philosophy. If this was true, I would have been in trouble. But, of course, it was not.

Let me explain this point a bit. Some of the skills you have are derived from your particular field. For example, a friend of mine, a former ethnographer, is now applying her knowledge of the discipline in helping companies design their products (and making a good living in the process). My own background in the philosophy of language (which included a significant amount of linguistics) was certainly essential for me to get a position in artificial intelligence and later find work in a company that specialized in an English interface to databases. But apart from such specific skills, there are other abilities that may be just as useful. For example, if you are a good teacher, you have good communication skills, which are always in demand. If you happen to have organized a conference at your institution, you can be sure that most organizational tasks at an average company will be simpler than that. Just by finishing your thesis, you have shown that you are an independent thinker who is experienced in focusing on a problem, searching for possible solutions. Such a skill is highly valued in many workplaces.

Recognizing the type of skills that you may have and that are relevant to nonacademic employment is a crucial step if you plan to leave academia. But after years of having the university as your only professional frame of reference, this is a difficult task. Fortunately, there are good books that help you in this process, and I would highly recommend using them (I did). Apart from helping you see your abilities in a new perspective, the recognition of the valuable skills that you already possess will boost your confidence. A particular book that was very helpful to me at the time was

How to Get the Job You Want in 28 Days by Tom Jackson (New York: E. P. Dutton, 1982). Of course, this book may be hopelessly outdated today (not a single Web site to be found there!), but its main points are still valid and helpful, I believe.

One thing that hit me in the face when I was about to leave academia was my total ignorance of the most basic and mundane realities of the business world. For example, I did not know the difference between an academic c.v. and a business resume. Nor did I know how to apply for a job in industry or what the difference was between an academic job interview and a business interview. This was a significant problem, and I solved it in a typical academic way: by searching for books to help me out. I used *The Perfect Resume* by Tom Jackson (Garden City, N.Y.: Anchor Books, 1981), and later I used *How to Have a Winning Job Interview* by Deborah Perlmutter Bloch (Lincolnwood, Ill.: VGM Career Horizons, 1988).

For example, when you are interviewed for a job, would you know how to approach the topic of a salary? This was not the kind of thing I knew anything about when I left academia, but I found a little booklet about the subject, *How to Make $1,000 a Minute: Negotiating Salaries and Raises* by Jack Chapman (Berkeley, Calif.: Ten Speed Press, 1987), and one of the simple, but extremely useful, insights I got from it was that it is *always* in my best interest to try to make the interviewers specify how much *they* are willing to pay first. It's kind of obvious, but with my mindset at the time, it would never have occurred to me. Moreover, the book provided simple and effective techniques I might actually use to do this in an interview. Applying what this book taught me made a significant difference in my income.

What most academics do fairly well is extract information from books quickly and efficiently. Make use of this skill. Of course, don't expect any intellectual depth from the "how to" genre. But on the other hand, don't let the all too frequent combination of academic arrogance and insecurity (especially when dealing with the business sector) prevent you from benefiting from such books.

Of course, books are not the only source for useful information. Friends outside academia, for example, can be as helpful, if not more.

If you can manage it, undertake some formal or vocational training before looking for a job: it could only help. Obviously, if you choose to be a lawyer, you need to go to law school, and if you want to be a doctor, you should go to medical school. You don't need me to tell you that. But the same is frequently true of other career choices. For example, the days in which you could have gotten decent on-the-job training in computers are long gone. A computer company may hire you as, say, a linguist, but if you don't have an independent knowledge of programming, your opportunities will be quite limited. In my case, for example, getting a master's in computer science proved to be very valuable, and similar programs exist for other fields as well.

On the other hand, avoid at all costs the trap of the perpetual student, no matter how good you are at being one. Make sure to take advantage of academic courses outside your department that you might be able to audit while still in academia. My very first chance to work with computers was a beginning programming course I took during my very last year as a Ph.D. student. In retrospect, this course simply changed my life. I also took quite a few computer courses while teaching philosophy at Cornell. This proved to be extremely useful as well.

Needless to say, I was quite a bit older than my peers when I studied computer science and when I joined computer companies. I am often asked whether I feel age was ever a problem. Well, not in my case, I don't think, although I was certainly conscious of the age difference. When you change course the way I did, you don't start from scratch. You bring with you a rich combination of knowledge, experience, and a degree of maturity that works much in your favor. So in the right context, age is an advantage. Of course, some kids were much faster programmers than I was, and that was occasionally hard to swallow. But there were other things I was better at precisely because I was older.

The issue of age is a complex one, both objectively and subjectively. A good friend of mine, also an ex-philosopher, stayed in academia much longer than I did, but eventually decided on a career in law. He was accepted to a top-notch law school, made the law review, and ranked very high in his class. Still, he did not get nearly as many job offers (or even interviews) as did younger students with lesser credentials. So I think age *was* a factor in his case. He didn't have any problem getting a job, though.

So how is life in the business sector different from that in academia? Well, if you leave academia for the business world, your monetary compensation is likely to be higher. Perhaps substantially so, if you are lucky. You will also be *much* more flexible in choosing where you live, what company you are affiliated with, for how long, and so on. My own first encounter with such flexibility was nothing short of exhilarating. While expanding your mind, academia can simultaneously narrow down your options significantly.

Another positive aspect of work outside academia is the chance for a more *immediate* sense of accomplishment and satisfaction. I am not saying that the academic life lacks these qualities—far from it. My own experience of writing a scholarly book gave me a tremendous sense of accomplishment, and I know many academics who find research very rewarding. But such activities take a long time, the results are rather intangible, and it is frequently difficult to gauge their impact. In the business sector, on the other hand, accomplishments and rewards are both immediate and concrete. You are given an assignment, and when you finish—say, three weeks later—then you are *done* and you have something both fairly concrete and immanently useful in hand. This is, indeed, a pleasant surprise: someone truly *needs* what you have just produced! Moreover, you have probably produced it as part of a team, which, if you are lucky, consists of a group of people who are both helpful and fun to collaborate with. Such experiences were in sharp contrast to my bouts of self-doubt when I was working alone on my book for months, occasionally wondering who the hell cared.

This leads to another point that is hardly ever mentioned nowadays, but is nevertheless very important in my view. Work outside academia is more likely to give you a chance to develop some sort of craftsmanship you can be proud of. I have tremendous respect for people who have mastered a craft: carpenters, drummers, trapeze artists, computer programmers, cooks, or what have you. If academia is mainly about knowing *what,* work outside academia is to a very large extent about knowing *how* (a great oversimplification, but bear with me for now). Whether you help design a successful product, win an important case in court, or put a new roof over a house, one aspect of your pride is your *craftsmanship.* And academia—especially the humanities—does not offer too many venues to show craftsmanship in this sense (teaching at a university is an obvious and important exception, but regrettably it is not valued nearly as much as it should be).

This was the good news, but the business sector has a down side as well. One of the most significant differences between the business sector and academia is simply this: in the business sector, the sole purpose of whatever you are asked to do is *to make money.* With rare exceptions, money is the ultimate criterion by which the value of your work is to be judged by your managers.

You already know that, of course. But until you actually experience this reality, I assure you that you don't understand what it really means. Let me tell you, it takes getting used to. The academic world is very, *very* different.

Is making money a bad thing? Of course not. But accepting the goal of making money as the ultimate criterion, to the exclusion of everything else, has some definite consequences. For example, even if you were denied tenure under the most reprehensibly political circumstances, you were in all likelihood given close to a year at full salary during which you could contemplate your next move. This is a luxury that is unheard of in the business sector. In most layoff cases, you are given about *two hours* to clear your office and leave the premises. This happened to me once (although I was just a consultant at the time), and I have seen it happen to about twenty coworkers. Until you see with your own eyes what this does to people, you don't fully understand what the absolute commitment to maximize profit might mean (incidentally, the United States is the only country among the industrially developed nations where surprise layoffs on a large scale with no severance pay are tolerated).

There are other, more benign consequences of the mythical *bottom line.* For example, in academia you are expected to produce the very best quality of work that you are capable of. In the business sector, on the other hand, you are expected to produce the very best quality of work that you are capable of *within a rigid time frame.* The difference is significant. Of course, academia has its own pressing deadlines that force you to compromise: book reviews, grading periods, letters of recommendation, search committees, publication dates, and on and on—not to mention the tenure clock. But in the area that matters most—your research—deadlines are usually measured in months, if not years. Moreover, if in the end you remain unsatisfied with the results of your research, you can almost always decide not to publish. Such a decision may have consequences, but it is nevertheless entirely up to you. You are the final authority on your own professional integrity.

In the business sector, on the other hand, deadlines are typically a matter of weeks, if not days, and quality compromises are by far the rule rather than the exception. All too often quality is not even the primary goal. That's the down side of the craftsmanship issue I mentioned earlier. You are given the chance to exercise a craft, but frequently you are not given enough time to do it right. If you are like most people—that is, if you'd like to take pride in your work—that's a significant issue.

This is related to another significant difference between academia and the business world. Both universities and corporations are fairly rigid, top-down, hierarchical institutions. But obviously there is a significant difference between academia and the business sector regarding power and autonomy at the bottom, or even in the intermediate level. Even if you don't have tenure yet, you probably have some flexibility as to *which* classes you teach. You are granted still more freedom in deciding *how* to teach these classes, and you are entirely autonomous in deciding what problems your research is about (well, not quite, especially if you depend on grant money, but let's ignore this for now).

In the business sector, the situation is different, of course. You can be reassigned to a different project at any given moment or be moved to a different department at the drop of a hat. There is no denying that this uncertainty is part and parcel of the work environment. Some people adapt better than others, but all must deal with it. Having said that, however, I would add that there were extended periods of time in which I managed to achieve a significant degree of autonomy, working on projects that I initiated and developed. And I was not alone in this by any means. Even in the business sector, there are areas of stability where you can find your niche and enjoy a fairly rich and productive professional life.

The fact is that most people work and live within this framework, and if they are privileged enough to possess the educational level and background that readers of this book are likely to have, they frequently thrive in it. It is the academic world that is the exception.

So what's the upshot of all this? In a nutshell, you have many more options than you might think. If a university setting does not work for you for any reason, it does not mean that your professional life must be second rate. Not by a long shot. I should also add that the business world is certainly not the only alternative. I have focused on the business side because this is where I had the most experience outside academia. But nonprofit organizations, government agencies, political groups, and other noncorporate entities may offer work opportunities every bit as interesting and rewarding.

Part
Two

The Academic
Profession

6 | The Life of the Assistant Professor

Tell us what it is like to be a brand new assistant professor beginning that first job.

John Goldsmith: Of all the transitions that we have occasion to discuss in this book—and there are many—the transition from being a graduate student to being an assistant professor is the most difficult. This is truly the moment when one becomes an adult in the academic world, and fully responsible for one's actions. The assistant professor is suddenly in unfamiliar territory, without a very good road map.

Some of the problems the assistant professor is likely to face are normal by-products of a move, a change of locale, and she is likely to feel how anyone leaving one city and one job for another will feel. She is likely to need to find a new home to live in, to become oriented to a new city and region of the country, and to find new friends.

John Komlos: Indeed! Many new and major challenges lie ahead. This is independent of the kind of institution you've joined because it is surely going to be different from what you are accustomed to. However, you should take comfort in your demonstrated ability to persevere and succeed. After all, you do have a full-time academic job, and not everyone can boast of that. Graduate school was undoubtedly a major challenge, perhaps even a grueling experience at times, but you had the inner strength to persevere and the talent to complete the program. That automatically puts you into the top few percentiles of the intellectual community.

While it can, and usually does, provide a truly rewarding experience, academia ought not be idealized: it has plenty of surprises, and many similarities with how other bureaucratic systems function. It is perhaps worth repeating that even though you have joined this elite group, you should not expect your salary to reflect it. You need to obtain your satisfaction from your teaching, your research, and the esteem in which you will be held by those around you, and not from your income.

John Goldsmith: Many graduate students will have had some experience teaching undergraduate courses—expository writing courses or introductory courses in their particular area. Most of the time, this experience will have been under the direct tutelage of an overseeing professor, and the student will have had little experience putting together a syllabus, for example, from scratch.

John Komlos: Or in conceptualizing a course from beginning to end.

Penny Gold: You are now both an adult professional, fully responsible for your own work, with virtually no direct supervision, and a neophyte in a totally new environment.

It doesn't help that your adaptation to a new situation takes place when you are probably the most overwhelmed you will ever be. All your course preparations will be new (a situation you'll never have to face again), and you might be trying to finish your dissertation at the same time as well as beginning to publish. Introductory courses, where you may be teaching material way out of your specific field, can be especially challenging. I remember hoping, that first year, that no student would ask me a question in class because everything I knew about the subject I had just told them in my lecture. I also remember a colleague comforting me with the information that some years down the road the time I would spend on teaching would be the least of what kept me busy. I had trouble imagining this, but it is certainly true that the balance of activities changes over the years.

How do you juggle the various responsibilities—teaching, research, and service?

John Goldsmith: There are two especially severe problems facing junior faculty members that deserve our special attention. First, how should she deal with the transition from being a researcher under someone's direct supervision to being an independent researcher? And, second, how should she determine the best way to distribute her time and energy among the competing demands that she faces in the job, demands involving teaching, research, and service? We will take these up in turn.

The juggling problem is the single most difficult problem that a junior academic has to face. If all has gone well in graduate school, you have already learned how to do research, but now you have to learn how to do research while being an assistant professor. That's like learning how to balance a stick on your nose and then learning how to do it while riding a bicycle.

Each person has to decide for herself, of course, how she wants to develop her life and her career. There is no particular recipe regarding how one ought to balance teaching, research, and service. Each course offers certain rewards and demands, varying sorts of involvement and activities. Teaching can be a very social activity, in which there is much interaction with young people; service is social as well, though perhaps a bit less; research tends to be a good deal less social. But while each person has to make her own decisions based on her own strengths and personal values, there are a number of traps and potential difficulties that it is worthwhile pointing out. Behind any discussion lies the following fact: the years as an assistant professor lead inexorably to a decision that will be passed regarding one's professorial activities, the tenure decision. In most cases, assistant professors believe that they are working in a fashion designed to help them pass this critical examination. But in far too many cases, they make choices—not randomly, but in a consistent pattern—that make it difficult or even impossible for them to get tenure.

The biggest issue is one that is simple and well known, and that goes by the name "publish or perish." Spelled out in full, at most universities, if your publication record is not satisfactory, nothing else will save you when it comes time for evaluation for tenure. Tenure and evaluation for tenure are a subject we'll take up later (see chapter 8); for now, we may just take our problem to be what an assistant professor should (and shouldn't) do in order to produce a satisfactory record in research, teaching, and service so as to not have a rude shock at tenure time.

John Komlos: Because each person's situation is unique in important ways, it is possible only to make vague generalizations about the way an assistant professor should allocate time. Ultimately, you should be comfortable with it, but do make sure that the sum of the daily demands on your time does not exceed twenty-four hours. Often they do. And do keep the tenure clock always in the back of your mind. The rule is that years will always fly by much quicker than you anticipate, and you cannot afford to put your research agenda on the back burner. Of course, the degree to which teaching matters varies across institutions, but be aware that at research universities it does not actually count toward tenure. It is taken for granted that you will do an adequate job in the classroom. At most liberal arts colleges, however, teaching is most important because these institutions found their niche in higher education by attracting students through their reputation for good teaching.

Teaching is your most immediate responsibility and, together with class preparation and research, will consume about 85 percent of your working hours or even your waking hours (see table 7 in appendix 3). There are a number of additional claims on one's time, including giving papers and attending conferences, but these occur at irregular intervals. There are also responsibilities that are of negligible importance at the outset of a typical academic career, including dissertation advising and peer reviewing (i.e., making recommendations for grants and promotions and reviewing manuscripts for journals and publishers). At small colleges, you will be expected to do some community service or talk to local newspapers about current events pertaining to your discipline so that the college will gain some valuable publicity.

Penny Gold: The ratio of time spent on various activities changes significantly over time. In my first year of teaching, I did little besides prepare for class, eat, sleep (not enough), and bring my new "lemon" of a car in for repairs. Now, twenty-six years later, I spend as much time on administration and service as I do on teaching prep, and I get significantly more sleep (though still not as much as I would like).

Can you help me to sort out what my priorities should be?

John Goldsmith: Consider the three fundamental laws of academia: (1) you must be in your classroom at the hours when your classes meet, (2) your participation in various service activities will often be sought, and (3) no one will ask you to do your research until it's too late. I hope that most people would think these rules so natural as to not need saying. But I am amazed to discover that many people think that even these simple rules do not apply to them. They do.

Most of us will be asked to do more than we can possibly manage. It's often necessary simply to say "no" in the face of requests and demands on junior faculty members' time. The burdensome requests all too frequently take up time and energy for functions that are of relatively low priority in the larger scheme of things at the university, and all too frequently those long-term projects that are, indeed, high on the university's scale will suffer: to wit, research and publishing. Remember that just because you're asked to do something doesn't mean it has to be done—or done by you. The world might just get along without you. If there's a job that no one has been willing to take on, it just might be for a good reason: the job might not be worth taking on.

It is also the case that if you're from a group that is traditionally underrepresented in the profession—if you are a woman or an African American, for example—you will be disproportionately subject to recruitment, and the opportunities for involvement in truly worthy causes may well be quite significant. You will be asked to be on more committees and task forces in order to make for a "balanced" group. An African-American faculty member at an institution with few African-American colleagues will understandably feel a responsibility to spend time mentoring African-American graduate students in her department, or even in other departments, when a white colleague will most likely feel no parallel responsibility. In the best sense of the term, the young black assistant professor is now a role model, and there's a lot of pressure (internal and external) to live up to the burden of that responsibility. Each person must follow her conscience in cases like this, but it would be an enormous loss all the way around if she were to let those short-term opportunities have a serious negative effect on her early research program. I in no way want to send the message that these opportunities to help others should be passed by, but simply bear this in mind: don't count on anyone looking over your shoulder to tell you that you are or aren't doing enough research—you've got to take that responsibility on yourself, and you'd better listen to what your internal voice says on that score.

Penny Gold: Sorting out these multiple requests is an ongoing challenge. Our institutions cannot function unless we say "yes" to any number of things beyond our regular schedule: things like search committees, ad hoc task forces, independent study courses, student group advising, and presentations to an admissions function or alumni group. And quite a few of these tasks are interesting and rewarding. But you will be asked to do many more things than you can do. Take the time to figure out if this is something that (1) you have the talent or skill for, (2) you have a strong interest in or commitment to, (3) you think has a good chance of bearing fruit, and/or (4) will help you connect with other people you're interested in working with.

What keeps us from saying "no"? The pressures are somewhat different for untenured and tenured professors. Untenured faculty may be concerned that one has to please tenured faculty, the administration, and students at every turn. Tenured faculty sometimes think the institution's welfare demands that we do everything we possibly can. Yes, the health and welfare of the institution depend on each one of us contributing beyond our teaching and research to the service of the institution. But the institution will be best served by having faculty who contribute out of commitment and interest in the ways best suited to them. It's not well served by having faculty worked to a frazzle doing tasks beyond us or whose value we're not sure of. Here are some ways to say "no": "I wish I could, but I really don't have time for a formal commitment. Maybe we could just talk once or twice." "I'm afraid I'm not the best person to help you with this. Have you thought about asking Professor N.?" "I'm sorry, but I've just got too many other commitments right now." "That sounds interesting, but can I call you back tomorrow? I need a little time to think about it before I decide."

People in shared appointments are in a particularly difficult position in this regard. You will probably be asked to do just as many extra things as full-time faculty, but in keeping with your contractual obligations and in fairness to your sanity, you should say "no" twice as often as other people. This is hard! And people—both faculty and students—may forget (or not realize) you're half-time and may be frustrated that you don't seem to be in your office very much. I suggest you tell students at the beginning of every course that you're half-time and that they may have to wait a bit longer for an appointment. (If you can offer phone or e-mail contact during stretches you're not at the office, this can help.) And it doesn't hurt to remind colleagues on occasion as well, in a matter-of-fact way.

On the other hand, there are some people who don't say "yes" enough, who somehow think that their time is more important than everyone else's. Their withdrawal makes life even harder for people who do say "yes," as we're asked to do all that many more things.

Why should I begin to think about tenure now?

John Komlos: The tenure decision is the next important step in your academic career (see chapter 8). Suffice it to say at this point that you should be thinking about it from the minute you arrive on campus. In setting priorities, it is essential to realize that getting tenure is not going to be a snap. Landing a job is, of course, an achievement in itself, but you still face further hurdles to gain permanent membership in the community of professional scholars. You do not have much time, and you need to think about viable strategies not only to make it through the first year, but also to achieve tenure six years down the road. A good rule-of-thumb to follow is that projects usually take twice as long to complete as initially thought, and do not forget that overcommitment will affect your overall performance. One easy way to keep commitments manageable is to avoid accepting summer teaching assignments. (They are paid at the meager part-time rate of $2,000–$3,000 a course, which will rarely compensate for the loss in lifetime earnings that results from your diminished research productivity.)

You probably broached the topic of tenure during the job interview, even if only in passing, but upon arrival on campus, you should discuss it again more fully with your chair (and with your colleagues in turn) until you have a good idea of the actual departmental expectations for promotion.[1] She cannot possibly give you a firm commitment because there are so many variables involved, and requirements are always ambiguous and flexibly applied. The criteria for tenure generally entail meeting local standards of scholarship, teaching, and good citizenship, generally in that order, though at liberal arts colleges, teaching is taken more seriously than research. The better-known colleges, such as Carleton, Dartmouth, and Amherst, for example, will also require a respectable publications record for tenure, though, as a rule, they are not as strict about making the distinction between original research and synthetic works. A textbook, for instance, even a good one, would not suffice for tenure at a research university, but may serve you well at a small college. You might be expected to write a book in a history department, but how long it should be, or where it should be published, or just how good the reviews are expected to be will remain open. Because of the vagueness in the criteria to obtain tenure, you will need to be on the lookout for information to help you interpret the standards to which you will be held at your institution. You need to sort out what the criteria will mean in your case, and talking about it with your colleagues over coffee can gain you a more nuanced understanding of it.

John Goldsmith: I am reminded of one difficult case, where a linguist was hired by a computer science department on the basis of his strong background in computational linguistics and a Ph.D. in linguistics. While the university in question was primarily a teaching university, the chair of the department wanted to develop a strong core of researchers who would teach less and publish more. A number of young scholars were hired under the banner of more research, less teaching, but when these scholars began to come up for tenure decisions, the scholarship issue was so downplayed compared to teaching load and ratings that tenure became a difficult matter for the researchers.

Penny Gold: One of the biggest joys of getting tenure is that you don't have to think about tenure anymore. I didn't even realize the weight of the ever-looming decision until some months after the granting of tenure, when I realized the relief of its absence. The pressure is very hard to avoid. But that doesn't mean it has to totally dominate your life. Don't compromise on your principles, even if you sometimes compromise on matters of desire. And try to find some friends outside the academy with whom you can have conversations about something else!

Getting good information about past decisions may relieve anxiety by helping you deal realistically with the tenure situation at your institution. Asking about the reasons for recent past denials of contract renewal or tenure should yield helpful information. But beware of uninformed (even if strongly opinionated) nonauthoritative sources. Negative decisions can lay down a wide train of paranoia—sometimes deserved, but not always. Here's one instance where department chairs are an important source of information (concerning people in their department), but not always an entirely reliable one, depending on what side of the issue they were on.

How about getting along with my new colleagues? I'm a little worried about that.

Penny Gold: Much depends on getting to know the culture of the institution you've joined. Get to campus at least a few weeks before the semester begins so that you can scout out the place and the people before you're swamped with work. How does the institution work? Who are the key players? What values characterize the place? What intellectual approaches are dominant? What interpersonal styles? And the same for your department. You will have brought bits and pieces of information about some of these things back from your job interview, but this is the time to really develop your knowledge. Whatever observational and analytical skills you've developed in your graduate education should now be trained on this place and these people. While your main long-term professional goal may be framed in terms of your individual success, that success is possible only within the context of a good working relationship with your institution. And the longer you're at a place, the more likely it is that one of your professional goals will be to contribute to the development and success of your institution. This can even become a quite rewarding aspect of the job—the chance to become an effective member of a complex institution. If you're lucky, your first place of employment will be one with which you feel your own goals and style are compatible. (Would that finding a teaching job were like finding a college to go to, where you can shop around for just the right one for you within your competitive range.) But even if you feel at cross-purposes with the institution, you'll need to develop congenial and effective enough working relations so that people will recommend you when you want to move elsewhere.

Life in the academy will be easier if you can get along with a wide variety of people, including some you're not particularly fond of. In a large university, the arena of concern is predominantly one's department. In a smaller college, departmental relations are crucial, but interactions will spread much more broadly through the institution. The more you know about how the institution works and who the main actors are, the more effective you can be, and the less you will feel at the mercy of unknown forces.

How does one learn all these things? Some of what you need to know is available in writing (for example, in the faculty handbook—very dull, but required reading). But most things you'll need to learn through observation and through active questioning. Hook up with a variety of people to whom you can turn when you have questions about things. Why did Professor X and Professor Y flare up at each other like that in the faculty meeting? Why wouldn't anyone talk about issue Z at the department meeting? Why didn't Professor A get tenure last year? One of your main goals for your first year or so should be to get to know a fair number of people on campus. This is for the purpose not just of making friends, which is certainly important in any new environment, but also of finding people who will be good sources of information and advice for you. One or two of these people will, with luck, turn into mentoring figures, without which your travel through the institutional thicket will be much harder.

Your department chair will be an important source for some information and advice, and should certainly be your first stop for information about anything at all technical about your employment (e.g., how to propose a new course, how to arrange for leave if one gets an outside grant).

But aim for a wide set of working relations within your department. These are often the people who can help you the most in the daily dilemmas you will face in your job. And, of course, they're the folks who will be voting on you for tenure several years down the road.

Look for people outside your department as well. Even if your department relations are thoroughly congenial, you'll want to be able to get perspective on your department. It could turn out that your chair has given you a distorted picture of past developments in the department or that an outside perspective can help you understand the complex personal relations within a department. You'll also just want some folks with whom you can blow off steam about departmental matters, something you should restrain yourself from doing within the department. One of the main advantages of having a spouse or partner at home is that you have such a sympathetic ear immediately. (That is, if they're not also a member of your department. If the two of you are in the same department, beware of the possible magnifying effect on any perceived problem.) But don't rely only on those at home. Seek out ways to see your situation from the perspective of other people within the institution. For several years, I had a colleague, a somewhat younger contemporary of mine in another department, with whom phone conversations would routinely begin: "Do you have any stories today?" Talking out the day's events with her was enormously therapeutic. Connections with people entirely outside your institution can also be useful, not only for advice about your research (more on that later), but also, once you know someone well, for discussion of comparative institutional politics.

Yes, it's an issue of politics. That is, some people in the institution have more power than others (whether from tenure, longevity at the institution, gender, personal relationships, or whatever), and power is not always used in the most rational ways or for the greater good. How to navigate the waters? The first thing is to work on charting the waters—the better you know the placement of shoals and submerged rocks, harbors and islands, the better you'll be able to make your way safely. And, of course, you'll do well to have the advice of someone who's made the same trip. But the landscape changes, new situations arise, and you'll have to go it on your own sooner than you think. I recommend five keys helpful to success in the academy, and necessary to the maintenance of self-respect. If you build relationships with colleagues on these five foundations, life will be easier. There's nothing special about these—they go into any set of long-term relationships. And that's what you hope collegial relationships will be—long-term!

1. *Tact:* If you're on a search committee and a senior colleague makes a strong pitch for a weak candidate whose only apparent virtue is that she is the student of a close friend, restrain yourself from calling your colleague on the carpet. Rather, make a convincing case for a candidate you know to be stronger; it's likely the other people on the search committee will join you in the vote. Later that night you can call up a confidant in another department and rail about the episode. This strategy of public tact combined with private stress reduction will serve you well. There's no need to embarrass anyone in public. If the matter under dispute is of no consequence, you should consider ignoring it. But if it's a matter of some significance and it's something you care about and have some knowledge of, go ahead and say something. Just have it be calm, rational, and persuasive. Your colleagues—some of them perhaps too timid to speak themselves—will be grateful.

2. *Integrity:* Tact does not mean misrepresentation or deception. You need to develop decent working relations with a wide variety of colleagues, and it's difficult to do this without a good measure of trust. Speaking and acting with integrity is the best way to gain that trust as well as to live happily with yourself.

3. *Sense of proportion:* Maybe it's true in other kinds of institutions as well, but sometimes huge controversies can develop over very small things. There will be many battles in which to engage. Choose the ones that really matter—to you and to the institution—and let the other ones run their own course.

4. *Humor:* Closely related to a sense of proportion is a sense of humor. If you can't see the humor in some of the situations you'll face, life will become very grim, indeed. And if you can help others lighten up occasionally, all the better.

5. *Follow-through:* If you say you're going to take care of something, do it. You want people to know they can rely on you—just as you want to be able to rely on them.

It's not easy to keep all these things at the center—I can think of perhaps one colleague over the years who acted consistently on all these principles, all the time. He was respected enormously on campus, and when he spoke at a faculty meeting, everyone listened—and mostly voted with him. We can't all be like that, but it is well worth the try.

John Komlos: This is all good advice, but an assistant professor will need time to learn where the boundary between tact and integrity lies or how to calibrate her sense of proportion. She will need time to learn how the issues play themselves out within the institutional framework. If she concentrates on the political side of academic life at the outset, her prospects for tenure might well be jeopardized at a research university.

I think, for example, it would be risky for an assistant professor at a research university to give specific advice on hiring decisions. This is particularly the case if senior professors are of a contrary mind. To take a particular stance could be costly at tenure time. At the beginning of her career, she should have the utmost concern for obtaining tenure for herself before she attempts to change the world around her. What does it help if one gains even a valued colleague at the expense of one's own tenure? Even later on in one's career, going to the mat on appointments is not always a rewarding experience because there is no assurance that one's assessment of particular candidates will turn out to be correct. I have erred many times on strategic issues to which I was completely oblivious at the time the decision was being made. It is also a bit presumptuous to think that at the start of one's career one's judgments are reliable. On the contrary, I have found that experience hones one's decision-making abilities. At other times, candidates whom I've supported have turned out to be subsequent adversaries. So it seems to me that hiring issues are generally much too complex for a freshly minted assistant professor to sort out with any degree of confidence. This is obviously different at small colleges, where more involvement is expected from the start. But it will be small consolation to you that your timid colleagues appreciate your speaking out on their behalf on controversial issues if those same timid colleagues remain too timid to speak out on your behalf at your tenure-decision time.

What about the institutional bureaucracy? I understand that can be a challenge to deal with.

John Komlos: You need to accept the institutional framework as it is. You have become part of an impersonal bureaucratic structure, similar to that in the corporate world. My advice is to avoid becoming actively involved in departmental politics for the time being and, above all, to avoid trying to influence major decisions. The institution is bigger than you; it is bigger than any single individual. There are myriad reasons why things are done as inefficiently, or illogically, as they appear. Accept them as givens, and if you do not particularly like them, simply do your utmost to leave on your own terms as soon as possible. It takes an immense amount of effort to reform an institution consisting of thousands of people with disparate needs and interests. If you attempt to do so, you might be caught in a bureaucratic squeeze. Leave that for later: once you have tenure, or even farther down the road, or never at all.

Penny Gold: As you might guess, I have a different take on this. It's true that colleges and universities are bureaucratic institutions, not easily changed. On the other hand, they are also changing all the time, and active participation in this change—helping an institution set and carry out a new agenda—can be tremendously gratifying. While untenured people should certainly give their teaching and research commitments top priority, there still can be room for significant participation in institutional change. The task force charged with drawing up a proposal for a new curriculum at Knox, for example, had three untenured and four tenured faculty on the committee. It would be awful for the institution to consider fundamental curriculum change without involving new scholars closest to recent developments in their fields. And I would guess that the individuals involved have found their work interesting and gratifying, even while time consuming.

John Komlos: However, for untenured faculty, I think it is safer to steer away from academic politics. You will have plenty of new responsibilities to which you need to become accustomed anyway. Concentrate on the crucial aspects of your job, such as getting tenure, by teaching, by publishing, and by gaining a foothold in this unfamiliar, and hence in many ways mysterious, world.

You need to know how the various parts fit together, how the system works, before you can begin to feel comfortable in it or before you can start to influence your environment for your own purposes. It is to your advantage to act from knowledge based on experience rather than from assumptions about how the system seemed to work while you were in graduate school. The social dynamics might be very different, partly because the people are different, partly because your position—hence vantage point—is different, and partly because the institutions are different.

Your colleagues have the advantage of considerable experience and will know how things work there. Who makes the decisions in particular cases? How is power distributed?[2] Who is part of which network, and how strongly are they connected to each other? How do the networks interact? Who talks to whom, and who listens to whom? How openly do your colleagues communicate with one another? What are the relationships among your colleagues' spouses? Consider the relationships among the spouses of your colleagues as an indication of factions within the department. If the spouses are on good terms with one another, the chances are that your colleagues will be as well. In addition, listen to what the spouses are saying because often they are conveying messages that your colleagues may not want to relate to you themselves. How are coalitions formed and decisions made? What is the history of relationships within the department? Who is beholden to whom? Who holds animosities toward whom? These factors will determine the dynamics of your department, and you are not likely to know much about them at the outset.

Assume a wait-and-see attitude. Be skeptical of appearances. Do not presume that everyone will always be guided exclusively by the most rigorous moral and legal principles. All social groups have their folkways—unwritten rules of conduct. Although the facade of propriety is often maintained, people nonetheless act differently in an organizational role than they do in private, particularly if responsibility can be passed on to someone else or if they perceive the risks of a particular act to be minimal.

You have essentially four tasks ahead of you regarding your professional career: to become a successful teacher, to establish and slowly build up your scholarly reputation, to work toward obtaining tenure, and to do all this while avoiding being overwhelmed by the organization. It is possible to succeed only by developing effective strategies to publish, to teach, and to get along with your colleagues and administrators. Though this is by no means easy, if you pay attention to how your department functions, you can learn on the job, upgrade your information set in the process, and adjust your actions accordingly.

One reasonable strategy that will help you to avoid becoming too involved or entangled in institutional politics is to assert forthrightly that you are not interested in such matters. Your primary goal is to obtain tenure. Such a strategy can get you off the hook to some degree, particularly in the beginning. However, you should attend departmental meetings. They will be educational because you can get to know your colleagues much better in that setting. Caution is, however, warranted. People often argue obliquely or strategically, or they do not mean what they say, or what they say has various interpretations that are not immediately obvious.[3]

Each department has its own idiosyncratic ways to channel differences and arrive at a decision. There might be a lot of open conflict, in which case you will have difficulty staying neutral. And there might be many controversial issues that have to be decided in some form by people who have not been selected on the basis of their diplomatic skills. Hiring and tenure decisions tend to be the most contentious ones, as they determine the future course of the department. On the other hand, the absence of overt discord does not necessarily mean that decisions are made harmoniously. It could also be an outcome of strong and successful leadership by the chair.

Your relationship with the senior colleagues will undoubtedly influence how departmental standards for tenure are applied in your case. The chair has considerable flexibility in this regard. For instance, if you are well liked, coauthored publications might be treated as though you had written them by yourself. If you are popular among tenured members of the faculty, the fact that your publications did not appear in refereed journals could be overlooked. The publication of your dissertation by a minor press might be viewed as though it had been published by major university press.

Once you've been in the department for awhile, the existence and composition of factions will become apparent to you. Keep to your own business by remaining noncommittal. "It sure sounds plausible, but I would like to find out more about the issue." You can always nod while saying "maybe." "It is fine with me to hire another econometrician." "It seems perfectly reasonable to. . . ." "I have no strong opinions on who the next chair should be." I am reminded of Polonius's advice to his son, Laertes, as the latter is about to set off for France. In the same breath that Polonius urges, "To thine own self be true," he also admonishes, "Give every man thy ear, but few thy voice."

This does not mean that you need to remain completely silent on committees or at departmental meetings. If you were to do so, you might convey the impression that you do not care at all about the department. But you should certainly choose noncontroversial issues on which to express an opinion. It is usually safe to talk about the inadequacies of the department's or the library's budget, for example. And do not press the issue if you were disregarded. The chances are that it was not accidental. In short, you need to demonstrate willingness to be a good citizen. In any case, politics is usually one of the most unanticipated and unsavory expects of academic life.

What if I am unable to stay out of the fray?

John Komlos: A department that does not allow its assistant professors to remain apolitical cannot be a healthy place to put down roots, and you should avoid making a long-term commitment to the institution.

Penny Gold: It's certainly true that some departments are snake pits and that survival at the institution will mean constantly guarding your tongue, watching your back, and checking out key information with multiple sources both within and outside of the department. But other departments are dominated by senior faculty who care deeply about the success and professional growth of untenured faculty as well as about the educational mission of the department. And others, of course, are in between. In some departments, a studied avoidance of controversial issues will be interpreted as a lack of backbone or of commitment to the institution. Would you want to rely on someone who never risks a stance on a significant issue? You need to figure out what the character of your own department is and then do your best to accomplish your professional goals in that setting.

John Komlos: Exactly my point. But for most people, it will take several years to figure out what the lay of the land is, and by that time, you will be close to your tenure decision anyhow. In the meanwhile, Polonius's advice should be heeded. An unnamed member of Yale's history department paraphrased it with much less eloquence: "it's perceived wisdom that when you're a junior faculty member, you keep your mouth shut."[4]

Penny Gold: The size of the institution (and hence your department) will affect the nature of collegial relations. Politics within a large department at a university is usually more complex than within a small department at a college, where it is much easier to get to know all your colleagues and to develop working relationships with them. On the other hand, there are pitfalls in such a small environment as well. If one or two of the people in the department are difficult personalities or disdainful of the kind of work that you do, it is virtually impossible to avoid them. In a large department, a tenure vote of thirty-two to three will probably not endanger a favorable decision, while in a small department, where the voting members may number only three, one or two negative votes may well determine the outcome. And the pressure to conform may be greater in a small place than in a larger one, where diversity of lifestyle and intellectual position (not to mention race, gender, ethnicity, sexual orientation, and religion) may be taken for granted. The five principles of tact, integrity, sense of proportion, sense of humor, and follow-through will be of service to you in any of these environments. Just because others lack integrity doesn't mean you should lose yours! You have to be able to live with yourself, knowing that you've done the best you could.

Doing one's best matters in more than one arena. The central arena is, of course, one's own personal accomplishments in teaching and research—the core of academic work. But there is also the larger institutional arena, in which one should be, as John Komlos says, "a good citizen." The university or college is the community we've become part of through employment, and its success is dependent on each of us being willing to think beyond our own little niche to the larger issues of departmental/institutional functioning, such as curriculum, searches, educational policies, and the like, which keep the place running and carrying out its mission. I don't see the logic of waiting until one is tenured to participate actively in this larger arena. Yes, the extent of the time commitment can reasonably be less when untenured, but institutions cannot thrive if only a small handful of people do all the work of maintenance and change. I would hope that you want your institution to thrive and so will contribute to the effort it takes to make that happen. And if you want to find a cynical reason to do this related to the bottom line of your own chances for tenure, you can factor in that senior colleagues may be resentful if you're not doing your share. In some institutions, that share will be very small; in others, it will be larger. Another thing for you to figure out!

John Komlos: I can see that working in a small college setting, but the untenured professor at a research university is going to run into serious problems unless she concentrates on research and teaching during the first five years. One has to be aware of the fact that at a research university being a good citizen is not going to count one iota at tenure time. In fact, one has to be very careful how one allocates time even after tenure. I'll give you one example at a major department vying for top national ranking. A tenured faculty member was effectively booted out—not given any raises at a time of sizable inflation. Her only sin was writing a textbook—it was not considered original research! Admittedly, this might seem like an extreme case, but it isn't. The general rule at a research university is that the pressures to publish original research can be very strong.

If I want to become involved in changing something at my institution, how should I do this?

Penny Gold: Here are some thoughts on how to enhance your effectiveness as you seek improvements or new directions in your department or in the institution as a whole.

1. *Work with other people.*[5] We each have our own pet peeves and ideas about what may need to change at the institution. The key to successful change, however, is to find those nodes around which a "critical mass" of faculty interested in the particular problem can be gathered. An initiating idea may come from one person, but if it's to have a chance of success, it needs to be bounced around, reshaped, and perhaps rejected for a better one that arises in the discussion. If you're the only person who cares, it won't happen—even if you're right. If you want to effect institutional change, you've got to be prepared to work with others. And, of course, to work with others, you have to know them—another reason to network both within your department and beyond.

2. *Avoid self-righteousness.* As one of my colleagues has said, "Today I cringe when I recall how ferociously my flaming sword burned." An impatient, self-righteous, or hostile attitude will prejudice your position, not help it. Learn about the institutional history and context for the particular problem that interests you. The solution you seek may have been considered before and defeated. Maybe now the time is ripe, but you should know the past history, seek out those who participated in the previous discussion for information and advice, and then consider your path of action.

3. *Choose your battles.* Take into account which issues and principles are most important to you, which ones are also likely to engage a good group of colleagues, and which have at least some chance of success in the current institutional environment.

4. *Use appropriate channels.* Every institution has a governance structure, one of the main purposes of which is to generate, discuss, and move along ideas for change. Find out what committee oversees the area of your concern. Talk to the chair of the committee to see if your item can be put on the agenda. Depending on the nature of the proposal, approval at the committee level may then mean that the item is brought to the whole faculty (or a faculty senate) for consideration and final approval. Sometimes committees are unresponsive, and other routes should be looked for. But you'll generally get a better reception if ideas have been passed through the structure in a standard route. And don't go over people's heads without very good reason. If something can be settled by your department chair, go there rather than to the dean.

5. *Talk out issues ahead of time.* Before the meeting at which a decision is going to be made, talk with your fellow change makers and others about the issue that is going to come up. This will help you see the lay of the land, from which you can refine your own positions. And if you see ahead

of the meeting that there's no way the proposal will pass, you might want to drop it or hold off until another time.

6. *Learn Robert's Rules.* Be observant at meetings run by Robert's Rules so you can pick up on how procedures like amending a motion, tabling a motion, and calling the question can be used to move an issue in a particular direction.

7. *Do the work.* Proposals need to be written by someone. There were two key policy changes at Knox that all concerned agreed upon (a reduction of teaching load and the introduction of a parental leave policy), but weren't happening because no one was writing up the prose. I volunteered to write up drafts of the policies, which then were revised in committee and implemented. Doing the work is an effective strategy for change!

John Komlos: Remember, though, that you are an assistant professor on a short-term contract, dependent on the approval of your colleagues and hopeful of tenure, and that your influence will remain very limited for the time being. If you are unhappy with the politics, make plans to leave. But do not spread the word that you are unhappy as a consequence of the politics of the place because that will diminish your chances. The grass may not turn out to be so much greener on the other side of the fence, and people do not like to hire unhappy people in any event. And people may well interpret your unhappiness as being caused by your inability to get along in any impersonal bureaucratic institutional setting.

What about long-term goals?

John Komlos: How to allocate your precious time among your competing responsibilities will depend on your aspirations and on such other factors as how far away you find yourself from your ultimate goal, your degree of commitment to reaching it, and how much time you are willing to give yourself to reach it.

Your longer-range plans depend on the degree to which you are committed to your current institution. It is possible that the offer you accepted is one that matches your aspirations and those of the department. It is possible that you have good students and like the courses you are teaching. Perhaps you always wanted to teach at a small liberal arts college, and you finally have an opportunity to do so. Great! You can consider yourself among the lucky ones. Since you are not concerned with job mobility, your main task will be to keep your job by fulfilling the expectations of your colleagues with your teaching and publications. In such a case, you would devote relatively more of your time to your immediate responsibilities than to tasks that might increase your ability to move.

You should periodically reassess how realistic the goals are that you have set for yourself. In the academic world, known for its mobility, it is rather exceptional for a professor to retire from the institution in which she started her career. For many, but not for all, mobility is in an upward direction. One could debate whether it is harder to work one's way up or to start high up in the hierarchy and worry about sliding down. I suspect that there is not much difference. Both have their own problems and challenges. I have seen people succeed and fail in both situations. I believe that the most important factor is self-confidence. In the long run, competition usually works in such a way that people will reach their own level of excellence at the college or university where they will do the most good for themselves, their institution, and the scholarly community. I know of only very few exceptions to this ambitious generalization.

John Goldsmith: One of my teachers reminded me, in just this context, of what Danton is reputed to have said when Paris was being attacked: *il nous faut de l'audace, encore de l'audace, toujours de l'audace, et la France est sauvée!* He agreed with you very much: what we need is audacity, more audacity, still more audacity, and France will be saved!

Penny Gold: Even if you're very satisfied where you are, it doesn't hurt to think about mobility at the same time. For example, I was entirely satisfied with my job situation at Knox, but two things led me to work on publishing a book early in my career, something that would not have been necessary for tenure at Knox. The first thing was that my dissertation had the potential to be a book, and I was interested, for my own sake, in making this kind of contribution to my field. The second thing was that while I knew that I liked Knox, I couldn't be entirely confident that six years down the road Knox would want me, and in my field (history), I would have needed a book to find another job.

The degree of your mobility depends a great deal on the type of institution in which you begin teaching as well as the kind of institution to which you aspire. It is difficult, though not impossible, to move from a small liberal arts college to a major research university. And mobility from one college to another is even more rare, as colleges do not commonly make appointments at the associate or full professor level. Research universities, on the other hand, often seek to bring in scholars with rising or very established reputations, and hence there are opportunities for movement at that level of the profession. If you are not interested in or cut out for a job in that stratosphere, your main chance of moving will be at the beginning of your career, when you can still market yourself as an assistant professor, rather than later on. Your field will also be a factor in your chances of moving, with some fields quite desperate for qualified people willing to teach (computer science) and other fields oversupplied with highly qualified people (English literature).

John Komlos: Although it might seem as though it is better to start near the top of the academic hierarchy, I have my doubts about it. In fact, it is easy to become overly confident and not work with sufficient intensity to maintain the position. I have seen a fair number of incredibly intelligent scholars fail for this reason. The problem is that they see their slide down the institutional hierarchy as a failure rather than as a new beginning with lots of new opportunities after a pleasant sojourn at the top; then the slide can turn into a free fall. To be sure, it is also possible to find the initial conditions so daunting that one despairs and either gives up or sets one's sights lower than is reasonable. So I urge you to stay calm if you are below your long-term goals and to try your best to avoid being too confident if you find yourself at or above them.

You should formulate your goals before you have received your first job offer. Admittedly, the market will provide an initial evaluation in the form of the jobs you are offered, but there is much more to success in the academic world than that. Some factors will not be revealed for some time, such as your ability to get along with colleagues, your perseverance, and your ability to publish. That is not to say that the market's initial evaluation is to be disregarded. Not at all: indeed, the market can be right, but it can also err. Your accomplishments during the first couple of years on the job will provide further valuable information to refine and reconcile your own and the market's evaluation of your long-run scholarly potential. If you started at a first-rate institution, you will be immediately tagged as a promising scholar, and that alone will open doors for you that otherwise would have remained shut. However, you will have to deliver on that promise in haste, that is, from the very beginning. Otherwise, your market valuation will be quickly revised—and not in your favor. This, needless to say, could easily develop into a stressful situation for you, even if you are a very competent scholar, for creative insights are produced not continuously, but rather in fits and spurts. In addition, keep in mind that research initiatives do not always pay off, and even the best of minds can find themselves in a dead-end project on occasion.

Starting at a less-prestigious institution does have the disadvantage that initially the profession will have lower expectations of you. As a consequence, doors will not open automatically for you. However, this handicap can turn into an advantage because you can take your own time to develop your own agenda—that is, to get your research revved up—and if your own confident assessment of yourself is correct, there will be plenty of opportunities to prove yourself. Over time, your colleagues will pay attention to your achievements, and the market will revise its judgment of your academic worth. I do remember that one of the referees of my first grant application to the National Science Foundation, which was turned down, did point out that she noticed that I was trying diligently to "write my way out" of the institution where I was at the time. I admit that it did impress me considerably that there was someone who noticed and confirmed my strategy to do just that. In short, regardless of where you start, you will have to work pretty hard to end up in one of the top 100 colleges or universities.

We will not have much to say about how to arrange your personal life until later (see chapter 10), except to mention the obvious—namely, that you should keep in mind that you ought not overlook your health and family commitments. I have seen academics neglect their health and let their eating and sleeping habits deteriorate in order to increase their productivity. While in the short run such compromises may be necessary to meet certain deadlines, it is equally self-defeating to practice such self-abuse over the long term.[6]

What else do I need to think about?

John Komlos: In contrast to your earlier experiences, your raw intelligence will not be a binding constraint on your success. Instead, other attributes become more important, such as your creativity, your perseverance in the face of uncertainty or adversity, your ability to develop a convincing research program, your ability to publish, and your willingness to get along with others. Now that you have a job, you will have to demonstrate within a few years that you can teach satisfactorily and that you have the potential to make a contribution to scholarship.

Penny Gold: If you are at a primarily teaching institution, the expectations with regard to publishing will be less, but can vary greatly. At some institutions, expectations are very low, and there may even be suspicion of scholarly ambitions as something that will take you away from teaching. At other institutions, expectations are very high, based on the assumption that active scholarship is necessary to good teaching and/or on a concern for the external reputation of the faculty. The quantity of publication expected will be less than at a major research university, but quality will need to be high, and your material will be sent to outside reviewers at tenure time. In the middle would be institutions where work that would not count as real scholarship further up the scale—papers at conferences, essays published in unrefereed collections, a textbook—would be seen as sufficient. Ask around, see what other people are doing, and aim for the high side.

Teaching institutions will generally also appreciate activities that contribute to the community beyond the college or university. Town-gown relations are important, and one way to keep them healthy is to have faculty members involved in community activities. Talking to local service clubs; participating on the boards of cultural, charitable, or service agencies; running for the school board; serving on a political task force—these are some of the ways in which you can make a contribution beyond the campus.

How do family considerations enter into my academic commitments?

John Komlos: Family life is a key consideration in your academic career. That is why we devote chapter 10 to it. Children, for example, will demand much of your time, and there are not many opportunities to cut corners that won't have psychological consequences. Thus, when you are formulating your aspirations, you will need to keep your private commitments in mind: your personal obligations should not conflict with your professional ones, and vice versa. (If I sound like an economist here, it is because I am one.) Obviously, the less stressful and complicated your social and family circumstances are, the more you can concentrate on your professional endeavors. You should avoid overcommitting yourself at all cost. That would only become a self-defeating trap.

Penny Gold: Family commitments are not always something you can plan. Your wife, content to manage the home in the early years of your marriage, may now decide to go back to work, leaving a newly enlarged share of child and house responsibilities to you. Your aged father may need to move into your home. Your obedient, well-behaved child may turn into a juvenile delinquent. You may find yourself going through a messy, stressful divorce. This is life!

The conflict between family and professional work is real, and the pressure to put work first is enormous; we will be saying much more about this later. There is something profoundly wrong with our society when the "ideal" professional worker is someone who is expected to devote themselves totally to work, with no extraneous, "time-consuming" commitments like children. And yet this is the institutional expectation into which professionals (not just academics) are acculturated. Many feminists hoped that when women entered previously male-dominated institutions, we would be able to effect changes in how those institutions are run. But universities—as well as law firms, medical practices, and corporations— have been resistant to the fundamental change it would take to put family and work on a level playing field. I hope the next generation will move this agenda along.[7]

What about job satisfaction?

John Komlos: It is amazing how much actual dissatisfaction there is even among new assistant professors. Expectations were apparently too optimistic: perhaps we regularly overestimate our strengths or underestimate the competition, or we do not consider that the number of jobs available in the Ivy League is far less than the number of scholars who aspire to teach there. You should not expect the academic job market to welcome you with open arms with full-time tenure-track positions in the part of the country in which you prefer to live and in the type of institution in which you prefer to teach. Hence, there is considerable dissatisfaction with one's current status at the beginning of one's career. Though a negligible number of Ph.D.s are unemployed, many seek jobs outside of academia, while others find only temporary jobs at first. Even if we do not count postdoctoral positions, the proportion of non-tenure-track appointments recently ranged from 10 percent in engineering to between 27 and 38 percent in mathematics, chemistry, physics, and political science (in increasing order). The persistent oversupply of aspirants has led to an amazing increase in part-time positions in recent years. A 1997 survey of new assistant professors indicates that 11 percent of those in permanent positions are actively seeking alternative employment. Combined with the numbers in temporary positions, this implies that a "sizeable mismatch exists between employment expectations and market reality for many doctoral graduates."[8] Note, moreover, that the above report did not include the humanities, where unemployment and dissatisfaction are more pronounced.[9] Hence, the realities of the job market are such that you should expect to struggle through the initial years until either you lower your sights and admit to yourself that your prior expectations were unreasonable or your talents are "discovered" and appreciated sufficiently for you to win a certain degree of job mobility.

It is also important for your self-esteem that you not equate your personal (or intellectual) worth to the ranking of the college or university where you are employed. For one thing, our worth is intrinsic, and your own perception of yourself ought not depend on academic factors or, for that matter, on external factors alone. Your contribution to family, friends, and community should not be overlooked. In addition, the satisfaction gained from just doing a good job—from learning, exploring, and developing yourself—should be sufficient reward to keep your ego from wilting. Focusing on external factors instead of doing a good job that you enjoy and are good at is unhealthy and counterproductive. Teaching is an important vocation, and one can get considerable satisfaction from knowing that one has made an honest contribution to the education of students, regardless of external factors. It is also my opinion that our colleagues can err and that significant contributions to scholarship are made every day outside of the Ivys. We cannot be sure which ideas held in high esteem today will be forgotten by the next generation and which ideas overlooked today will be held in high esteem in the future. I have encountered very clever, knowledgeable, moral, helpful, intelligent, good-natured, creative, serious scholars at all sorts of institutions.

Penny Gold: Job satisfaction can be elusive, even if there is a good match between you and your institution. I don't think anything prepares us for how difficult this job is. All of us have gotten this far because we were very good students. But being a good student does not necessarily mean that you will be a good teacher—the roles and responsibilities are very different. And if we think of our students as duplicates of ourselves, we're also doomed to disappointment, since the vast majority of our students will not be going on for professional training in our disciplines. So teaching does not come as naturally as one might think, the students are not the same as one might expect, and if you add in a difficult person or two in your department and the continual pressure to do whatever you need to do to get tenure, the job can be pretty stressful.

But then there are all the things we've talked about earlier: the satisfaction that comes from being paid to learn a subject one loves, the satisfaction of seeing students light up as they come to a new understanding of a subject, the satisfaction of making a contribution to one's field, and the privilege of working for an institution where the mission is education, not profit. Indeed, according to a recent poll of the U.S. professoriate, over 90 percent of faculty members express a clear satisfaction with their career choice and with their current position, with key factors being the attraction of teaching, the love of learning, professional autonomy, and intellectual freedoms; the attraction of a flexible work schedule as well as job security is also important.[10]

7 | Teaching and Research

Do you have a philosophy of teaching?

John Goldsmith: There are many books on teaching, on how to do it, how to be better organized, and so forth. I'm going to leave those more concrete topics to others and get down to what it's really all about, in my opinion.

I'm more and more convinced that the real teaching I do consists of getting up in front of a class (note that I didn't say a classroom: it's the people, the class, that matters and not the place) and thinking out loud about a subject that I know well. The physical trappings help, to be sure. (I have become a convert to, and a great fan of, using PowerPoint presentations for virtually all my classes. The truth is that they probably help me more than they help the students.) But what gets through to the students, I think, is the thought process. I'm not a substitute for the reading; I'm the voice of the thoughtful critic. The students never pay more attention than when I get very irritated at what the author of an assignment—especially a textbook—has said. Occasionally, I have gone so far as to e-mail the author to rap him on the knuckles for something dumb he has written, and when I get an answer (usually a sheepish one) back, I share it with the class. That's my function: to ruminate, and criticize, and try to put together a reasonable position.

I hasten to add that this philosophy (that is no doubt too highfalutin' a term) is not a justification for lack of preparation. To say that it's my public thinking that matters the most is not to say that I don't have a perfectly clear understanding of what I'm going to say, step by step. That goes along with preparation of other media, to be sure. But I listen to myself as I lecture, and part of me is listening from the (idealized) student's point of view. And many is the time when I have laid out what I thought was the right answer on some subject, paused, and said, "You know, what I just said is not as compelling as I thought it was. Because one could reply. . . ." Then I'll point out a weakness in what I had presented. It's not the time then to work out all the details in front of the class; that is to be done in private before the next class.

Of course, the same thing goes for questions and criticisms from students. There will be times when a student's question does lay bare a weakness in a position that I have prepared. There's nothing to be done for it but to acknowledge and underscore that fact! Acknowledge what has just happened, and either deal with it on the spot or work it out after class for presentation at the next class.

What a professor is supposed to have about his subject is a firm grasp of—well—everything. Obviously, that can't mean knowing everything, but it does mean a perspective on everything that's out there, being done or already done, in an area. If you have a discussion with a nonprofessor friend about elementary particles, or unemployment rates, or Greek roots in English vocabulary, or van Gogh's style, you're likely to run to the ends of your information sooner or later—more likely sooner than later. The professor is supposed to know not only what he knows, but also what it is that other people know and how to get a hold of it. He is also supposed to be able to hear a half-baked idea and recognize it as a variant on something that is known and to show how these two formulations are related to one another.

The belief I spoke of a moment ago—that teaching is about thinking out loud for the students—is confirmed when I think about some of my own teachers. I had the great fortune to have four teachers in college who had an enormous impact on me. Four seems like a large number, and I think myself very lucky indeed. What they had in common was that—as the expression goes—they made their subject come alive, and, of course, the way they did that was to live and breathe, to incarnate, their subject. They also plainly cared for their students and for their students' welfare and future.

These four college teachers were quite passionate about their subjects, which ranged over mathematics, linguistics, economics, and philosophy. I don't suppose I ever stopped to wonder how much they really knew about their subjects; from where I stood, their knowledge might as well have been infinite. But I remember watching both the mathematics and the philosophy teachers struggle with the materials that we were reading in our seminars. That was an eye-opening experience. In the case of the philosophy teacher—and remember that this was during the Vietnam War— he was trying to come to grips, along with the rest of us in the seminar, with, on the one hand, the attraction that he felt toward John Dewey's pragmatism (which has always been willing to prove itself in the red-hot furnace of reality) and, on the other, the ease with which pragmatism had seemed to align itself over several generations in this century with a peculiarly American style of imperialism, or at the very least an aggressive foreign policy. He was trying to come to grips with a question to which there might not even have been an answer, but, boy, it brought the passion home to us students.

Mathematics would seem to be an odd place to watch a teacher struggle, but I had the good fortune to take a couple of advanced courses with a teacher who was agreeable to taking on some subjects that were relatively new to him and reading along with us some rather difficult texts. We went through them line by line, quite literally, and he made sure that we understood how the argument advanced step by step.

The two other teachers who made a deep mark on me were people that I got to know better—one a teacher of economics, the other of linguistics. Both are uncannily good teachers, and yet it's not at all obvious why. In retrospect, I think that part of it is their style of speaking to a class, which is not particularly different from their style of conversing one on one. There is no artifice to it; there is no sense of performance. In conversations, both in the class and out, they listened carefully to what the student said, and with genuine interest, but without giving the sense that it would be easy to convince them of something.

John Komlos: Teaching at its best is not only the conveyance of information. Rather, I see it also as the act of helping the students make new connections, see concepts in a new light. Hence, the teacher's enthusiasm for the subject matter is an important element in his ability to accomplish this task. Unfortunately, teacher evaluation protocols can measure this aspect of the quality of teaching only imprecisely.

John Goldsmith: I'd like to turn now to more institutional considerations. My own personal experiences have largely been at research universities, especially during my adult, job-holding years. It is important to bear in mind, however, that among all universities the research universities are in a small minority. There are only about sixty research universities, out of about four thousand institutions of higher education altogether. The most common, and practical, definition of a research university in the United States is one that is a member of the American Association of Universities. These universities are the ones that gain most attention, though; the research universities include such private institutions as Harvard, Princeton, Yale, Stanford, and the University of Chicago and such large public universities as the University of California at Berkeley and at Los Angeles, Indiana University, and the University of Michigan. Virtually all research universities have an important undergraduate teaching function in addition to their graduate and research units (the only exception being Rockefeller University in New York).

By and large, the other colleges and universities beyond the sixty are teaching institutions and require much less independent research on the part of the faculty, but correspondingly impose much greater teaching loads. By and large, too, these teaching institutions do not teach graduate students at the Ph.D. level. Colleges may or may not offer master's degrees (Swarthmore does, for example), but they do not generally provide the research environment for either the faculty member or the graduate student that is necessary for research at the doctoral level.

What is expected of the faculty member at a research university?

John Goldsmith: Quite simply this: at the research university, the professor is expected to undertake and to publish research throughout his career and to take his teaching responsibilities seriously. Teaching loads are generally in the area of three to four semester-long courses per year or four to five quarter-long courses per year (bear in mind that a semester is fifteen to sixteen weeks of teaching and a quarter ten weeks, both followed by a week of exams; some universities use the one system, some the other). In my experience, all faculty members are expected to contribute equally to graduate and undergraduate teaching. In a few rare cases, there is a tacit understanding that a certain outstanding scholar simply isn't a good classroom teacher, and that person may simply never be expected to teach undergraduate courses. But that's quite rare.

But the most important expectation is in the area of research. This is, in my opinion, an eminently Good Thing. The development of knowledge is a very valuable and worthwhile project, too little undertaken in today's busy world. And it is extremely difficult. Alas, the world at large has blessed little understanding of how difficult it is to come up with new ideas that are worth anything. The amount of time spent reading, thinking, and writing to come up with just a small bit of worthwhile research is enormous. When we read criticisms of university professors and the system that they function in, we find that in case after case the critic thinks that the primary job of the university professor is to teach and research is the pleasure-filled dollop of whipped cream thrown on top.

Not so! Research is the primary task of the professor at the research university, and it is a tough job. Do not be fooled by the advocates of what I call the Cabbage Patch Theory of Research. The Cabbage Patch Theory of Research is like the Cabbage Patch Theory of where babies come from: research, served up in articles, monographs, and books, arrives—like magic and with no labor—one fine day, just under the cabbage patch, nicely packaged in a neat ribbon. Don't ask who produces it, or when, or at what personal expense. And it all looks so straightforward, so obvious, so easy, once we have the results and the issues have all been resolved.

Was ever a theory so wrong! The truth is that research is like any major undertaking in life—raising a child, starting a business, or writing a novel. It is guaranteed to be at times a miserable experience, demanding time and energy just when everything seems to be going wrong. It requires confidence in the ultimate value of the enterprise because, without that, the researcher just has no reason to keep on going. And yet, of course, there are many of us who are willing to keep going on, doing research and writing books and papers, because in the long run the process is a rewarding and exciting one. But it certainly is not easy and typically requires many of the personal characteristics of the entrepreneur. And something we must never lose sight of is that (1) research takes a lot of time and (2) you must carve that time out for yourself because no one will do it for you.

That is a theme that I keep coming back to again and again, and it is worth putting it in neon letters—research is the essential aspect of being a professor at a research university; it is the creative and entrepreneurial side of the job. By and large (and with some blessed exceptions), no one will help you with this side of the job: it is your responsibility to find the time and energy to do it, and to do it well.

John Komlos: At the minimum, it requires a fair amount of self-discipline, self-confidence, and ability to persevere. Let me venture a simple generalization about the quality of teaching and how much time to devote to it: all is well until students complain about you. Students choose to attend a particular institution in large part because they have a set of expectations about the quality of teaching there. You should know what those are and try to live up to them, regardless of how much time that takes. The rest of the time can then be yours to use for research and community activities.

What is expected of the faculty member at a teaching institution?

Penny Gold: As we have mentioned earlier, the expectations about the nature and quantity of publication vary significantly from one teaching institution to another. You'll need to find out what those expectations are and do your best to fulfill or exceed them. In general, the higher the teaching load is, the lower the expectations are for publishing, but even this is not consistently true across institutions.

The expectation you can be sure about is teaching. The mission of these institutions is defined by teaching, and you'll be expected to do your part to sustain that mission. Your contribution may be assessed rigorously, haphazardly, or not much at all. You should find out early on what teaching evaluation system is used at your institution. The quality of your teaching, difficult as it is to assess (more on this below), is of great importance. The quantity of your teaching (how many students you are teaching) is much easier to assess, but may or may not be a central concern in your institution or for your particular department. (Introductory courses in ancient Greek, for example, are not expected to have as many students as introductory psychology.)

How do I go about preparing a syllabus?

John Goldsmith: By and large, the first year or two of teaching for an assistant professor will be limited to courses for which syllabi already exist in one form or other, but it may not be easy at the start to find helpful new colleagues who are gracious enough to share the materials that they have—materials such as syllabi, handouts, problem sets, and sample examinations.

Penny Gold: I have taught at four institutions, including introductory courses at each, and nowhere was I expected or even encouraged to teach a preexisting syllabus—which I was glad of, as I find the crafting of a syllabus (thinking up the goals, content, and shape of a course) to be one of the ongoing pleasures of academic life. Certainly there are some courses that I teach (for example, the European survey, an introductory religious studies course, a course on the Holocaust) that many others have taught as well, either at my own institution or widely across the profession, and I routinely ask colleagues for syllabi so I have the benefit of seeing what others have done. Syllabi from colleagues at your institution will tell you a good deal about expectations of reading load, kinds of writing assignments, and so forth. You can also ask people in your field at other institutions. Subscribe to a teaching e-mail discussion list in your field, and put out a query for relevant syllabi.[1]

There are many challenges to making a good syllabus. One of them is to wean yourself from the courses you had as an undergraduate and to think in a fresh way about what *you* want to accomplish. It may also be difficult to shake loose from a core list of books and topics that seem "essential." My approach to syllabi changed dramatically some years back when I attended a workshop on course design sponsored by the Great Lakes College Association (GLCA).[2] My standard approach to preparing a syllabus had been to think of all the texts I wanted students to read, to mark up a pad with the date of each class, and then to try to squeeze all the readings into the given time period. At the workshop, I learned instead to think first of my most basic goals in the course. Try this: if you were to meet up with one of your students ten years from now and he said to you, "I'm really grateful that I took your course because . . . ," what would you like to hear that student say? If you then match up possible readings and assignments with your underlying goals, you'll have a much easier time selecting material for the syllabus.[3]

John Komlos: The preparation of clear syllabi for the first day of classes is crucial for attracting students into your class. It should specify not only the prerequisites, contents, readings, and order in which you propose to cover the material, but also the weights you attach to the various assignments and examinations in computing the final grade. This document is your commitment from which you should not deviate later except by unanimous consent, which usually means in the direction of relaxing requirements. If you committed yourself to giving 5 percent of the grade to class discussion, for instance, you should not change it to 10 percent during the course of the semester. Look at the syllabi of colleagues for the same class.[4] Reassure students about the fairness of tests on the syllabus.

One goal is to retain students who are willing to meet your requirements. In turn, that will make for happier students and thereby improve your student evaluations. As a beginning teacher, you might not be able to gauge precisely how much material you can cover in a term, and hence you should be flexible in adjusting your pace. If you see that students are not able to absorb the material, you might have to slow down or backtrack. It is always easier to decrease the amount of material you actually cover than to increase it. And remember that the ultimate goal is not to merely cover the material, but also to do it in such a fashion that the students comprehend it.

You might also make previous examinations available to students or give them a sample exam to take home. A flexible policy pertaining to make-up examinations is useful to have from the outset.[5] And do not forget to clarify your policy concerning plagiarism and laboratory work. A working definition is a good place to start because in my experience many students are not familiar with our honor codes. These practices will lessen student anxiety about exams and will improve both your communication with them and their perception of you as a caring and fair instructor.

Penny Gold: I can't help but cringe when students ask the question "Will this be on the exam?" since it seems to presume that nothing is worth learning unless it will appear on a subsequent test. But so long as we give exams, we have to expect this question or else preempt it with the strategies John Komlos recommends.

Yes, the syllabus is a kind of contract, and the expectations you lay out in writing at the beginning of the course (including things like penalties for late assignments and your class attendance policy) provide important information for the students and protection for you. On the other hand, even legal contracts can be renegotiated if both parties are willing. If you see that you've assigned way too much reading or too many short papers, students will generally be appreciative if you are flexible enough to cut back.

What are the pitfalls that the neophyte teacher needs to be aware of?

John Komlos: It is common for beginning teachers to misjudge the length of a lecture. Make sure that you have enough material for each lesson by being at least one lesson ahead of the class in the preparation of lectures.

Join discussion groups on teaching in your discipline,[6] consult guides on teaching, and exchange experiences with colleagues.[7]

How do I learn to teach?

Penny Gold: In some ways, our academic habits prepare us badly for learning to teach. We're used to learning primarily from books. There are, indeed, a great many good books about teaching, and I strongly recommend that you read a variety of them. Some are practical manuals, some personal thought pieces. I have found both types to be very helpful.[8] But one needs to learn through other, less private methods as well: talking with others who care about teaching, observing others, and trial and error. There are some folks who don't care about teaching; I suggest not spending much time with them on this subject—it will only contribute to cynicism and complacency. But there are many who do care, even at the most research-oriented universities. Ask about general issues and specific problems, and ask more than one person. Ask if you can sit in on a class or two to see what other people do. And be open to learning from your own mistakes in the classroom. Take stock of what works and what doesn't as you move through a course, and right after it's over, make notes as to what you might try differently next time. Sometimes professional conferences have sessions on pedagogical issues—attend some. They'll put you in the company of other folks interested in teaching, and one is sometimes freer to express frustration and despair away from campus than on.

There are some things about the teaching environment at your own institution that you'll need to familiarize yourself with quickly. You'll want to learn about your students. Who exactly are you teaching, here at this place? Students are not the same everywhere, and they're not the same at one institution at different points in time. (I don't, by the way, give much credit to the notion that students are less qualified today than they were twenty years ago. I think this is a trope of academic life—students are always worse now than they were in yesteryear!) Try to avoid comparisons. You may be more or less happy with the students in your classroom, but that's who's there, and you need to be teaching them, not some imaginary students.[9] How to find out who your students are? Ask them questions, and be observant. Ask your colleagues. Ask someone from the admissions office. And there are even some good books on this subject.[10]

The better you know your students, the more closely you'll be able to adjust your expectations to their capabilities. Surely you'll want to have high expectations, but if the amount of work you assign and/or the standards of work you set are beyond what a sizable proportion of the students can accomplish, you'll be creating a situation of great frustration, not only for the students, but for yourself, too. If you find yourself complaining a good deal about the students in general at your institution (rather than just about individual students, who can be trying for all sorts of reasons), it may be a sign that you haven't yet adjusted your expectations to ones appropriate to the institution you're now in. These may not be the students you would wish to have, and previous experience with more well prepared or intellectually eager students may make the adjustment especially difficult, but we'll do a better job of moving our students along in their educational growth if we start by knowing where they are and teaching with that in mind.

How about exams and writing assignments?

Penny Gold: When I first began teaching, I assigned each class a midterm, final, and paper, following the model of my own classes in college. My initial stimulation to rethink these assignments was a casual comment by a colleague at Antioch College, who mentioned that she always gave take-home exams, never in-class exams. This comment caused me to think about exams as learning experiences rather than simply as chances to assess how much students had learned. The GLCA workshop on course design provided further prodding. Now the assignments I give differ significantly from one class to another, there is more variety within each course, and each assignment is tied to one or more learning goals. The variety of assignments is also connected to my growing recognition that students need more help than I originally imagined they would to meet the expectations I have for them in my courses. In some of my courses, I break out the various skills needed for historical analysis into a series of short assignments, which then are brought together at the end of the term in a culminating paper.

You may well find that the teaching of writing becomes a significant component of your assignments. Many institutions have writing-across-the-curriculum programs in addition to or in place of specific courses in expository writing. But whether mandated or not, if you want to receive well-written papers in your classes, you'll probably need to spend some time working with students on their writing. This can take various forms: providing handouts on writing, devoting in-class time to brainstorming ideas for an upcoming paper, having students submit an outline sometime before the paper is due, and so on. Perhaps most helpful—but most time consuming for the professor—is the offer (or requirement) of a rough draft and/or the possibility of revision for a new grade. Many institutions have writing centers that provide help to faculty as well as students, and you should find out what resources are available at your institution. Faculty development workshops on teaching writing can be very helpful and are offered at many institutions. And there are good books, too.[11] Yes, I'd prefer a situation in which students were accomplished writers before they entered my classes, but since many of the students I have are not, it's more satisfying to me to help them write good papers than to read what I receive without such aid. More work, to be sure. But there is an additional side benefit—my own writing has improved greatly from learning how to teach writing to my students.

What should I do on the first day of class?

Penny Gold: The first day of class is an opportunity to show students something about who you are as a teacher and what the course will be like. Try not to spend the whole time just going over the syllabus. If your teaching style is to lecture, the task is straightforward—give a representative sample of your lecturing. If your classes are predominantly discussion, the task is more difficult, as the students have not yet done any reading that can be discussed. But it will be helpful this first day to give them a taste of what the class will be like and what you expect in the way of student participation. The sooner each student speaks in class, the more likely it is that they will continue to speak throughout the term. Figure out a way to spend at least part of the class with students talking. You might inquire into their preconceptions about the subject to be studied. You might ask what brought them to the course. Bring in a short text or some data relevant to the course that you can discuss together. If nothing else, you can ask them to give some introduction of themselves for the benefit of their classmates as well as you. If you spend the whole first class speaking yourself, this is what you'll set up students to expect for subsequent classes.

Could you say a little more about using computers in the classroom?

John Goldsmith: My working relationship with syllabi has undergone revision in the last few years, with the rise of the World Wide Web. I begin a course with a syllabus placed on a Web site particular to the course, and I revise the site constantly over the course of the quarter. There is some learning that needs to occur on the professor's side to become comfortable with the steps it takes to save a document as an HTML file and to upload it appropriately to the computer that hosts the Web site, but it's truly within the grasp of anyone who uses a word processor. I think it is a skill that simply must be learned at this point. There is something comforting, for both me and the students, when I can answer a question by simply saying, "It's all on the Web site," or I can add, "If you want to know more about this question, I've put a couple of good links to sites on the Internet on the course Web page."

A few years ago I became a sudden partisan of using transparencies and an overhead projector in many of my classes, and more recently I've transferred this allegiance to using computer presentation software (such as Microsoft's PowerPoint) for all my classes. I find that it takes no more time to prepare my notes for class the first time I put them into Power-Point, the classroom presentation is better organized (or at least easier for the students to follow), the slides are always available to be used again in this course or another future course, and I often put the whole thing up on my Web site for the students afterward.

How do I learn how to evaluate students' work?

Penny Gold: It helps to divide this subject into three parts: determining the basis of evaluation; learning how to write constructive, helpful comments on student work; and grading. Sure, students may look first to the "bottom line" of the grade and perhaps not read our comments with any care. But our assessment of student work should be seen as part of teaching, and the rewards of insightful assessment will be the subsequent success of the students who take our criticism to heart.

Teachers have a great deal of freedom to determine the particular qualities on which student work will be graded, with the exception sometimes being multiple sections of one course.[12] The clearer you can be to students at the time the assignment is made, the better chance there is that students will meet your expectations and that they will accept in good spirits your assessment based on those criteria. For example, I have received very few complaints about grades on papers, since I have shared with students beforehand the criteria for grading. On a 100-point scale,

I count the introduction to the paper for up to 10 points, argumentation for 60 points, style and grammar for 20 points, and the conclusion for 10 points. I use a grading sheet with these criteria listed, with the earned points at the left, and written comments specific to each aspect of the paper in their own section. This makes it easier for students to see how a confused introduction and multiple grammatical problems can hurt the grade of a paper even if the main ideas presented in the body of the paper were extremely interesting and convincingly presented.

John Goldsmith: Grading is feedback to the students—and that's perhaps the most important function of grading, in the final analysis. But our usual categories for grading are not set up terribly well for that function. In one class I teach, I have set up a list of about 10 categories, ranging from 1 to 10, in which "10" means "so good that I don't expect to give anyone a grade this high," "1" means "you put your name on your paper, and that's all," "5" means something like "you carried out the steps of an analysis in a coherent way, but that coherent way had virtually nothing to do with the particular problem we're looking at," and so forth. I give the meanings of the categories out with the syllabus at the beginning of the year. But what I'd really like to find is a way to tell students that they need to be more creative. I've never written "Boring!" on a paper, and I wouldn't. But I'd like to find a way to use grades—especially on papers—to get across the idea that the student should try to be more creative.

Penny Gold: Writing comments on student work is itself an art. I received an important lesson about comments when I was sitting on a plane next to a colleague of mine who was grading essays from a composition course. She had a very strong reputation as a teacher, and I was curious to see how she graded, so I looked over her shoulder for awhile. I saw her mark up the paper with comments like "Good idea here!" "Watch those comma splices," "Nice way of expressing this," "I'm confused about the main idea of this paragraph," and "Convincing argument here." And then she gave the paper a C. I was surprised, given how many positive comments were scattered through the paper. This made me realize that I saw the task of commenting on student papers as one of justifying the grade I was giving, which was probably going to be lower than the student had hoped for. So the worse the paper was, the thicker my comments would be, as I piled up notes on all the visible weaknesses. Suddenly, I understood that such comments were not likely to motivate students to do better work, since they were so discouraging to read. About the same time, I read a pedagogical piece suggesting that teachers abandon red pens for grading and that they consider judiciously the extent of comments written. The symbolic connection of red with blood is strong in our culture, and the impact of receiving back a paper covered with such comments is rarely the positive one we intend. This doesn't mean you should forego comments! But, rather, you should realize that less can be more: concentrate on a limited number of key problem areas, make constructive comments on how improvements might be made, and praise wherever you can.

The third area of concern is the actual grading. Again, I would encourage you to seek out others in your institution, particularly those teaching similar courses. Ask to see some sample graded papers from one of their courses so you can get an idea of grading standards at your institution.[13] Students are understandably concerned about the fairness with which they are graded. Grading is, at best, an imprecise art. Put these two facts together, and it's not difficult to understand why grades provide for some of the most uncomfortable teacher-student interactions.

John Komlos: Establishing clear standards from the very outset, ones that are in accord with the caliber of your students and with common practices at your institution, is important not only for your own interactions with students, but for your reputation with your colleagues as well. It is best not to deviate significantly from the average standards prevailing at your institution. The main reason is that, if your requirements are far below the average set by others in the department, your teaching will be considered inadequate, and as a consequence, you just might experience difficulties at the time of your evaluation for promotion. It is hardly worth the risk. Analogously, standards well above those prevailing in the department will have two immediate unwelcome consequences: students will tend to avoid your courses to the extent possible, and they will start complaining about your teaching and grading to the chair. While initially you might not consider this much of a problem, it can easily become one if it imposes a heavier workload on your colleagues or if a decline in enrollment in your courses begins to worry the chair, who wants to show to the dean that there is a substantial demand for courses taught in the department in order to justify the number of faculty on the staff. Thus, you may be seen as not pulling your share of the load.[14]

Though you might expect that academic freedom would protect you from student complaints, it will not do so if it becomes a big enough nuisance for the chair. It is well known that students seldom complain if courses are too easy, and never if they receive a higher grade than they deserve, but there are always a few in a class who are prone to complain if your expectations are higher or if the grade they received is lower than they anticipated, based on their encounter with other members of the faculty. Students might even complain about a B if they expected to receive an A. Consider that even if only one or two students per course were to complain about you to the chair, that could add up to as many as six to twelve students per year. You can easily see that even at such an insignificant rate the accumulation of complaints by the time of your review for tenure would put unacceptable burdens on the chair. Spare him these unpleasant moments if you do not care to jeopardize your promotion.

Penny Gold: In my experience, most students will come to me first to complain about a grade, and if I am able to give them some satisfaction in the ensuing discussion, they are unlikely to take the complaint further. What does it take to make this a satisfying conversation for the student? Evidence that you take their concern seriously. Who knows—it's even possible that you were so tired when reading that last paper in the pile that you really weren't paying enough attention to the argument! This said, I have to admit that I have almost never changed a grade. There's nothing fun about having students come in asking why they got the grades they did, especially when you've done your best to give helpful comments on the work. I think there are a few students who do it routinely, just on the off chance they can get a few points out of it. But I try to deal with the question as though the student had said (as some of them do): "I'd like to learn from this so I know how to write more effectively on the next assignment." Then you can make the interchange into an occasion for teaching instead of a session of self-defense or attack.

John Komlos: Though you may find it difficult, you need to do your best to disregard the standards that prevailed at your graduate school. You might well wonder why you bothered to go through a rigorous graduate program if you are now being urged to be flexible in setting standards, adjusting them to the ones prevailing at your current institution. The answer is, however, less baffling than you might think, given that you are likely to be at an institution with students who aren't as capable as those at your graduate school. It does makes sense not to expect identical accomplishments from students with a combined SAT score of 1000 and from those with a score 30 percent higher. Hence, "good teaching" is not defined identically everywhere. Rather, it is defined relative to local custom, that is, as meeting the standards prevailing in the department. At most teaching institutions, you will not be expected to set achievement standards as high as they are routinely set in the Ivys. That would not work either for you or for the students. "Good" teachers must take into account two factors: the capabilities of the students and the effort their colleagues expect them to expend. I recommend a strategy of seeking an acceptable (good enough) solution when you are faced with a highly complex task that is full of uncertainties.[15] Hence, be a good enough teacher, or a good enough shopper, or a good enough friend. Striving to achieve more would be as frustrating for you as for the students: you would encounter substantial student resistance, thereby counteracting the satisfaction that you seek in teaching.[16]

Note that students have a large incentive to invest heavily in lobbying for a higher grade. Their potential payoff is much higher for them than it is for you. You are defending your own values for nonpecuniary gain, and often by imposing additional stress upon yourself. They, on the other hand, are fighting to stay off probation and therefore to continue to work toward a diploma, or to qualify for a scholarship, or to go to professional school. Often even a B or C can be damaging to the student's future career and can trigger as much resistance as a D or an F normally brings forth. As a novice, you may be surprised and unprepared for this resistance, which can lead to unpleasant and distressing encounters.

This reasoning can also explain grade inflation: the main factor behind it is that the average standard is actually not easily ascertainable. Consequently, in an environment of uncertainty with asymmetric payoffs, it is easier for the teacher to err on the side of caution and set expectations slightly below average. The outcome is that the average standard declines over time in the absence of countervailing forces. And there is no institutional structure exerting an offsetting influence. Meanwhile, the higher the standards according to which you grade your students are, the greater the probability is that some of the students will be dissatisfied.[17] In contrast, you will rarely be rewarded for setting rigorous grading standards. Infrequently, a student or two might compliment you for it, but they will almost never tell the chair. The rewards have to be internal. These would have to be substantial in their own right: you know in the bottom of your heart that you are making a contribution to the formation of the next generation. But that may not suffice to keep you going through the years.

John Goldsmith: My experience has been different than yours, John. I do have the impression that what people call "grade inflation" is a real phenomenon: that over the last several decades the average grade has risen. Just what to make of that is not so obvious, and it forces us to think about some basic questions, like what the point of education is in a society such as ours, whether a major function that university educators play is to evaluate their students for other downstream institutions (such as medical and law schools), and whether students, on the whole and in the long run, get more from the educational process if their short-term motivation can be whetted and honed by the opportunity to do well on next Friday's exam. I myself am not a strong partisan of grading in courses, being convinced neither of the importance of doing the evaluation for professional schools nor of the educational value of threats from regular examinations at the university level. I want to be careful of what I say: I know that, in fact, the amount of time that students put into studying is enormously affected by exams and grades, and I also believe strongly that part of my job is to motivate my students to study and to learn; I would be denying reality if I overlooked the use of exams as a means to encourage students to study and learn. A teacher should learn how to use both the carrot and the stick sides of grade assigning, and there's surely not just one unique and optimal way to do that. So it seems to me that grade inflation is a problem, from that point of view, only if it marks a decrease in the effectiveness of teaching in the long run.

By the way, I'm more of a believer than most in the value of frequent pop quizzes, taking five to eight minutes at the start of class. I don't care about the grades that individual students get so much as being sure that most of the students have actually internalized some material that I think is crucial. I'll repeat the same quiz several classes in a row, telling people that it will continue until everyone (more or less) gets it all right.

In my experience, young teachers have not been penalized for having especially rigorous standards, whether this is in their manner of giving course grades, exam grades, or amounts of work expected of the students in a course. To be sure, the tougher the grading is, the more complaints there may be, all other things being equal, but I think that the assistant professor who lowers his natural expectation of what his students should achieve is likely to suffer other sorts of problems that may well be worse in the long run—the chief of these being a kind of disillusionment with the education biz. But I can see that there is a range of opinions on this question, John—regarding what I think of as the *Realpolitik* or, rather, *Realpedagogik* of our profession.

How do I know if I'm a good teacher?

Penny Gold: It's much more difficult to know how one is doing as a teacher than as a researcher. With regard to the quality of one's research, there are external measures readily available: Is your work being accepted for publication? By good journals and/or presses? Are you receiving grants? How frequently is your work cited by others? How are the reviews of your book? Does a presentation at a conference yield requests for your work? External measures of one's teaching are much more limited, and the ones that exist are more likely to be of perceptions of one's teaching rather than of the teaching itself.

Many institutions routinely administer student evaluations of every course taught by untenured faculty. And many untenured faculty live in terror of the results. It is tempting to try to "teach to" the evaluations, hoping that you can manipulate student response to up your numbers. I think faculty discomfort with these evaluations—and with the feeling that one's job is hostage to student opinion—is unavoidable. But there are also some ways to use the evaluation process constructively. A key thing is to remember that these are measures of student *perceptions*. For example, you may be inclined to dismiss a low score on the question "Was the course well organized?" because to you it is self-evident that the course was clearly structured, with a syllabus that laid out all the assignments and how they fit together. You may be baffled as to how students could judge the course to have been disorganized when all this was made clear. But since they did have the perception of lack of organization, despite your efforts, it's worth trying to figure out what may have given them that impression. Perhaps you made several last-minute changes in the syllabus, which, even though done with good reason, were disorienting to them. Or perhaps many individual classes were disorganized, with students unable to follow what was going on. And since there is no question on the evaluation asking "Was the instructor well organized in class?" the negative impression will come out in the question about the course instead.

Or here's an example from my own teaching. In the first years of teaching, students gave me low ratings on the question "Is the instructor enthusiastic about the material being taught?" This seemed odd to me, since I knew that I was deeply enthusiastic about the subject. But when I finally made myself consider why they might think I was not enthusiastic, even though I knew I was, I realized that other things were getting in the way of conveying that enthusiasm to my students—in particular, my insecurity at the time in feeling woefully underprepared for each class, given the breadth of material I was teaching.

One more example: the evaluations at my institution have a cluster of questions I think of as "approachability" questions, which get at issues of the students' comfort with asking a faculty member for help and the students' sense of faculty concern about their progress. Again, early on I had low scores on these questions, despite the fact that I had office hours, encouraged students to come see me, and consider myself a friendly and approachable person. But since students didn't perceive me as approachable, I needed to change something—not just for the sake of better evaluations, but because it bothered me that students would perceive me this way. A simple change in my practice has had a large effect: in the week or so before a paper is due, I make out an appointment sheet with available time slots and bring it to class with me. I send it around the room and encourage students to sign up. (And if the class is small, I might ask them all to sign up.) This gives students the tangible sign they seem to need that I really do care about helping them with their work.

Don't suffer through your evaluations in isolation. Seek out a couple of people who are in a position to know how the evaluations are used in faculty assessment, and ask them to look over yours with you. They will be able to help you put your evaluations in the context of institutionwide performance, and they may be able to tip you to questions that tend to receive particular attention. (At Knox, these are the general questions on "the effectiveness of the instructor" and "the quality of the course.")

The other source of imposed external evaluation takes the form of peer evaluation by colleagues. At my institution, the chair is mandated to sit in on some classes before contract and tenure reviews. At some places, all tenured members of the department will troop into your classes. In the best situations, this is helpful information to add to student perceptions (although faculty may be less willing to view their observations as "perceptions"). The problem is that institutions don't often give training to department chairs on how to perform fair and constructive evaluations. It should be a matter of course that the observer will gather materials from you beforehand and sit down with you afterward to discuss the class(es) observed, but this doesn't always happen.

You may have the opportunity to submit materials about your teaching at the time of contract and tenure reviews. At Knox, we ask for a teaching statement (as well as one about research) and sample syllabi and assignments. These materials should be carefully considered—it's your one chance to provide actual content from your courses for the review. Publications, of course, can be judged on the publications themselves. But your teaching is—aside from this material—judged not on the teaching itself (since one can't capture all those classes and present them as evidence), but on secondhand information from students and colleagues.

There's one other rough measure of your teaching—the number of students who sign up for your courses, in comparison to the numbers who sign up for comparable courses in your discipline. If you can't attribute low enrollment to extraneous factors (e.g., an 8:00 A.M. time slot), you should consider it as a warning sign. Difficult to interpret, yes, but not to be ignored. Sometimes small changes can help enrollment—perhaps coming up with a more appealing course title or dropping a prerequisite. But if you are developing a consistent pattern of low enrollments and these are in conjunction with problematic teaching evaluations, it's time for help!

Besides the resources mentioned in our earlier section on learning to teach, here are a couple of other suggestions—ways of adapting evaluative procedures to your own desire to improve your teaching.

1. Get feedback from students well before the end of the term. This way, you can use their responses and suggestions to make adjustments in this very course rather than waiting until the next time it's offered. Students also appreciate your seeking their suggestions. The caveat is that, once solicited, you need to take their suggestions seriously and show that you've done so. I usually hand out a list of such questions in the fourth or fifth week of our ten-week term. The questions don't need to be elaborate. The "survey" can be as simple as handing out a sheet of paper with one question at the top: for example, "What do you think I need to know about how this course is going?" Giving the students class time to write their responses is essential—you won't get many back if you ask them to write out of class and send them in. Such qualitative evaluations are also useful at the end of the term and can be tailored to specific things you want to know about (responses to individual readings, to a guest speaker, etc.).

2. Get peer feedback by asking another faculty member to sit in on a number of your classes. This should be someone outside your department, a person who will not be a part of any formal institutional evaluation of your work. This kind of class visit is private, for your own efforts at self-improvement. There may be a teaching-learning center on your campus, with a roster of people willing to do peer visits. If not, seek someone out on your own. Best to have it be someone whom you trust and respect and whose basic teaching values and style are similar to yours. If you teach

mainly through discussion, having someone in who relies primarily on lecturing will not be so much of a help. Give them course materials before the visit, tell them some things you're particularly interested in feedback on, and then, when the visits are over, do your best to listen receptively to the comments. Watching a videotape of yourself teaching can also be very instructive, particularly if done in conjunction with a peer who also observed the class.

John Goldsmith: I suppose we teachers need to have it brought to our attention that we're not teaching well when we think we are and that we are actually having a positive pedagogical impact—it was a good class!—when we think we've really messed up (so to speak). In all my years of teaching, I've never been approached after a class by a student who wanted to tell me, "That was a particularly bad class; please do better on Wednesday." If I've explained something poorly, I'll have to figure that out for myself—by listening to myself lecture (with a third ear) or more likely by seeing homework and test answers that are not sensible by my lights. But many are the times when I was very discouraged by a particularly bad class—the level of presentation was, I felt, too high, too low, too confusing, too obvious, too disorganized—when a student has come up to me and said what a particularly good class that was. I draw two conclusions from this: first of all, I (and am I really different from others in this?) should not trust my judgment too far on how good a class was, and second, it's possible that some kind of window of accessibility opens up for the student at the time when I, the teacher, feel something slipping out of control. That doesn't add up to a very useful piece of pedagogical advice, I realize, but teaching is not writing. Teaching is getting into some kind of a personal, human relationship with the people listening to you, and the goal of the teacher is to demonstrate the character of getting into a certain relationship with knowledge and scholarship.

Speaking of a relationship with the people listening to you—there's another aspect of decent behavior that needs to be mentioned: punctuality. For most people, getting to the classes on time, every time (barring extraordinary circumstances), is not an issue, and, indeed, it should be unthinkable to be five minutes late to class on a regular basis (and students will consider it a "regular basis" if it happens three times running). When I'm occasionally late, I apologize to the class, and I truly mean the apology. But if you are someone for whom punctuality is something that you feel can be, and should be, and inevitably will be, something that is sacrificed for some other reason (like talking to interested students at the end of the preceding class or getting the homework assignment finished up just so), then wake up and hear the message: don't be late again; make yourself get there five minutes early if you must, but be there. If you know you tend to be late, then my advice is not to trust your own judgment; try to get more than a little bit obsessive about getting to your classroom a few minutes before the starting bell. Believe me, this is truly important.

What about teaching at the graduate level?

John Komlos: Graduate students require a greater personal commitment from you than do undergraduates, even if they are fewer in number. The general rule, to maintain average standards, applies to the graduate program as well. The chances are that you will not be expected to teach at the graduate level at the beginning of your career, and it is good this way. You should become involved in the graduate program only to the extent your senior colleagues desire you to. Your main goals are to get a handle on a few standard courses you will teach repeatedly and to get some publications under your belt. Mentoring takes much time, for which you will not be rewarded at tenure-decision time. In addition, graduate teaching often carries more prestige, and your colleagues might not be willing to share it with you immediately, especially if they feel it comes at their expense.

Graduate students can be useful to their dissertation advisors by doing work that complements their own research, by spreading and supporting ideas that are congruent with their research program. There is also some prestige in having the best graduate students in your department choose you to work with. You will be seen as having won in a sort of contest of ideas.

John Goldsmith: My experience has been different. Especially in a field where a new fashion is changing (or seeming to change) the complexion of the field, the junior faculty member will likely be sought out by graduate students. Imagine a field where gender studies or chaos theory is a really hot topic and the faculty is open enough to it to decide they want to hire someone in this field. It's likely that the students are every bit as aware that this is an area where hiring is going to continue to be done — or better yet, they may be fired up and enthusiastic about it for intellectual reasons!

You've mentioned the business of fighting among faculty members for graduate students. Clearly, this happens in some departments, but I'm able to report that I've never been in a department in which that occurred.

It would be interesting to try to get some data on how widespread a phenomenon that is.

John Komlos: Another issue has to do with the caliber of graduate students at your institution. Be forewarned that the most talented students have enough sense to enroll in the top graduate programs. If you are at a less well known institution, the chances are that the overwhelming majority of students are not talented enough to go beyond the M.A., and usually a lot of disappointment is associated with students' attempts at cashing in on the implicit contract they have with the institution to obtain a Ph.D. degree. It takes a fair bit of effort to help average students to write a thesis. As a consequence, some students at the ABD stage at such institutions have difficulty finding someone to work with them. Yet even such programs provide a certain amount of prestige for the faculty because Ph.D.-granting institutions generally have a higher relative standing in academia. At the same time, graduate students are needed as teaching assistants for the discussion sections of the large lecture courses. Without them, these courses, which are often the backbone of their programs at large state universities, would not be possible. In other words, the system of mass education is predicated to some extent on the services rendered by teaching assistants whose future in the academic community is rather dubious and who often harbor false expectations as to the probability of their success.

How do you deal with ethical issues in the classroom—and outside of it?

John Komlos: It is a commonplace that the bottom line matters at many institutions. To be sure, this is not the case at colleges with an oversupply of applications, but even there, admissions officers are quite eager to maintain the reputation of the school in the face of stiff competition. At most institutions, administrators are anxious about enrollment numbers, and financial considerations drive much of policy. Indeed, enrollments come to be of paramount importance in many cases. There is no way of getting around that. One should not ignore that in one's dealings in the classroom, particularly in offering courses that will attract students or in setting standards that will be considered fair. Suppose you have very high standards, and you hold strong convictions on what you should expect from the students. You might even consider it immoral to pass students who have not done as well as you think they should have. They are not doing college-level work in your opinion. Now, if you begin to fail a significant proportion of your students in a mandatory freshmen survey course, the administrators might well be displeased with the result, and understandably so. They might think that your job is to teach those students on campus and not those in a university in wonderland. In this respect, the institution expects you to show more respect for the abilities of the students as you find them and to adjust your own grading criteria accordingly. You can make an ethical issue out of it, but it will not necessarily be the right thing to do. By accepting a job at a that particular institution, you have implicitly accepted the standards that the reputation of the institution reflects.

A similar case can be made about plagiarism. The problem has worsened noticeably during the last decade.[18] It would be, again, very difficult to go against the grain and decide single-handedly to change the tide. It would be an uphill battle, and administrators have little patience for quixotic crusades. They, too, want to (in fact, have to) maintain their sanity, and having to deal with unexpected controversies can rapidly increase stress levels. What can one do? It might not make sense to assign the kinds of term papers that can be easily purchased through the Internet.[19] If the students do not have the skills to write them, you should make your assignments simpler: ask the students to write book reviews in areas in which you are well informed. On the other hand, if the students have the ability to write term papers, you should structure the topic in such a way that they cannot easily purchase a paper on the subject. In addition, it is useful to assign several deadlines for different parts of the paper so as to be able to see it evolve over time.

Penny Gold: In some ways, one can feel on moral high ground in academia. We're not selling formula to Third World mothers who should be breast feeding, and we're not pushing violent computer games (or other despicable products) to our youth. We're selling knowledge, and we don't even have to get our hands dirty collecting the money. And yet our life is run through with ethical decisions, whether we are aware of them or not. The production of knowledge in our research, and the subsequent use of that knowledge by others, can have profound ethical implications—from helping to develop the atom bomb to contributing to civics curricula in public schools. Many ethical choices come in professional dealings with our colleagues: for example, knowing how to deal honestly and fairly with colleagues in a variety of situations or having the courage to speak our minds when we know it will annoy or anger people with whom we have to work and who may even be in a position to determine our ultimate job security. And there are institutional policies and decisions that we have to decide whether or not to speak up about, like the balance of athletics with academics, the role of fraternities and sororities, and unionization on campus, to name a few. And with our students: Do we discuss the ethical implications of the subjects about which we teach? To what extent are we putting into practice our ideal—that education will make students better people, more responsible members of our society?

This seems a little overwhelming. How can I possibly accomplish all this?

John Komlos: You will most certainly feel overcommitted at the beginning unless you are extremely adept at managing your obligations. As far as teaching is concerned, you will have a lot of decisions to make, and experience to acquire, before you will find a comfortable routine. This will take time, but in the beginning, try to avoid locking yourself into a set schedule. You will need to choose courses to teach in consultation with your chair. At the time you were hired, the department probably expressed its preferences, and some of those courses are probably not renegotiable. Yet rarely is it the case that you have no leeway at all at this point. To the extent possible, I suggest that you try to teach courses that are a natural outgrowth of your own graduate education, including, of course, your thesis. Try your best to avoid extra preparations, and, instead, try to teach multiple sections of the same course: one during the day and one in the evening, for instance. It is also a good idea to repeat courses from one semester to the next. This will give you some opportunity to set aside some time for scholarship. Of course, if you are at a teaching institution and you are satisfied with your current position, the pressure on you will be much less to do research and publish.

Penny Gold: If you have some choice over the time slots in which you teach, try out a few different combinations to find what works best for you. I like to teach in the morning, keeping at least a couple of afternoons each week clear to come home and work on my research.

John Goldsmith: A friend of mine gave me some good advice once: never teach a course for the first time. He meant that, obviously, with tongue in cheek. The first time you give a course can be quite a nightmare, with an enormous amount of work involved, far more than could be reasonably expected of one. (That's how it seems, at least!) In the best of cases, that creates an atmosphere of excitement, and it can make for a very good course and a very stressed teacher. It's ironic that one of the few conventional criticisms of college professors is that they can trot out the same old tired course notes, year after year after year, using the same jokes at the same places. While that is undoubtedly a problem in some cases, this is just an example, taken to extremes, of a strategy that makes sense all the way around: a person who knows well how to teach second-semester phonology (let's say) is the person who should teach it, and the way to know how to teach that course well is to have taught it several times.

I can be a good scholar without publishing, can't I?

John Komlos: Yes, but being a good scholar does not suffice. You also have to demonstrate it to the satisfaction of neutral observers. Until you do that, you are alone in your conviction of your own excellence. There are many institutions that concentrate primarily on undergraduate education, where one does not need many publications for promotion. Hence, if you do not want to subject yourself to the pressures associated with extensive publishing—and these can be substantial—you should aspire to a position at one of these colleges or universities. You will be happier there.

John Goldsmith: In all fairness to those institutions, I'd like to add that they're looking for a different kind of scholarship and research. Everyone knows the old joke that copying from one person is plagiarism, while copying from five is scholarship. All joking aside, that remark does suggest a truth, which is that one part of research is reading a lot and basically keeping up with what's happening in one's field. That's a lot of work, though it's less work (by a long shot) than reaching beyond the limits of the known to develop new ideas, formulate and test them, and publish them. Teaching universities are willing, by and large, to have scholars who keep up with what's happening in their fields, and they expect their faculty to produce the kinds of publications that demonstrate an ongoing familiarity with the current literature.

Penny Gold: As someone at one of "those institutions," I would say that faculty are expected to make a contribution to their fields through publication, but are not necessarily expected to be leaders in their fields (though some of my colleagues are). It is understood that publication has repercussions for one's teaching as well, in addition to being a sign that one is up to date with the field. To publish, one has to be willing to work on something until it is polished and convincing and to be willing to take the risk of putting one's ideas out in an arena where they can be criticized. We ask our students to do this all the time, so it's important that we do it also—at the very least, it gives us some additional sympathy for the challenges they face to complete and perfect their work.

Is it fair to perish if I do not publish?

John Komlos: At a research university, yes, because research and the dissemination of the results of that research are an integral part of our job description, and legitimately so. The profession benefits from communicating one's thoughts and ideas to other colleagues. Thus, even though publishing is in one's own best interest, it is at the same time an act of sharing. One is opening oneself up to criticism, and that prospect is so uncomfortable to some that they become unable to proceed. What might I have overlooked? What is missing from the paper? Be that as it may, I do believe that one ought to be expected to publish; otherwise, research can become a narcissistic activity whose goal is self-gratification.

Thus, research cannot and ought not suffice by itself. This statement might well appear odd, but I put it this way in order to emphasize that the belief that publication follows naturally and automatically from research is incorrect. The publishing process has its own separate challenges.

Penny Gold: I very much agree with John Komlos on the value of publishing. I would just reiterate that lack of publication puts one at risk of "perishing" in teaching institutions as well, as research and publication are seen to be linked to good teaching. This is certainly fair, so long as expectations have been made clear.

How should I begin to publish?

John Komlos: Publication of articles from your dissertation should be your highest priority as soon as you have your Ph.D. in hand. You do not have time to start new research just yet. Having just completed a major research project, many will, of course, feel that they deserve to sit on their laurels for awhile. There is really not much time for that, however, as the tenure clock is running. Others will find that they are really anxious to get on to new discoveries and will find returning to the dissertation somewhat tedious. Yet another possibility is that they might have become addicted to doing research to such an extent that it begins to interfere with the next logical task, namely, the publication of their results. So you may find taking this next step difficult, particularly since it is not much fun and you have so many other new responsibilities, such as lecture notes to prepare and committee meetings to attend. But don't allow yourself to become trapped in the research phase of your scholarship. You must let others know about your work.

John Goldsmith: It is quite common in my field for students to publish a chapter of their dissertation during the period that they are writing up their dissertation, I might add.

John Komlos: Whatever form your first publication takes, this is your chance to profit from the years you've invested in your thesis, and you need to put your mind to doing just that. The name of the game is to "beat the clock." To maximize your advantage, you need to first extract chapters that you think ought to be disseminated to a wider audience. By and large, this should be the case for most of your dissertation. Obviously, these chapters will have to be rewritten to some degree because articles have to be self-contained, whereas a chapter of a dissertation can draw upon information presented in another chapter.

A standard article obviously varies across disciplines, but "the principles of good writing—simplicity, clarity, unity—are universal. . . ."[20] An article develops a single theme, and it does so by addressing itself to examining an unsolved problem or a controversy, to presenting a new way of looking at an old problem, or to opening new avenues to explore. It might, in addition, propose a new conceptualization, synthesize a fragmented literature, or analyze new data. Most articles need an introduction, which gives an overview of the literature on the topic: What is the received wisdom on the issue you are discussing? What has been written about it lately? Why should people be interested in it? How does your approach differ from those of others? Do you have new data, new materials, new sources, new ideas? You might continue by presenting the main issues to be considered. You need to explain your methodology and the data and facts upon which you are building an argument, followed by the main body of the paper. The conclusion sums up the argument, perhaps qualifies the findings, and points to future directions for research. It is appropriate to discuss the strengths and weaknesses of your evidence and the possible alternative interpretations, if any. Why is your approach superior to that of others? In sum, an article usually has one strand of thought leading from the introduction to the conclusion, must be self-contained, and has to be understandable by the specialist in the discipline.[21] Because the dissertation is likely to be made up of a number of interlocking arguments, an article cannot be lifted straight out of the dissertation. With practice, writing an article can become second nature to you, but the first time around can be a challenge.

Penny Gold: There are also significant stylistic changes that need to be made if one is revising material from a dissertation for publication as a journal article (or a book, which we will discuss later on)—they are very different genres, with different audiences and different purposes. For a dissertation, the audience is the three or four people on your committee, and the purpose is to prove to them that you can do research and that you have read all the relevant scholarship in your area. The audience for a journal article or a book is obviously much broader (how much so depends on your subject and intentions), and the purpose is to give people who will be interested in your ideas access to them. Footnotes, beyond the simple ones of citations, should steer other interested people in useful directions, not prove how much you know.[22] Felicity of style is, for obvious reasons, more important in a book than in a dissertation. A publisher is hoping your book will earn money for the press; you want someone who reads the first page standing up in a bookstore to want to read more.[23]

How should I find the right journal for my article?

John Komlos: Advice from your mentor can be useful while you are in graduate school. In the sciences, graduate students frequently coauthor with their advisor, so they will have hands-on experience on how the thinking unfolds in the process of creating a publishable product and how to steer it through its course of publication, but those in the humanities and social sciences will not have had this experience as a rule. You might ask yourself (after making sure that you know most of the main journals in the discipline) which journal has published similar articles recently. Weigh the alternatives by analogy: if a particular journal has published an article on such a theme, perhaps the editor(s) will be willing to do so again on a similar topic. Look at the frontispiece of the journal. Many journals have a statement of philosophy on what kinds of themes they will consider. You also need to think about the audience you want to reach and, not least of all, make as objective a determination as possible about the importance of your article to the profession at large. How good is it? Which segment of the profession would be interested in it? Is it essential reading for all, or is it aimed at a niche of the discipline? How original is it? Is it path breaking, or is it essentially derivative (that is to say, does it derive its inspiration from the work of others)? What is the reputation of the journal? What about its methodological orientation? These questions are by no means easy to answer, but over time you will develop a good sense of which articles are appropriate for which journals. However, even the experienced hands will make mistakes in thinking that there is a match between an article and a journal, while the editors and referees see it differently.

There is also the issue of prestige to consider. Generally, the higher the rejection rate of a press or journal is, the more prestigious it is to publish with or in it. As far as books are concerned, the presses of the elite universities are considered a bigger feather in your cap than those of the minor ones. This is the case not only because the manuscript goes through a more stringent screening process, but also because such presses devote more attention to editing and advertising the book. Moreover, more libraries order regularly from them, and consequently they guarantee a larger circulation. Hence, the publisher is similar to a warranty that influences the extent to which the book will be taken seriously by the scholarly community and the extent to which it will be read, reviewed, and cited.

There are similar considerations among journals, where prestige often also depends on circulation. Top journals have a rejection rate as high as 90 percent. Generally speaking, the more prestigious the journal is, the more attention your article will get, and it is more likely to have a higher impact on future research, that is, to be cited more often by other scholars. Because such citation rates are available in all disciplines[24] and because they just might influence your promotion through the ranks (and not only the granting of tenure), you will benefit from a publication according to the prestige of the journal in which it appears.

Publishing in refereed journals tends to be more important than publishing in an anthology because standards of inclusion in anthologies are less stringent than in journals, insofar as an editor often has difficulties finding enough submissions to complete the volume.[25] Anthologies are also more difficult to publish and have a smaller circulation as a rule. Thus, essays in a collected volume seldom receive the attention that journal articles generate and are less frequently cited. Publishing in a foreign language is considered to be another market and is generally not taken seriously by American departments.

Penny Gold: While it's true that publishing in an anthology will earn you fewer "points" than publishing in a refereed journal, that doesn't mean you should reject an opportunity to do so out of hand. If you haven't published anything, or not very much, yet, it is a way to begin to get your work out there and to have some publications on your c.v. And if the anthology is one to which interesting people in your field are contributing, it will help you to be in their company, and just having these people know of your work is a good thing. One caution is the time to publication. Journals are not speedy, but they are on some kind of regular schedule. Depending on when you come on board to an anthology, you may have a very long time to wait before publication.

John Komlos: Good point. Publication of an anthology is determined by the slowest contributor, and consequently a delay of several years is not unheard of. The length of your article is another important factor to keep in mind. Editors are extremely conscious—in fact, ridiculously so—of keeping articles to the absolute minimum length. Hence, you should pare down your paper to the bare essentials, given the argument you are making; you should justify to yourself the inclusion of every sentence, every word. In an anthology or a book, you have much more leeway, and you can stray away from the main argument without facing much resistance from the editor.

Journals usually specify the length of articles they are willing to consider, and it is advisable to hold to that range precisely. If you do not think that you can meet the length constraint, you had better try another journal.

How do you know when an article you're working on is ready to be submitted?

John Komlos: The art of good writing is not a mystery: "Good writing requires revising, revising, and revising again." So you need to give the paper a little time to mature: "Let time elapse between revisions. If your paper is . . . familiar to you . . . , you will never discover your mistakes. You need to let it sit in a drawer for a while. When you pick it up again, it will have a freshness that will allow you to see immediately where it can be improved."[26] Ask for as many comments as possible, and wait for feedback. You can never have too much of it.

Penny Gold: Think strategically about whom to get comments from. Different people can help you in different ways. You need comments from someone who knows your field well, as they're in the best position to assess the strength of your argument and save you from some later woe with a journal's outside readers. Such a person may also suggest relevant work that you haven't incorporated into your article. Perhaps you already know well someone who fits this description—preferably someone other than (or in addition to) your graduate advisor. But if not, that's OK. This is an opportunity to introduce yourself to other scholars in the field. Send a note to a person whose work you admire and who you think is in a good position to critique your work. Ask if they would be willing to read a draft of an article. If yes, that's great. If no, then try someone else. Another type of reader is someone who can help you with your prose style and matters of structure and argumentation. This needn't be someone in your field, but should be someone conversant with academic writing. This is something a generous friend can do for you; consider a reciprocal swap with an academic pal.

John Komlos: I presume that you have sent your dissertation to all those in the field directly interested in it and that you have already incorporated their suggestions, insofar as they were relevant, into the first version of the article. You should also send the newly finished article to the same scholars, asking them for further comments, if any, but you should not wait until their responses arrive before submitting the article for publication. Let it go! Don't let yourself lose sight of the goal of submitting the article. You have entered dangerous territory just as you are completing the article—when too many authors begin a self-defeating process of soul-searching procrastination. After a month or six weeks of waiting for feedback and of revising and polishing, submit the article forthwith. See what anonymous referees really think of it. Waiting for a complete set of comments from colleagues would now delay the publication process unacceptably. As the colleagues' comments do arrive, however, they should be incorporated continuously into the manuscript. In fact, you should return to the article occasionally to polish it, even while you are waiting for a response from the journal.[27]

Do not spend more than a couple of weeks thinking about which journal is the most suitable for the article. If you are torn between various options, just make a random determination. You should not wait until you deem the article to be perfect and its acceptance by the journal of your choice a certainty.[28] If you have reached that stage, you have no doubt already spent too much time on polishing it. The key now is to avoid getting stuck.

Further delay is not helpful because you are not likely to obtain additional useful information on your own about the quality of your article. To be sure, you are very much in need of information, but only the review process can convey it to you realistically and credibly. You are left no choice but to form a subjective opinion about how probable it is that certain journals will accept your article and weigh those against the desirability of having your article appear in them. The referee reports you will receive will enable you to revise your prior assessments as appropriate, and your future assessments should be that much more accurate.

The same holds for being pedantic about details before submission.[29] Excessive polishing of an article may make it more pleasing to you, but it is not likely to impress the referees because they will have a different point of view in any event. They will be less critical than you in certain respects, but more so in others. Hence, the winning strategy is to find out—as soon as possible—what a set of referees thinks about the article. After all, their opinion is the one that matters, and not yours.

When will I receive an answer?

John Komlos: You should have two (occasionally three) anonymous referee reports on your desk alongside the editor's decision in about five months (with a standard deviation of approximately two months).[30] If you are much past six months of waiting, you can inquire at the editorial offices if anything has gone awry. All sorts of unexpected things might happen: editors can change, and your manuscript could have gotten lost in the shuffle. Hence, it is advisable to make some informal inquiries after awhile.[31]

You will get one of three kinds of responses from the editor: rejection, a request to revise and resubmit, or acceptance with minor modifications. If the article is rejected outright, you still have gained important information about your subjective evaluation of the match between your article and the journal's editorial policy. Do not despair. Do not take the rejection personally. There are other journals with other editors and hopefully a different set of referees. This is an idiosyncratic process. One journal's rejection is another's acceptance. Do not make the mistake of filing the article away in a drawer. If you have not learned much from the referee reports, it is better to send the article out again the same day to another journal than to brood over the disappointment for an extensive period. To be sure, it is possible that the referees misunderstood some aspects of the article, in which case you might be tempted to explain the discrepancy to the editor, asking for his opinion on what could be done about it. However, my experience is that such objections are rarely useful.

You should profit from the critical opinions of the referees (who, in a sense, are surrogates for the profession at large) even if the article is rejected. The referees' remarks should be considered carefully, even if you intend to send the article to another journal, because that can only improve the article and because it might just land on the desk of the same referee again. Though unfair to some degree, referees are under no obligation to disqualify themselves (though some do) just because they have already rejected the article for another journal! I know because that has happened to me on occasion.[32]

Alternatively, your article might be accepted outright, which unfortunately happens very seldom. Then there is nothing more to be said. Congratulations on being on the way to becoming a published scholar! You can move the article in your c.v. from the "under consideration" category to the "forthcoming" category. Another possibility is that the editor will ask you to make only some minor revisions, which is generally tantamount to an acceptance without explicitly stating that. In such cases, the article will not be sent to the referees again for their consideration. Rather, the editor will peruse the article in order to assure that you have followed his (and the referees') earlier suggestions. You are then very close to success. You only have to make those minor changes requested, and your article is finished. The real danger in such cases is that you do not read the editor's letter carefully enough and you fail to see that the requested revisions are more or less pro forma.

How should I read the referee reports?

John Komlos: By far the most frequent editorial response is a request to revise and resubmit. You (and the manuscript) have now reached a crucial juncture because, in some sense, the article begins to take on a life of its own. Academic freedom notwithstanding, its fate is no longer entirely in

your hands, as the referees and editor assume the important (and sometimes intrusive) function of seeing the article through to its final publication. It will take a little practice to get used to reading the referee reports
and the editor's summary and judgment correctly. Their intentions can be
easily misunderstood. Frequently, an editor's revise-and-resubmit letter is
read by an author as a letter of rejection; in fact, the editor might well have
implied that he wants to publish the article, without saying it outright,
provided the author can respond in a positive fashion to the referees' remarks. Other authors may be so overwhelmed with the prospect of a
lengthy revision that they are flustered, while still others feel their ego
trampled on with all the criticism. These are not helpful emotional reactions. Referees almost always seem more critical than warranted or anticipated, so you should not think that you are alone in receiving acerbic reports and should not take their criticisms to heart.

   In fact, referees have little or no incentive to respond quickly (or at
all). Often the editor does not even inquire if they are willing to serve in
that capacity, and suddenly an article lands on their desk for judgment.
While the recipient could return the envelope, it takes too much time out
of the day's activities and is not considered good form. It is much easier to
put it aside. Then a few weeks later it is still on the wrong side of the desk,
and he realizes that he would lose face if he returned it to the editor at
such a late date, and he owes him a favor anyhow, and the topic sounds
interesting, so perhaps he should move it to a different pile. In the mean-
time, the author is anxiously hoping for a quick turnaround. Well, it is
easy to see that it is a miracle that the refereeing process works as well as
it does, and generally it does work acceptably.

John Goldsmith: I'm pleased when an editor asks me ahead of time whether
I'll review an article on a given subject, and this ask-first policy seems to
be happening more and more with the rise of electronic mail. The response I give most often is that I'm not sure, but I promise I'll let the
editor know within twenty-four hours of receiving the manuscript if I
won't do it. This seems to ensure that the editor's worst nightmare won't
happen, and it gives me the opportunity to look briefly at the paper before
deciding.

John Komlos: The only reward the referees receive is the satisfaction of
knowing that they have made a contribution to scholarship and have had
an opportunity to impress their views on others—and thereby exert an
influence within the discipline, even if in a small way. These incentives

suffice to make the system work relatively well. Referees do not feel like they have done their job unless they have added at least a few critical remarks to their report. It is important for novice authors not to become discouraged, and to consider every single one of the referees' comments. Generally, their advice is helpful in providing new perspectives on the issue. If you disagree with some of the criticism, make it clear to the editor in your letter accompanying the resubmission. If the referees disagree with one another, the editor should give you some hints about which of them you need to take more seriously. If the editor overlooks some aspects or if some of the referees' comments are not entirely clear to you, you need to contact him for further guidance. As a matter of courtesy, you should certainly not ignore any suggestion from either the referees or the editor. If you disagree with a referee and you are not able or willing to make the requested changes, you should let that be known to the editor as well, though it is in your best interest to be flexible because the editor is likely to give the referees the benefit of the doubt. Of course, some referees will want you to write another article entirely, though you shouldn't consider doing so for the present. The editor might be willing to guide you on how to respond to such critiques. In rare cases, the critiques will be unreasonable, and you should consider sending the article to another journal immediately. However, even in such cases, it pays to consult the editor first.[33]

Penny Gold: One warning: anonymous reports on articles can be dismissive, nasty, even brutal.[34] Comments of this sort on the first piece I ever sent out might have discouraged me from ever trying to publish again but for the fact that I shared my distress with a colleague. She told me that she had received comments in a similar vein on an article, that it was quite common, and that I should just turn around and submit it again elsewhere. I did, and the piece was accepted with no requests for revision.

When responding to readers' comments, I suggest setting up three categories: the suggestions for change that you agree with and that you will implement, the ones that you disagree with (and why), and the ones that you agree with in principle, but are unwilling to undertake (and why—because they would take too much additional research, take you too far afield from the central argument, etc.).

John Komlos: After your resubmission, the editor will again send the article to referees—most likely the same ones—and the process will repeat itself. With any luck, your conception of the article and that of the referees will move closer to one another over time as the referees run out of objections.

The need for one or two more such cycles is common, and if you are flexible, time is on your side. If, however, the editor is uncertain about your article or not favorably disposed to it, he also has the option to send the article to a new set of referees. This makes your task more difficult, inasmuch as you need to respond to an entirely new set of critiques the next round, and the process of asymptotically converging to an agreed version of the manuscript becomes more unlikely. After a couple of such futile cycles, it might be well worth trying another journal. With competing schools of thought in most disciplines, it is unavoidable that at times you will run into referees or editors who are completely unsympathetic, perhaps even hostile, to your article. Though unfortunate, there is nothing to be done about that. Worthy papers do get published eventually.

Editors tend to be cautious about accepting an article whose merits they are uncertain about—especially when it does not fit easily within the accepted paradigm; that is, it is iconoclastic, controversial, or too far from accepted norms. If they reject it and they are wrong in doing so, only a handful of colleagues will find out about their error. In contrast, if they accept an article that turns out to be a dud, then everyone will find out about it. There are plenty of examples of path-breaking publications that were initially rejected.[35]

It should be clear that publishing is a rather tiring process, without much intellectual satisfaction. Having a good paper is a necessary condition, but not sufficient for publication. You also need patience, lots of perseverance, and tolerance of referees' and the editor's idiosyncrasies to succeed. The principle is rather simple: submit, revise, resubmit, publish. It is not fun. Research is fun, but publishing is tedious.

Is coauthoring a good idea?

John Komlos: In the laboratory sciences, research is often a collaborative effort, so that there are inevitably numerous coauthors of a publication. In other disciplines, this is not standard practice, yet coauthoring often makes sense because you are likely to get slightly more credit for it toward tenure than your share of the input warrants. In order for the relationship to be satisfying, the coauthors should complement each other in some way; that is, there should be some advantage conferred on each of the collaborators. This would entail a more than proportionate decrease in the effort needed to complete a project. One of the authors might possess some skills that the other lacks, such as a language, mathematics, or computer know-how.[36] In order to avoid bad feelings later on, it is desirable to agree in advance on the broad outlines of the project, the delegation of responsibilities, the journals that you will consider for publication, and the order of appearance of the authors' names.[37]

John Goldsmith: Coauthored publications can raise questions during the tenure review in some disciplines. It is best not to have too many co-authored papers before tenure—or, rather, it is best to have a sufficient number of single-author papers by that time.

Penny Gold: It will be very helpful to the people considering your dossier at contract and tenure time if you explain briefly the nature of your contribution in any coauthored work. (Your internal curriculum vitae is being read by people outside your field as well as within it, so it is, in general, a good idea to give brief explanations of the significance of any item that is not self-evident.) The range of actual contribution to a coauthored piece, especially one with several coauthors, is so large that you're best off owning up candidly to your part in the work, even if it's small. Saying nothing risks getting you little credit when you actually did a great deal.

Are there additional ways to bring attention to my research?

John Komlos: Self-promotion is important because there is no formal mechanism to advertise your ideas. So you yourself need to see to it that your ideas reach as wide an audience as possible. Bear in mind that there are economies of scale in the dissemination of ideas. With interdisciplinary research, you automatically have several audiences worth addressing. Every time you can get your name in print, you add to your visibility. More people see and read your work. It is analogous to advertising. The profession notices that you once again made it through a screening process. Although initially your contribution might go unnoticed, after awhile, as you develop a research agenda and profile, people's propensity to read your writings is likely to increase.

As a rule, academics are overwhelmed with commitments. But those busy people—coping as best as they can with information overload—are exactly the opinion makers you would like to reach. You cannot expect them to go too far out of their way to learn about your work. That is why publishing does not, by itself, guarantee that your article will be read, understood, cited, and discussed. To be sure, it will be read by those directly involved in the issues you raise, but that might be a small group, and you'll want to reach out to a wider audience to attract more attention to your research. Networking can help develop a coterie of followers—friends and acquaintances—who read your publications regularly. These will be the people to whom you send your working papers before publication, and your offprints thereafter, and they will be the ones who come to your presentations at conferences.[38] Such networking is likely to help spread your ideas. In addition, if you come across an article close to your field and you find no evidence that the author knows of your work, it can be useful to establish contact with him by introducing yourself and by attaching an offprint of one of your articles.

What about publishing a book?

John Goldsmith: In some disciplines, such as mine, assistant professors have to consider whether they should try to publish a revised and expanded version of their dissertation as a book or split the dissertation up into separate articles and publish them individually in journals. One can do only one of the two because a publisher will recoil from a manuscript of which several chapters have been published as articles. Which strategy is better? There is no hard and fast answer, but I think that the advantage goes to the side of publishing the chapters as articles in journals, preferably the best journals possible. On one's c.v., publishing a book with an excellent press looks very good, and perhaps even better than the separate articles, but one's work will be seen and read by far more of one's colleagues if it appears in serious, mainstream journals. So I would recommend taking that route, all other things being equal. But among the things that are not equal is what the expectations are in one's specific field, so one must inform oneself.

In my experience, by the way, those making tenure decisions generally view manuscripts that have been accepted for publication on an equal footing with those that have actually appeared in print. That only seems fair, I should think, and to my knowledge, that's a principle that is regularly held to.

Penny Gold: My own decision on book versus articles was just the opposite of what John Goldsmith recommends. But this depends entirely on your discipline. In my field, history, books count much more heavily than articles and are also more widely read.

John Komlos: I advocate not viewing the publishing endeavor as an either-or proposition because it is very often useful to find multiple venues for an idea, and one way of reaching different audiences is to develop a book from a set of published articles. Scholarly discourse obviously varies by discipline: in economics, publication of a book at the beginning of one's career has become completely discredited, while in history it is indispensable. Competitive history departments expect substantial progress on even a second book by tenure time. Though it may seem odd, at research universities journal articles carry much weight toward tenure in economics and little in history. How such tribal habits come into being and serve a discipline is obviously not our subject here, but they highlight the idiosyncratic nature of the scholarly endeavor. One should obviously have a clear idea of the expectations at the very beginning of one's career and adhere to them religiously.

It is advantageous to first publish several articles from your dissertation, even if you are hoping to publish it as a book as well, in order to begin disseminating your ideas quickly. There is no reason to delay until the whole manuscript is complete. With some luck, you can conceivably have an article appear in the second year of your first job, whereas the appearance of a book will probably take years longer. If appropriate in your field, you should begin working simultaneously on the publication of the whole manuscript, revised, enlarged, and polished sufficiently so that it no longer reads like a dissertation. The publication of a book advances scholarly discourse, independently of the articles that have appeared from it as segmented ideas, because it reaches a somewhat different and perhaps wider audience and because it conveniently collects your arguments so that their relationships are more obvious. Consequently, the arguments in a book-length manuscript are much more complex than in the articles taken together. It is also important that books are usually reviewed in journals. This implies that other scholars will go on record about your work, which (provided, of course, they are positive on balance) will become useful at tenure time. Articles do not automatically elicit a similar public response. To be sure, articles are cited, and you should (years later) find out who is actually citing your work[39] because that will enable you to learn who uses your research in their own publications and which segment of your intended audience you have not succeeded in reaching.

John Goldsmith: In fields where publication of a book is critical in obtaining tenure, the acquisitions editor at the press plays an extraordinarily influential role in the academic process. Just like a journal editor, the acquisitions editor selects the referees chosen to review a manuscript, and this choice can be critical in the decision, up or down, on a manuscript. While most journal editors hold academic appointments—that is, they are regular professors somewhere—acquisitions editors are not. Different university presses have different policies with regard to vetting and to faculty oversight of the publications of the press, and, of course, nonuniversity presses, which are for-profit organizations, have no faculty oversight.

John Komlos: Publishing your dissertation means substantial rewriting. One way to find out the difference between the two is to take a recent publication by a first-time author and compare it in detail to the dissertation from which it was developed. A dissertation can sound more tentative and might have more detail than a book. In the book version, you can also cite your dissertation, so that you can shorten some aspects of your thesis or skip some evidential material.

Simultaneously with the rewriting process, you need to embark on a search for a suitable publisher. This process is analogous to finding an appropriate journal for an article. There has to be a match in quality as well as subject matter. University presses tend to have favorite subject areas, and you will have a better chance of having a manuscript accepted if it fits into the market segment in which the press has already developed a certain visibility. This is important for its marketing success. The best way to begin your search is by talking to editors or other press representatives who attend conferences. They will be able to give you an overview of their publishing strategies, connect you with the right people in their organization, and give you an off-the-cuff impression of how your manuscript is likely to be received or possibly suggest more promising options.

Once you have this information, you should have a list of half a dozen prospective publishers, and you can start making preliminary formal inquiries about their interest in your manuscript. Send along a c.v., a table of contents, and perhaps a synopsis or an introduction to the manuscript. If you have some positive responses (usually in about a month), then you will be asked to send the whole manuscript upon completion. If you have more than one editor interested in your work, then you need to set your own priorities, and you might ask them if they mind if more than one press reviews the manuscript simultaneously. This would be of considerable advantage to you for obvious reasons, but some presses are reluctant to accept such a procedure. If you do not have positive responses, then you need to widen your circle of choices, lower your expectations, and repeat the process until you are successful. My experience is that most people who are unsuccessful are so only because they give up too early.

Penny Gold: I would recommend a somewhat different order for determining prospective presses, saving conference talks with editors until the initial sort is done. Here is how I've found a press for two books: First, I made a list of a dozen or so presses that looked to be likely prospects. I judged suitability by looking over publishers' catalogs, book displays at conferences, and my own book collection to see which publishers had a line of books into which my own might fit. I also noted which books were attractively produced, which publishers advertised prominently in the journals I read, and which had a series into which my book might fit. I included in my list a range from the most prestigious presses to ones that might be a little "hungrier" for manuscripts. I then sent a prospectus to each of these publishers. In addition to the elements John Komlos suggests, I included a paragraph discussing the audience/market I anticipated for my book, and I included a sample chapter.[40] In the cover letter, I also mentioned that I would be at the American Historical Association meeting that year and would be happy to talk with the editor at that time. (I sent these letters out in early fall, with the conference coming in December–January.) Both times this solicitation yielded several expressions of interest, some of them warmer than others, and a few meetings at the convention. I then used the convention meeting not to assess interest, which I already knew of, but to get a better idea of how the press saw my book as fitting in with its list and to assess whether or not I would feel good about working with that particular editor. "Acquisitions" editors have a somewhat misleading title. Yes, they are the ones who are responsible for the all-important decision on whether or not the press should consider your manuscript. But they play a central role in shepherding the manuscript well beyond its acceptance, into the production and promotion process. The more confidence you have in your editor, the happier the publication process will be.

John Komlos: Once the editor has decided to put the manuscript through the review process, he will send it out to two referees, whose reviews will probably be longer, but otherwise similar to referee reports for journal articles. One important point to inquire about is whether the press will send the manuscript to the referees simultaneously or consecutively;[41] that is to say, if it will send the manuscript to the second referee only in case the first one's report is positive. Insofar as the latter procedure is almost twice as long as the former, you should avoid such a submission if you have the option to do so. If you submit the manuscript in the third year in your tenure stream, for example, you could be well into your fourth year before you receive a decision from the press of your choice. And if there are problems, you could find yourself in your fifth year, when your tenure dossier is being prepared, still without a book contract. So if a book-length volume is expected from you for tenure, then you should start early looking for a suitable publisher, revise the manuscript quickly, find a press that will not referee consecutively, and make sure you are not aiming too high. Novices at book publication do not have it easy: it took me six years before my dissertation saw the printer's ink!

The procedure with regard to responding to the referees' comments is the same as that with article submissions. You should expect that meeting the criteria set out by your editor and referees will take an additional six months. Once your manuscript is accepted, you will receive a standard contract.[42]

Once the book appears, you need to make sure that it gets reviewed. You ought not leave it up to the publisher because its staff have so many books to worry about that they will probably not be able to tailor their efforts to the specific needs of your book. You should ask the editor to send you a list of the journals that received your book for review purposes. You should be given a chance to suggest some additions to that list. Make sure that the addresses of the journals' book-review editors are correct. In an amazing number of cases, presses will not have updated their files and will send books to incorrect addresses. However, your job is still not complete. You should write to the book-review editors to find out if your book arrived because in my experience the post is not always reliable. The book-review editors of the journals will write back to you with an appropriate response. My point is that it is your responsibility, and not that of the publisher, to make sure that the book gets to the book-review editors of the journals you deem appropriate for a review of your book. Of course, the number of appropriate journals may well exceed the number of review copies the publisher is willing to devote to promoting your book. In that case, you might have to send some of your personal copies to be reviewed by some of the journals that were left off the publisher's list.

With the book published and well on its way to being widely reviewed, you should be in a good position for your tenure decision. It only remains to celebrate and, yes, one last thing: you should still consider the prizes for which your book is eligible and submit it to the appropriate committees on time.

Penny Gold: Much of the above should be discussed with your editor at the time you are negotiating the contract for your book. Ask how many copies the publisher is willing to send out for review (and the press, in turn, will ask you for a list of journals to which the book should be sent). Ask how many copies the publisher is willing to send out to prominent scholars. And ask about the advertising plans. If the scope of any of these seems too small, argue for more. Much of this can and should be included in your contract.

How do I fund my research needs?

John Komlos: Keeping oneself informed of the changing opportunities for grants and fellowships is extremely important in all disciplines, not only in the laboratory sciences. It is a continuous process and can be done effectively only by maintaining and regularly updating files in which announcements are kept.

Besides funding research expenses and travel costs to conferences and to research sites, grants can provide you with summer salaries, as well as with released time from teaching obligations, so that you can dedicate not only more time, but also solid chunks of time to research. In many fields, applying for and receiving fellowships will be seen as an integral part of your professional development. You must keep abreast of new work in your discipline as well as in your subspecialty, which is extremely difficult to do during the academic year, given all your other obligations. Hence, released time gained through grant support is almost the only way to ensure that you will have the chunks of free time available to focus on the frontier. The summers, of course, are useful, but generally insufficient by themselves because you also need to continue your course preparations and research. That is the reason why you should avoid teaching during the summers at all cost unless you can trade such an assignment with your chair against teaching at other times of the year.

Fellowships confer prestige on the recipient in the same way that prizes do in other segments of society. Successful grant applications also make administrators happy because they may pay overhead costs to the university, some of which could filter down to the dean and the department.[43]

The Inside Track
Publishing the First Book
Colin Day

Colin Day is director of the University of Michigan Press.

The first question you must ask yourself is rarely mentioned and somewhat painful: how good do you think this manuscript is? An honest answer to this question can save a lot of time, and heartache. A related question is: how much more work do you want to do on it; is it something that you are prepared to revise and revise, or do you want to move on?

So the first task is to position this manuscript in the hierarchy from the epoch making to the useful contribution. Submit to the highest-caliber publishers if you truly think your manuscript is first rate and of importance to readers well beyond those who work in your particular subfield. But in truth, few books from young authors are of that standard. A realistic matching of quality—aim a little high, but not off the map—will get a good decision more promptly. Aiming too high and getting a crushingly negative review is a risk that only those of robust self-confidence should take.

However, there are, of course, multiple dimensions to the choice of publisher. The most important is that it publish in your field. Recent publications on topics close to yours are a signal that the publisher is active in your area and likely to welcome another such submission. There is no point in offering your work to one who is not already active in your field or whose books take an approach that is opposed to yours. Inspect your own personal professional library (if you are not buying books in your field, why should your colleagues buy your book?), the relevant sections of a good academic bookstore, and your school library. The imprints you see on those shelves are the ones to consider for your manuscript.

You now have identified four or five publishers of the right stature and active in your field. What do you do now? It is perfectly all right at this stage to send an inquiry to a few publishers. Tell each that you are consulting others at this stage. Always be open: publishers are tolerant of missteps, but not of misrepresentation.

The books referred to below will give fuller advice on what to send at this stage. However, the overall purpose is to say what the manuscript is about, what is special about it, and, where relevant, what philosophical or methodological approach it takes. Your task is to sell—gently, not stridently—your project to the editor. You should be trying to persuade her that your manuscript is special, intellectually significant, and likely to arouse wide enough interest to be economically viable. But nothing deters like wild claims of broad popular readership or automatic classroom use. However, it is valuable to explain why people in your discipline, but not in your precise subfield, will be interested. If you are working across disciplinary boundaries, do define the readership you envision for your work. This not only indicates the size of the market, but also helps the publisher think about reaching that readership. But if you have chosen your publisher wisely, and even more certainly if that publisher is a university press, it is the scholarly contribution that will weigh most heavily and that you should emphasize.

If it is your dissertation that you are aiming to publish, there is no doubt that a major rewrite will be necessary before publication. Your initial contacts with publishers may be made when you have a clear plan for revision, but before your revise. But expect that good publishers may not do more than offer encouragement and suggestions until a substantial revision has actually been made. The better stage for initiating publisher contacts would be when you have done a first revision.

A few do's and don'ts: Don't write asking in what form the publisher wants a submission. Just send a well-thought-out and small package. Do not send in the full manuscript. A sample chapter is perhaps worthwhile including. However, be sure it represents your work well. In particular, introductions are often unhelpful to your case: convoluted in structure and style, and burdened with relics of the work's dissertation origins.

Remember that each letter that lands on the editor's desk is unique, is often long, and takes time to read and think about. Give the editor a month or so to read your letter and decide on a response. Then a polite inquiry is all right—but do not harass! If you have sent out several inquiries, give a reasonable time for all to respond before you move ahead. Call the laggards to give them a chance to reply. Then choose one publisher who has expressed interest and send the material the editor requested. Write to the others asking their forbearance and expressing a wish to reopen the conversation if the first publisher chooses not to accept.

The review process takes time. Finding reviewers can itself be long, drawn out, and difficult, as the right experts are busy and backlogged (offering suggestions of suitable readers is always welcome and helpful). Then reviewers are not quick: ask your senior colleagues how quickly they review a book-length manuscript. And treat their answers with some skepticism. Completing a careful peer review in less than three months is hard. Again, a polite, unpressing inquiry after a couple of months is acceptable, but frequent phone calls do not help your case. From that comes a last and very important point: getting your book accepted and then published takes time. Do not start the process when the tenure clock is at five minutes to midnight. If your university requires a published book, then you really need to allow two years from submission to publication. It probably will not take that long, but it will if you receive a few rejections or are required to make some major revisions. If a contract is sufficient, then twelve months is probably enough time to allow. But things can go wrong, so allow as much time as you can. Scholarly publishers are very committed to their craft. They are genuinely enthusiastic about disseminating important academic work. But they are looking after a large number of authors and their books, so their enthusiasm and time do have to be shared. Bear this in mind, and you will have an excellent experience as your book works it way to publication.

Useful references include Robin Derricourt, *An Author's Guide to Scholarly Publishing* (Princeton, N.J.: Princeton University Press, 1996); Eleanor Harman and Ian Montagnes, eds., *The Thesis and the Book* (Toronto: University of Toronto Press, 1976); Beth Luey, *Handbook for Academic Authors*, 4th ed. (New York: Cambridge University Press, 1995); and Christine S. Smedley, *Getting Your Book Published* (Newbury Park, Calif.: Sage, 1993).

Competition is extremely keen for the more prestigious awards. It has been my experience that the more knowledgeable the application reads, the more convincing it will be and the greater the chance of obtaining funding is. It generally does not suffice to have a good idea, or a plausible hunch, because referees usually do not grant you the benefit of the doubt on account of their very tight budgetary restrictions. Hence, they want a clear sense of purpose and a cogent and persuasive explanation of what is at stake in the project. They want to be convinced that you will actually accomplish that which you suggest. Writing a persuasive grant application, with lots of background reading, is tantamount to writing an article.[44] I find that I have been most successful when I was able to present at least a pilot study with preliminary results to convince the referees of the validity of my intentions. Consequently, many scholars in the social sciences find it appropriate to apply for a grant or fellowship only after they have done sufficient work on the project that they can write authoritatively about it. Although the project by then is well under way, and perhaps the funding is no longer indispensable for the completion of the project, the leftover funds can be used for the next project. This system of half-project-ahead financing is obviously inappropriate for the natural sciences, but it does have the extra advantage of ensuring that the project will be completed as promised. It has the disadvantage that the initial costs of the project might have to be raised from personal funds; otherwise, seed money might be obtained for the pilot project from smaller foundations or the home university's research office.

Penny Gold: Another element that can add to the success of a proposal is how much of a difference having grant support will make to the completion of your project. When weighing two proposals for summer research support, for example, a granting agency may prefer to fund a proposal that has a travel or an equipment component rather than one that can be accomplished at home. This doesn't mean you should pad your proposal with unnecessary trips. But it can help you be realistic in expectations of funding outcomes.

As you begin to think about writing a proposal, ask around for others who have submitted successful proposals to the granting agencies on your list. Often you will find such at your own institution; if not, seek further afield. Some agencies (e.g., the National Endowment for the Humanities) will themselves send you examples of successful proposals. Looking at these will be a great help to you in crafting your own proposal. Some agencies have program officers who will give you advice along the way, even read a draft of a proposal. And some will send you readers' comments once the process is complete if you ask for them. These can be especially helpful if your proposal has been rejected. But even if accepted, it's always nice to see what others have thought of your project.

And don't neglect sources of funding internal to your institution. Some faculty development funds may be highly competitive, such as for blocks of research leave over and above sabbatical time, and some may be relatively routine, such as for summer travel or requests for materials/equipment. Institutions vary in their support for travel to professional conferences, but most will pay at least travel for one or more conferences per year, especially if you are giving a paper. Take advantage of these local resources to their full extent.

What if I am unable to publish?

John Komlos: You have at least three choices: (1) teach in a college or university that does not expect publication, (2) leave academia for a job in industry or government, or (3) try to find out why you have this mental blockage. Most of the time research is not the problem because if you were able to write a Ph.D. thesis, you must have some results that it would be worthwhile to communicate to a larger audience. In almost all cases, the inability to publish is somehow connected to a perfectionism that prevents bringing the writing to a conclusion, an inappropriate choice of journals, or an unwillingness to pay careful attention to the referee reports. So if you have not been successful, you must ascertain as quickly as possible the source of the problem.

John Goldsmith: That is good advice. The task of writing for publication is an extension and continuation of the task of writing a dissertation, and many of the same pitfalls are waiting for the unwary. I think that we have touched on the principal ones along the way, but getting one's work out and published does require a kind of entrepreneurship that does not come easily to everyone—not by a long shot.

8 | Tenure

First of all, what is tenure?

John Goldsmith: Tenure is what separates the junior faculty—the assistant professors and some of the associate professors—from the senior faculty. Tenured professors are guaranteed a job until they retire, the only exception being those rare individuals who are terminated because of a violation of ethical or legal codes. But the differences between the two parts of the faculty go beyond job security, though this depends on the particular university. The junior faculty member is quite naturally in a dependent, even a defensive position, knowing that the work that she accomplishes in just a few short years—generally five or six—will serve as the basis for a very serious decision about her career. The junior faculty member may often feel like she has little choice regarding the teaching and service demands made of her; to say "no" may give the impression of not being a team player, or of not being sufficiently grateful for being at the university, or of simply being lazy.

    The tenured faculty member, on the other hand, has a great deal of freedom concerning what she chooses to teach and to do (or not do) research on. It's hard to imagine any other profession in which such freedom is offered to so many people for such a long period of time. It is a great opportunity.

Penny Gold: The significant differences in job security and evaluative scrutiny in the lives of untenured and tenured faculty inevitably make for differing attitudes toward one's work and toward one's institution, with stress and anxiety being unavoidable, ongoing hallmarks of life as an untenured professor. And yet the content of the job being done on a day-to-day basis is the same for most beginning assistant professors as for those at the height of their careers (except for those among the latter who are taking a turn at departmental administration). That is, all of us teach class, carry out research, and do miscellaneous administrative and service tasks. Some people prefer to avoid the terms "junior" and "senior" faculty for just this reason—the basic job expectations are the same no matter where you are in rank. Identifying the two groups as "untenured" and "tenured" is, in this view (with which I am sympathetic), more clearly descriptive of the most significant difference in the two groups.

John Goldsmith: It is often said that tenure exists largely to guarantee the professor a position from which she can explore unpopular positions, either political or intellectual—positions that might be so unpopular (and therefore risky) that, without this guarantee, it would be foolhardy to undertake such an exploration. There is undoubtedly something to this, but I think it is a fairly small part of the whole story. Very few in academia ever think of using the security of their position to voice unpopular political positions, and in general, tenure does not seem to be necessary to protect the vast majority of academics who choose to take unpopular positions. An unpopular position, defended well, is by and large to everyone's liking; a professor who publishes interesting work from an unpopular viewpoint is by and large thought well of, regardless of his tenure or lack thereof.

Penny Gold: While it may not be the reason tenure exists, I have certainly relied on the security of my tenured status on those occasions when I have opposed the dean or the president on matters of institutional policy or action. Faculty are reliant enough on the good will of these individuals (as well as one's department chair and other senior colleagues) that opposition is not undertaken lightly, and if one's job was at stake as well, dissonant voices would be even more rare than they already are. The constraints on dissent amongst administrative staff, who generally have year-to-year contracts and no possibility of tenure, are even more severe.

John Goldsmith: I'm not convinced, in all honesty. I've observed up close various kinds of internecine struggle in nonacademic, but professional organizations—places where nothing legal prevented someone from being shown the door at a moment's notice. But in my experience, people are let go for business reasons, not for being ornery. A manager, even a ranking manager, who solves her problems by firing will neither last long nor rise high. No, I see the existence of tenure in academia differently.

The question as to why there is such a thing as tenure should be approached just like any question concerning a large social unit: it is pointless to ask why it is the way it is if we expect an explanation like one as to why we put on a particular shirt this morning. The only explanation as to why there is tenure will be historical, or else it will be one that seeks to understand why the system as a whole functions better with tenure than without it. Tenure does not exist primarily to protect the individual (though that may be a salutary side effect); it is rather part of a functioning system.

A experiment some years back at the University of North Carolina (Chapel Hill) illustrates this point. The provost decided to offer two types of employment options for new faculty members: either traditional tenure-track lines or non-tenure-track employment (with potentially indefinite employment, to be sure) at a higher salary. The difference between the two salaries? $5,000 a year, as of 1989.

So one natural side effect of the existence of tenure in the academic system is that it helps keep salaries down in the academic world. It only stands to reason (and to economic common sense) that people will be willing to work for a lower salary if their job is guaranteed: that is, the guarantee of employment is worth a hefty decrease in salary. To put the same point in a slightly different way, any system or any enterprise hopes and expects its artisans to be enterprising, original, and creative. In the business world, this hope is expressed most commonly in the enormous opportunities open to the entrepreneur who undertakes to provide a product or service better than anyone else. The rewards available to her are virtually without economic limit. Academia has no such means available to it with which to reward—financially—the enterprising intellectual; it can offer only a limited amount of reward along such lines. Instead, a different series of rewards and opportunities is available, of which tenure is the central and spotlighted element. Tenure is, first, then, a benefit that universities can offer at relatively low cost to themselves and that is worth relatively more in an economy with economic insecurity than it would in an economy where all were guaranteed jobs. To put it another way, tenure is at least as much protection from being laid off as it is from being fired.

From another point of view, tenure is a way that the academic system has of acknowledging that its ability to evaluate the research capacities and activities of each member comes to an end at a certain point. The system no longer needs to undertake that onerous burden for each and every faculty member, or perhaps we should say that the system no longer wishes to undertake the overall expense of such reviews. After a person receives tenure, the circumstances under which she is evaluated by her university are few in number. There will probably be the matter of promotion to full professor at some point down the road; there will be the matter of salary increments each year. Promotion to full professor is a serious matter, but nowhere near as serious as the tenure decision. Salary increments each year are a relatively easy matter, as we have seen: there will be a default value (perhaps occasionally as much as 4 or 5 percent, but more often less, and very occasionally the value has been known to be negative) set by the provost for all faculty members, and then there will be some modest adjustments above or below that line for a few individual cases. The only other critical moment of readjusting the resources offered to a faculty member comes when an offer has been made by a competing university (the subject of the next chapter)—which is a moment of crisis created by a competitor attempting to encroach on a university's turf, a rather different matter, and one that is not typically going to occur for each and every faculty member.

How does the tenure review process begin?

John Goldsmith: The simplest case to discuss is that of an assistant professor who takes a tenure-track position immediately after graduate school. The "tenure clock" (as the expression goes) starts for this person when she begins at the university and typically runs without any delays. Toward the end of the fifth year, or the beginning of the sixth, a review procedure is undertaken about which we will have more to say shortly. This procedure will typically take up to six to ten months to complete, and at the end of this time, a decision will be reached by the university that will be either positive, in which case the candidate will be awarded a position with "indefinite tenure," or negative, in which case the candidate will have somewhere between six and eighteen months to find a new job elsewhere.

If this case involves someone who has come to the university from another university, where she spent (let us say) three years, then the decision regarding tenure may or may not wait for six years. The tenure clock may be started at three, or perhaps two, years, and when the clock hits the beginning of the third or fourth year at the current university, the tenure procedure might begin. But whether this pushing of the tenure clock forward is done or not must be negotiated by the new professor and the administration when she comes to the university, and it must be put on paper in black and white.

There are no definitive reasons why an assistant professor (or an untenured associate professor) should try to get a tenure decision made earlier rather than later. There are good reasons to have the decision made earlier; there are equally good reasons to delay the decision as long as possible. Most of the reasons are transparent. In favor of an early decision is the fact that it is more comfortable to be tenured, and a salary raise will come along with that landmark. On the other hand, the longer one waits before the tenure decision, the more time there is to write and to publish, thus strengthening the tenure dossier. Of course, if you have an overwhelmingly strong publication record, you may wish to come up for a tenure review as soon as possible. But any tenure reviews that are early—that is, before the tenure clock has come to the sixth year—are bound to be judged by somewhat stricter standards. It is a calculated risk. Failing to get tenure on an earlier-than-necessary review is not necessarily a sign that the case will be rejected again when submitted during the sixth year, but a rejected early-tenure case is difficult for all parties to deal with comfortably.

The details of the tenure procedure differ from university to university, and to some extent even from department to department. The first step is generally for the chair of the department to collect a dossier containing all of the candidate's publications and documentation concerning all of the candidate's professional activities that in one way or another bear on the tenure decision. The chair and the candidate may then together construct a list of six to ten reasonably senior people in the candidate's field of specialty who should be in a position to offer an evaluation of that work. A common pattern is for the candidate to offer the names of four people she would like to see asked and a list of about four names of people who she thinks might be unreasonably inclined against her work (rather like a lawyer's preemptive right to veto a potential juror). The chair will then go on to pick another group of senior scholars (as few as three, but more likely closer to six) whose opinions will be obtained.

It is not uncommon for this procedure to begin early in the fall semester of the candidate's sixth year; it may start earlier. More often than not, the chair will call the outside experts (or referees, as we may call them) on the phone to ask if they would be willing to write an evaluatory letter, explaining that the deadline for the letter would be, say, October 10. If the referee says no, this is in no way prejudicial to the candidate's case; no one but the chair will know. If the person agrees to do it, she is honor bound to provide the letter by the day of the deadline—this is one of the most serious professional responsibilities a professor has.

The referee may be someone who has worked closely with the candidate, she may be someone who has followed the candidate's work closely over the past six years, or she may be someone who hardly knows the candidate's work at all, but is willing to put in some serious time and effort to read the materials that the candidate has published. In any case, the chair will typically send a large package of the candidate's publications (it may be the candidate's complete set of publications, but it is more likely to be some important selected items), and the referee will be expected to offer two kinds of evaluations. First, she will offer a judgment on the significance of the kind of work that the candidate is undertaking and the success (or failure) of that research in accomplishing its goals. Second, she will offer a statement as to how the candidate's work stands when compared with others who have been in the field an equal length of time. It is the outside referee who can explain why certain invitations that the candidate has received actually signify an important international recognition of the candidate, and it is also the outside referee who can say that the candidate has no grasp of the big picture of the field in which she works. Most academic specialties are quite small, and a leading expert will probably know something about virtually everyone contributing to the area. The outside referee is likely to have encountered the candidate in her capacity as an editor, or as a speaker at a conference, or as part of an academic organization.

Oddly enough, the most helpful letters that a candidate gets are frequently from someone who holds reservations concerning the candidate's work. If the letter is nothing but two or three pages of elegiac praise, it is hard to avoid thinking that the minimal amount of critical thinking has not entered into the evaluation. However, there is hardly anything more impressive than a letter from a referee who says, first, that she thinks that the candidate's perspective is fundamentally misguided and, second, that she nonetheless acknowledges that every paper (or most of the papers) that the candidate has published present strong and even compelling cases for the position that she thinks is, in fact, wrong. Honest respect from an intellectual opponent is far harder to earn than copious praise from someone with whom one is in agreement, and the academics who have to read these letters are generally quite well aware of that fact.[1]

These half dozen or so letters from outside referees, collected by the

chair, form the most important core of the tenure dossier at a research
university. At some time early in the fall—most likely after most, but not
all, of the outside letters have been received by the candidate's chair—the
senior members of the department will gather to discuss and vote on the
candidate. Each of the senior members will have (or should have, at least!)
read the candidate's publications and all the available outside letters. Of
course, most of the senior members will have a specialization removed
from that of the candidate; how much of the publications they will be able
to judge critically will vary greatly from person to person and from field
to field.

The department will vote, then, on the candidate's case—more often
than not with the advice of a smaller internal committee that has been
set up to give an initial evaluation. The chair will then report that vote,
along with a description of the department's general view of the candidate's work, and complete the tenure dossier, which by this time will include all of the referees' letters, all of the candidate's publications, and a
statement by the candidate as well, concerning her teaching, research, and
service activities. The chair will also include a brief academic biography
of each of the referees, explaining why they were among the best people
available to provide judgments of the candidate's work.

The dossier will then go, perhaps in early November, to the dean,
though which dean receives the dossier will depend on the particular academic structure of the university in question. In some systems, it will then
be read by a standing committee that has been elected by the entire faculty
and that serves in an advisory role to the dean. This committee will read
the chair's report and the referees' detailed evaluations and consider all of
the other material in the dossier. It is no longer a matter of directly evaluating the candidate's work—the experts have already done that. Now it
is more a matter of weighing the alternative judgments that comprise
the dossier. In some cases, all of the judgments will concur, either for or
against the candidate. She may be the best young scholar in the field, with
a long publication list of important books and many grateful students; she
may be someone incapable of serious academic research and teaching. Either way, the positive or negative vote from the department will be easy to
support, and there will be little discussion in such a case.

The tough cases are those where there are conflicting judgments that
are passed on to the dean and the committee from the department and
from the outside experts. A department may vote in favor—even strongly
in favor—of a candidate whose research and publication record is weak,
perhaps because the candidate fits in well and comfortably with a depart-

ment that has become sleepy and less demanding in research. In a properly functioning academic scene, this will not happen, but when it does, questions may be raised at this first level above the department as to whether a sufficiently critical process has been undertaken to evaluate the candidate's work.

This discussion of the tenure decisions places a different emphasis than many that are offered, especially in newspaper accounts of tenure decisions, a difference that is worth a bit of elaboration. Tenure decisions are often viewed as primarily decisions regarding an individual's continued employment, and, of course, that is an important aspect of the process. At the same time, the evaluative side of the tenure process is the most important aspect of the university's attempt to form, model, and better itself. Some of the (perhaps brutal) aspects of the business world are not present in the academic world, especially in light of the job security possessed by the tenured professor. But complete job security would bring down the system as a whole if its end result was to decrease the general degree of competition and activity in the academic professions.

What are the criteria used for tenure evaluation?

John Goldsmith: This is the big question: what criteria will be used by the university to determine whether an untenured professor will be granted permanent tenure? The traditional answer is that research, teaching, and service are the grounds for tenure.

At research universities—more or less, by definition—research is by far the most important criterion. "Research" generally does not mean research—it means publication, as we have seen, for there is no other way that a legitimate and consistent system can be established to evaluate the quantity and quality of a person's research. Emphasizing publication as a measure of research also, in effect, recognizes the fact that knowledge is not an individual's private possession; the knowledge that one "has" is part of a larger social fabric of knowledge, and one does not add to knowledge in the larger, and more important, sense simply by adding to one's own personal fund.

What is a strong tenure case? That's like asking how long a piece of string is. It depends entirely on the standards of the university and of the field in which the candidate is working. In many areas, there is a simple rule of thumb: one must publish a book, and the condition is often added that the book must not be a lightly revised version of the Ph.D. dissertation. In other fields (philosophy, for example, or mathematics, or linguistics), writing books is quite unusual, and publishing in refereed journals is the normal way of demonstrating research activities.

John Komlos: Requirements for tenure vary enormously.[2] At the economics department of North Carolina State, for instance, one is expected to publish at least one article in one of the main journals of the discipline, and these journals are actually spelled out. A journal in your own subspecialty would not suffice. In other words, if you are an economic historian, it would not be sufficient to publish in the *Journal of Economic History;* you would need to place an article in a journal such as the *Quarterly Journal of Economics.* An awareness of these criteria—and they are supposed to be purely academic—will be useful for you, even if there are always exceptions. Friendships and other extraneous issues can play a role occasionally, and grievance procedures are always available in case of unfair treatment, but these are generally not at all reliable. It is best to perform so as to have a solid case by review time.[3]

To be successful, you should formulate your publishing plans on a relatively tight schedule, with a steady stream of output, because the years to the tenure decision pass very quickly (see table 8 in appendix 3). By the end of your sixth year, you should have published at least four or five articles along with (in some disciplines) a book, and you should have several papers in progress. That is no small achievement and can be accomplished only by focusing on the tenure requirements from the very beginning.

Penny Gold: I have to say that this schedule makes me very glad that I landed at an institution that weighs teaching more heavily than research! The down side is that excellence in teaching is even more difficult to assess than excellence in publication, and one's classroom performance and approach to teaching will be up for close scrutiny during the tenure evaluation. If research is expected as well, as it is at many of these institutions, it is likely that your publications will be sent out for external review, as has been described above, though the number of reviewers may be smaller than for a research institution. The evaluation of your teaching, on the other hand, is necessarily a matter for internal rather than external review. As we've discussed in the previous chapter, you need to learn about and be responsive to the processes and instruments in use at your institution. While you may be able to crank out sufficient publications in the last couple of years before tenure to meet the research criteria at your institution, teaching is necessarily judged over a longer trajectory, and one or two years of positive evaluations may not be enough to outweigh a weaker record from several previous years. The teaching statement that you will probably be asked to include in your dossier is a place in which you can address the changes you've made that have resulted in this improvement. It helps to know the changes were the result of thoughtful deliberations, and not of accident.

Your statements on teaching, research, and service should, indeed, be carefully crafted. As always, get one or two people whom you trust and who are in a position to have read such statements by others to give you some feedback. This is your big chance to present yourself on your own terms rather than being seen through the eyes of others. Don't be apologetic, but don't ignore problem areas either. Why the latter advice? You may wonder why you should bring up problems yourself. The reason is that the review committee will see these problems anyway, and it is to your advantage to give a brief, but frank, explanation of them and—most important—what you've been doing to address them. A person who understands their problem areas and is addressing them is a much stronger candidate for tenure than one who ignores or is unwilling to admit such.

Your statements should also look to the future: What new research is in the works or on the horizon? Where do you see yourself going in your teaching in terms of either new courses or new pedagogical strategies? The tenure decision is based not only on your past accomplishments, but also on a prediction of your future performance. Necessarily so, given that just five or six years of performance are being used as a base for assessing what you will do for perhaps another thirty years after tenure. There is always a risk involved—the institution cannot be certain that the track record you've established will be continued. But, understandably, it's in the institution's best interests to keep the risks minimal. So the best tenure dossier is one that not only demonstrates minimal achievement of the expected standards, but also gives the institution grounds for confidence that your achievements are not just last-minute or ephemeral, but will continue well into the future.

Isn't the system of tenure controversial? I understand it's under attack in some places.

John Komlos: There has been considerable discussion lately about the institution of tenure. The motivation is clear: many university administra-

tors find the system not a very cost-effective way to run their business and
are increasing the number of part-time instructors, advocating or adopt-
ing post-tenure review procedures, or trying to eliminate tenure entirely.
What the future of tenure is likely to be is difficult to say, but some adjustment is likely because tenure seems to have outlived its usefulness. Its
justification lies in guaranteeing academic freedom of thought so that politically or socially controversial ideas could find a haven within academia.
But if that is the case, why not guarantee that freedom of thought from
the very beginning of an academic career? The answer usually given is that
one first has to prove oneself worthy of such a status. But freedom of
speech is guaranteed by the Constitution anyway, so tenure seems to be
superfluous from a legal standpoint. In any event, the significance of this
particular function has waned, or all but disappeared, over the years, and
tenure has basically become one of the many fringe benefits we enjoy in
academia. Of course, there is a price attached to it, as John pointed out
above. The tenure decision within a relatively short period after becoming
an academic also has a hidden adverse effect on the research agendas of
untenured faculty. There is an incentive to start safe projects that are likely
to yield quick results within the accepted paradigm of the profession.

It is amazing how well job performance actually does hold up after
tenure. I know absolutely no one who has acted completely irresponsibly
after receiving tenure and has taken complete advantage of her newly
gained privilege. Most academics actually do not change their behavior
after tenure because they have internalized habits that put them almost on
automatic pilot. In addition, peer pressure often suffices to maintain performance levels at least up to a minimum standard: "academics care about
how other academics perceive them, and many are powerfully driven by
the desire to maintain self-esteem."[4]

Nonetheless, tenure does afford a handful of professors the luxury to
slack off. In colloquial academic parlance, they are referred to as being
"deadwood" or as having taken "early retirement," implying that though
they continue teaching full-time, they've ceased their research and publishing activity. This phenomenon has given rise to the current questioning of the privilege. Actually, I don't see much compelling justification for
the maintenance of the institution of tenure, as those in other professions
do not enjoy such security.

John Goldsmith: It's not obvious what the effects would be on academia
of eliminating tenure. Chances are good that, in the best universities, fac-

ulty with seniority—a lot of years under their belts—would simply not be fired. The policy would be to keep people on. Why so? The answer is simple. Look at industry-sponsored think tanks and research groups. People typically move there from academia and give up a tenured position to do so. The administrations of these groups then fire very few people. If they did, the chilling effect on their ability to hire would be far too costly. While many people would still move there, it would, on average, cost more to do so, and a noticeable number of people who otherwise would have gone there would decide not to, thank you very much.

It would be very good if we could figure out a way to increase mobility in the academic system. It's quite difficult for any but the very best professors with tenure to find a job elsewhere; universities typically want to hire junior faculty—in part, but only in part, for economic reasons. My impression is that most senior job openings are linked to a search for a chair of a department—typically, a troubled department. If the dismantlement of the tenure system were to lead to a system in which faculty of all ages could move around, and by moving around both create and fill job openings, we might all be better off. However, if universities linked a policy of hiring and firing without tenure to a policy of trying to hire young and relatively low-salaried professors (even as a mild preference), then there would be suffering of the sort that we have seen in other labor forces, with the brunt borne by older workers. Excuse me, older professors.[5]

What happens if I am denied tenure?

John Komlos: The denial of tenure is particularly traumatic because the person in question is obliged to leave the institution. In essence, she is fired, and not necessarily because of her not measuring up. Budgetary decisions or a change in departmental prerogatives might have forced the decision. The system is such that the university cannot keep her on the payroll thereafter, say, on an annual contract or at a lower salary, even if she were willing to accept such an offer. The whole process is a highly prescribed ritualistic event of great inflexibility. It is particularly crazy that small differences in your achievement might have such tremendous consequences for your life. I personally think we could use more flexibility in the system. But because we do not have it at this point, you have to aim for safety-first: try to accomplish more than the actual stated requirements needed to obtain tenure.

Penny Gold: Denial of tenure is always very painful. Here you are in your thirties or older, and someone is telling you you're just not good enough. If the institution has been clear in communicating its standards, and fair in the process of evaluating you, and effective in communicating its assessment of you, then the negative decision should not be a surprise to you, even if it is a great disappointment. You may already have been looking for jobs elsewhere or even exploring alternative career paths. Sometimes the denial of tenure turns out to have the positive result of pushing someone to look for a job situation more appropriate to their personality, talents, and desires. It's still painful, but in these circumstances, one can leave with a minimum of bitterness.

Unfortunately, there are some cases where bitterness or outrage is justified. Sometimes the institution has, in fact, done a poor job of communicating its standards, and the decision comes as a hurtful surprise. And sometimes the decisions are unfair. The people making the decisions are, after all, human. We have prejudices and personal preferences, which may not be sufficiently suppressed. Having multiple people and levels involved in the evaluation process usually provides protection for the candidate. But certain individuals carry more weight than others (e.g., key opinion leaders in the department, the dean, the president), and it can happen that people who really should have been tenured according to the standards of the institution are denied tenure. One only needs to follow the accounts of some of the successful suits brought against institutions to be convinced this is the case. So what should you do if you believe your denial is unfair? You should explore the avenues open to you to contest the decision, both internal and external. Every institution should have in place a grievance procedure to handle such issues, whether the contestation is on procedural or substantive grounds. You also have the option of pursuing your case through the judicial system or, if you suspect discrimination, through the Equal Employment Opportunity Commission (EEOC). If you are considering such routes, you should seek help early on from other people who have pursued similar cases and from groups who provide support to litigants. The American Association of University Professors (AAUP) is the national organization to turn to,[6] and it can help you find groups within your own discipline that may be of help (for example, the women's caucuses of major professional organizations).[7]

John Komlos: Life, of course, must go on in or out of academia if the tenure decision went against you. You will often have a year to find alternative employment. In many cases, you will be able to move down the academic hierarchy and possibly even obtain tenure elsewhere. However, lateral moves, across equally prestigious institutions, are extremely rare. In the top handful of research universities, it is often made clear from the outset that even though you were nominally hired in the tenure stream, your chances of actually being granted tenure are extremely slim. At such universities, you need to "hit a home run," as one senior scholar put it to me, before you will be tenured; that is, you need to make a unique contribution to scholarship by doing path-breaking work, and unless you are a Mozart, you are not likely to be able to achieve that within a few years of leaving graduate school. There is nothing wrong with the criterion itself as long as you understand the implied terms of your initial contract from the outset. As compensation for the additional uncertainty you face, you will be working with the top scholars in the field. In such a case, you should think of your position as receiving further on-the-job training, making you a better scholar in the process. As long as you accept the job with that attitude and don't tell yourself that the rule doesn't apply to you, the experience will be very rewarding. Thereafter, people usually obtain a good job at a university slightly lower down the academic totem pole, so your years at such a department will be an investment with dividends. It is in your best interest to put out feelers about opportunities elsewhere well ahead of your tenure decision because often departments need to plan considerably in advance of your actual availability.

There is no stigma attached to being denied tenure at such elite departments because it is common knowledge that they are not willing to grant tenure even to good scholars. Such departments are interested mainly in recruiting senior faculty who have already acquired an international reputation and whose research accomplishments have been amply demonstrated. These people play an extremely important role in the department because they are the ones who attract the top graduate students in the country, the competition for whom is extremely keen. Without these top students, the reputation of the department would not be maintained for long.

What about opportunities outside of academia?

John Komlos: If you have not received a very enticing alternative offer, you should think seriously about taking a job outside academia. Many skills that you have acquired are very valuable outside of the narrow field to which you have applied those skills until now. Analytical thinking, clear writing skills, organizational talent, ability to communicate orally, and experience in getting along with colleagues in a bureaucratic organization are as useful in government service, in the nonprofit sector, and in research organizations as they are in the business world. You just need to persevere to find the right niche for your talents. And the fact that you have acquired a Ph.D. is a certification that you do have these talents, in spite of the tenure decision not having gone your way. Going to professional school is yet another valid consideration. And you can take joy in the fact that your lifetime salary will be substantially greater than it would have been in academia. I know of persons who, after having been denied tenure, went to law school (at forty), became corporate lawyers, and had extremely successful careers. So there is life after a denial of tenure after all!

John Goldsmith: The question of opportunities outside of academia is one much broader than the question of what to do after not getting tenure, of course, and it is one that we have discussed earlier. Professionals in the worlds outside of academia have long faced the problem of what to do when fired, downsized, or laid off, and there are many good books in the bookstores suggesting what to do when faced with this challenge.

9 | Competition in the University System and Outside Offers

John Goldsmith: Let's talk about the forces that operate among universities that lead to competition and to movement of faculty members from one university to another.

As we have already observed, academia is as it is because within it lie all sorts of separate forces: it is the home of scholarly research activity, of teaching activity; the tableau against which personalities come to grips with each other; and—let us not forget—a business. It is a business whose goal is to make knowledge, make students, and sometimes even make money. Part of the job of the good administrator is to make sure that his unit of the university is doing the best job possible in these areas. And, like it or not, the best system that anyone has come up with for keeping a large unit in top running shape is competition.

Competition! This rings in free-market economics and all that the phrase entails. American academics are quite unusual, on a global scale, with regard to the amount of moving around that they are willing to put up with and that they even take for granted. French Canadians by and large will not leave Québec. A Frenchman in France may land a job in the provinces, but the center of his academic life and point of orientation will remain Paris no matter what happens. Americans, on the other hand, think nothing of moving from Brandeis to UCLA and then back east again to Johns Hopkins, moves on a scale that would be unthinkable in Europe, or anywhere else in the world for that matter.

One of the major factors that has led to that situation, in addition to the relative homogeneity of our national culture, is the fact that our university system is not centralized. There is no university system at the federal level; [1] a few of the biggest state universities are centralized to the extent that several important campuses respond to a single central administration, such as in California and in New York. But even in the case of the University of California system, the campuses maintain a high level of autonomy—which is to say, of competition.

The notion that the university works by responding to the forces of competition is by no means either venal or amoral. To be sure, it is not the only force at work within the university system; if it were, the results would probably be volatile and perhaps even tragic. But anyone attempting to administer a large institution must assign himself a set of goals, and in the case of a university, these goals will include academic ones in addition to the more mundane ones of raising $50 million for the endowment or for a new athletic or biology building. How can academic goals be set at an administrative level above a department? How can the number of theorems proven in the mathematics department be compared with the number of new grammars published in the linguistics department or with the number of new editions of Blake poetry from the English department? A way must be found because one thing is certain: if we leave a department to its own devices and offer it limitless resources on demand, it will sink into a torpor of self-satisfaction, an intellectual drowsiness in which everything and everyone produced by the department will seem to be of the highest quality and without imperfection.

The upshot is that criteria must be established for determining how well a unit is faring. It almost doesn't matter what the criteria are as long as they are established in advance, and not as a way of recognizing what has already been accomplished. There should not be just one single criterion. No single criterion expresses more than a portion of the value that a unit brings to the university, whether it be the total number of students enrolled, the number of books published per year, or the dollars brought in by federally sponsored grants. A healthy university recognizes that a raft of such criteria will enable it to pinpoint those units and departments that are intellectually alive and healthy as well as those that are moribund or in poor health. These criteria may include the following:

1. Teaching
   - Number of undergraduates enrolled (normalized per faculty member)
   - Teaching awards to faculty in the department
   - Number of graduate students enrolled (in total and per year)

- Number of undergraduate majors (again per faculty member)
- Number of master's and doctoral degrees awarded per year
- Types of jobs offered to recent graduates from the department
2. Research
    - Number of articles and books published per year, with some consideration to the degree of selectivity of the publisher or journal involved;
    - Number of invitations to faculty members to participate in conferences, workshops, and so forth;
    - Number and size of grants and of faculty fellowships (such as Guggenheim fellowships)

What can be galling for academics is an imbalance, a distortion, of these criteria. The most frequent distortion occurs when the number of students taught is considered: how many students are taught in a university, or in a department, per full-time faculty member? That figure is certainly important, and if it is strikingly low, there is undoubtedly a cause, which ought to be clarified; the reason may be poor teaching, but it may also be the relative obscurity of the subject matter (linguistics professors know from obscure subjects), and obscure subjects may not attract many students. Still, obscure departments can buck the trend and through dint of hard work become attractive to students, as seen at a number of universities whose linguistics departments have succeeded in getting large enrollments (Ohio State University and University of California at Santa Cruz, for example). A low student-faculty ratio may be due to a higher concentration of research, a smaller number of teaching fellows, or a range of other reasons. Equally galling can be the consideration (to the exclusion of all else) of grant money brought in by professors, in part because the level of support available through granting agencies varies so much from field to field.

But in no case will a healthy, active department score poorly according to all, or most, of the criteria which I just mentioned. There is no academic health that manifests itself in an entirely new and unexpected way.

So the logic is this: our university system is kept healthy in part by virtue of the will to compete, experienced by individual campuses and departments, and competition presumes some way in which comparisons can be drawn and quantified.

The principal way in which competition in academia plays itself out is through the effort to hire. This is different from the case of competition in business, say, where the bottom line is the profit figure and where profit can be increased by cutting in-house costs, by finding cheaper suppliers, by increasing demand by advertising more, and so on. In business, one can hire, too, but one can hire in many different ways and at many different levels on the corporate ladder. But in academia, the main commodity that one hires is professors.[2]

This side of academia is quite peculiar when viewed from the outside. By way of comparison, let's imagine what happens in a nonacademic situation when some hiring needs to be done. Suppose there's a growing company in the age of the Internet that realizes all of a sudden that it needs someone to be in charge of a Web page for the company. There's a chance that someone in-house can be transmoted to that position, and the company might broadcast a message internally to the effect that it's looking for someone to fill this new post. More likely, someone new will have to be hired who has the credentials to take on the job.

Hiring will not be done on the basis of the prestige that it will bring to the company: a salary level and a job description will be set out ahead of time, and people will apply who think that they can carry out the responsibilities that are set out in the description. A few years of on-the-job experience will count for a lot, for this is the clearest indication of a person's ability to get work done.

In academia, professors at all levels do roughly the same thing (I ignore here the case of a department making a hire to fill the chair's position): they teach courses, they advise students, and they publish books and papers. The job descriptions of the posts held by a junior and a senior professor are not particularly different. But the effort put into (and the results that flow from) a senior hire is quite different from that put into a junior hire. The senior hire is expected to be someone with a distinctly high standard of professional distinction and recognition, and it is expected that these qualities have in the past, and will in the future, demonstrate themselves in terms that are tangible and concrete.

And the driving force in this activity is the understanding that individuals count for a lot in the composition of the life of a department and of a university. Individuals count, in the sense that a small number (like one or two) of energetic and enthusiastic go-getters can provide a spark and a core of energy that make a big difference in the larger picture.

What does all of this mean for the individual professor?

John Goldsmith: From one perspective, it means that once you've landed a job, it may not all be over and done. It may well be appropriate for you, at the right time and in the right place, to consider applying for a job elsewhere.

There are all sorts of reasons why this prospect might be unpleasant. First of all, looking for jobs, deciding which ones one could realistically apply for, sending in applications, and asking for letters of recommendation—it's a big job that consumes a lot of time and a lot of psychological energy. It's not made any easier—to put it mildly—by the knowledge that as far as any single job is concerned, the chance of getting it is pretty small. Of course, all these considerations hold for the unemployed job seeker as well, but he at least has more of an economic gun to his head—he needs a job. The lucky professor who has a job already can't rely on that bit of motivation.

Other, perhaps darker, reasons lurk behind one's unwillingness to apply for a job elsewhere. If Jones is lucky enough to have found a job that he really likes, then it may seem to him that applying for a job elsewhere is a sign of disloyalty and that there may therefore be a price to pay if his chair, or his dean, discovers that he has applied for a job at Arizona Tech. In a word, Jones may feel guilt: the guilt of disloyalty.

Another reason that some people avoid applying for other jobs is that they do not want to have to face the possibility of making a choice if they're made a serious and attractive offer. After all, if Smith is happy where he is—or at least reasonably happy—it is likely to be quite a difficult matter to choose between what's home today and another, new campus.

But the fact is, as we have noted, most successful academics make at least one major move in their academic careers, and many make several; this is especially true at research universities. And (perhaps more to the point) part of the business of academic administrators is to deal with professors who are considering moving. They themselves are very likely to be professionals who have at one point or other considered an offer from a different university, and very likely accepted it. Putting it simply: it is easy—but wrong!—to think of an administrator as a surrogate parent who might react like a guardian scorned if faced with the possibility of a faculty member thinking about moving on. That is the wrong metaphor to use!

We all like to think that if we do our work well and carefully, we will be noticed and appreciated by those who make decisions concerning our well-being: our salaries, our positions, and so forth. This is, I think, largely an infantile wish—in effect, a regression to a stage of childhood in which we took it for granted that our parents would see what we were doing, appreciate it, and give us not only what we needed, but also what we wanted. As a model for how academia actually works, it is a remarkably poor model, and yet, despite all evidence to the contrary, surprisingly many academics, both young and old, cling to the perhaps comforting outlines of this view. If that view were accurate, there would be no need for this book, and you would certainly not have read this far. If you're with us up to here, it's because you recognize that that's not the right picture.

My remarks should not be taken in any sense either to overlook or to demean a sense of loyalty to one's institution. A person who has found a good place to work is almost certain to develop that warm sense of identification that we call loyalty. If the time comes when a professor has an offer from another university, this sense of belonging should certainly be a major consideration in determining whether to accept it or not. But it is a mistake to think that loyalty means not considering the possibility of being somewhere else.

Penny Gold: Speaking as a medievalist, I am uneasy with the term "loyalty" to describe modern ties between individual and institution. The word invites feelings of "betrayal" if one party doesn't come through in the way expected by the other. While John Goldsmith suspects that a faculty member may not apply for other jobs out of feeling "the guilt of disloyalty," I suspect that a more widespread inhibition is the fear that others at your institution will perceive you as disloyal if they find out you have made such application. Indeed, I know some of my senior colleagues feel this way, which I think is unfortunate. I think of a faculty member's relationship to an institution as one of commitment rather than "loyalty." And while "dual loyalties" are problematic, since the term "loyalty" presumes only one object, faculty members do, indeed, have dual commitments— a commitment to the institution and also to themselves, which involves finding the job situation best suited to their talents and ambitions. One can continue to be committed to an institution even if looking elsewhere.

If you do apply for other jobs, you should use discretion as to whom you tell about it. Some of your senior colleagues might not only feel abandoned, but also be disgruntled at the thought of the work involved in another search if they have to replace you. At some point, you will need to let folks know—if you need references or want to negotiate in the light of an actual offer. But you're probably best off not saying anything until you need to.

Are there differences between searches at the junior and senior levels? How does this work?

John Goldsmith: From the point of view of the university trying to fill a position, a decision has generally been made ahead of time whether a junior (i.e., untenured) position or a senior position with tenure will be offered. These two procedures are very different, so different as virtually to deserve different names. The search for someone in a junior position is more than likely to finish by finding someone; the senior search is just as likely to end without a successful catch, for reasons we will come back to in a moment. The junior search is more of a stab in the dark, and if the candidate chosen doesn't work out to the department's liking at the end of six years (and in worse cases, after three years), he can be let go. A senior, tenured professor in the department may be a colleague for life and is likely to have a serious impact on the complexion of the department. Such a decision is made with a good deal more exploration and circumspection.

The junior academic is less likely to consider applying for jobs when he already has a tenure-track position, and for good reason: unless the offer comes with tenure (which is unlikely), the process of moving will use up valuable time, while the clock ticks toward the time of the tenure decision. Similarly, if he has, say, four years invested at the University of Washington, and Michigan is considering hiring him, Michigan will most likely be expected to consider his tenure case after two years, which is in many cases just a bit too soon to get a clear sense of how well the person is doing in a new department. If after such a move an assistant professor shows an unimpressive record, should Michigan take that as the side effect of moving and a new set of teaching responsibilities, or is it a sign of a lack of energy at this crucial time in a young person's career? It is a hard call to make, and for this reason, many universities will hesitate to make junior appointments at such a point unless the assistant professor's record is already so strong as to virtually warrant tenure.

A senior appointment is entirely different. A professor hired with tenure is a known quantity, with a considerable record of research, and perhaps administrative experience, under his belt. The recruiting university will have persuaded itself that the chance to recruit Professor Apple is a chance too attractive to pass up, one that in no way could be matched by hiring, say, two assistant professors for the same price. Apple's presence on campus will make a real difference, perhaps because of the reputation he has established as a path-breaking researcher, or the important connections he will make between his department and another, or any other of a host of reasons. He will have been invited to give a lecture or two on campus and to meet the chair, the dean, and a number of faculty members. If he continues to express serious interest about the possibility of moving to the university, the administration will make discreet inquiries in the field to gather frank judgments on the quality and the future of his work. Questions will be asked as to why he might consider leaving his present position. Often a senior appointment is contemplated by the administration (that is, outside of the appointing department) because there are no acceptable candidates within the department to replace the current chair. In such a case, it will be important to figure out if Professor Apple's abilities extend to the realm of administration as well.

The search for someone to fill a senior position often begins with a discussion in the department concerning who would be the ideal candidate in the field to appoint among all the people alive and kicking in the profession. The discussion is colored by the knowledge that most senior people are unmovable: a job offer will not be enough to induce them to move. You might think that the way to deal with that observation is simply to advertise for a position and see who applies: a professor will apply if and only if he is willing to move. But that maxim is wrong on both counts. For one thing, people who apply for senior positions often are not willing to move, a point that they may (or may not) have been aware of when they applied; and in addition, targeted and proactive recruiting is very often the most successful way of obtaining the ideal new hire. A person may simply not have been thinking of moving or of making a move to the department that is now looking for a senior person.

These considerations will become clearer as a person moves down the road of his academic career, but these observations will hopefully be of use even to junior academics in coming to understand how the system works that they have become part of.

What should I do if I receive an offer, but I might prefer to stay in my current position?

Penny Gold: As we've mentioned earlier, getting an offer from another institution is the main way of getting a substantial salary increase from your current institution. That is, if you receive an outside offer, you can go to your department chair or dean and ask what the institution is willing to do to keep you there. Increased salary is usually the main negotiating currency, but other things can be put on the table as well, such as research funds, a promotion, a job for one's spouse or partner, or the like. If your home institution makes an attractive counteroffer, you can either accept it or go back to the other institution and see if it will match what you now have at home. Some individuals pursue external offers—even ones at institutions they know they'd never move to—just for the sake of getting more money at their current institution. I think this is dishonest and inconsiderate. At the other extreme are people who don't even ask their home institution for a counteroffer because they are so genuinely eager to leave. But there are a lot of positions in between these two. I would suggest two rules: (1) Do not approach your own institution until you have a firm offer. Just being considered as a candidate at another place is not grounds for asking for more at your current home. (2) Be honest and considerate. If you absolutely would not consider moving to a certain place, don't waste the time and money that institution may be willing to spend in courting you by letting it get as far as an offer. If you know in advance that nothing your home institution would offer could keep you there, don't postpone the process by requesting a counteroffer. Yes, you should use the opportunity of an offer to better your situation, but to keep your conscience clear—and to avoid making enemies in the process—you don't want to leave anyone else feeling "used."

John Goldsmith: I agree with you, Penny, but it seems to me that when the search, the application, the offer, and the negotiation have all been done right, it's usually not until the very end that the candidate knows whether or not he prefers to stay in his present position. Why do I say that? There are two cases in which the candidate may know before it's all over what he wants to do—the case where he knows he wants to stay and the case where he knows he wants to leave. If he knows he wants to stay, regardless of what the new job and new home have to offer, then, as you said, this is not the time for him to be applying for jobs. On the other hand, if he knows he wants to take the new job, regardless of what his home institution provides in a counteroffer, it's not clear why he should bother to negotiate.[3] But in every other case (and most cases will be *other cases*), it's necessary to find out exactly what the two possible future scenarios will look like, and that requires working with both sides to gain as much information as possible. Think of this as the *Casablanca* principle—for who among us has not felt the tension in *Casablanca*, wondering whether Ilsa would go back to Rick or leave with Laszlo, her husband? And much of that tension comes from the fact that throughout the filming of the movie, no decision had been made which way the final scene would go. In the end, Rick sends Ilsa off on the airplane with Laszlo and stays behind, but the decisions are not made until all the facts are in, and that is as it should be.

And hopefully the decision will be a hard one to make for anyone who finds himself in this position because a hard decision means that the negotiation has gone well, and as an economist might say, the market has done well at finding the candidate's current value, and the candidate has done a calculation according to which each of the two possible futures is equally attractive. And being faced with a hard decision means that based on current knowledge (such as it is, faced as we are with little knowledge of what the future will bring us), neither choice is obviously better than the other. So don't worry! You have only one life to live, and neither choice is a wrong choice. Pick one.

The Inside Track
Consulting and Intellectual Property
Pierre Laszlo

Pierre Laszlo is professor of chemistry at École polytechnique, in Paris, France. He has taught at Princeton, Chicago, Colorado, Cornell, and Johns Hopkins. His main research interest is the catalysis of organic reactions by inorganic solids such as the clay minerals. He has published over two hundred primary publications and fifteen monographs, textbooks, and essays in the popularization of science.

Once you have attained some stature in your field, you may be asked by people in private business to do some part-time consulting or other work for them. You may be promised significant financial rewards for undertaking this work, although at first there may be an attempt to obtain from you, free of charge, the information that you ought to be providing for a fee.

Before accepting such an assignment, you will need to know how much will actually be required of you and what your capacities really are. You don't want to put yourself in a position of compromising your full-time employment for a temporary, part-time assignment. You will also need to know what rules your institution has established concerning outside work. For example, at the University of Chicago, professors are allowed to devote up to a maximum of 20 percent of their time (one day a week) to outside work such as consulting or running a company.

You should be aware that you can't apply for most outside consultancies. You may be contacted by phone or through a personal visit to your office, but usually only if a decision has already been made to hire you. In some cases, a general inquiry is made to the department chair or your institution's public relations office, which might refer the caller to you if your expertise is known to fit the caller's needs.

You may be asked to consult in an area about which you feel you know nothing. This is not necessarily a disqualification, since your training as a scholar may enable you, with some hard research, to make the desired contribution. However, it is always better to confess your ignorance frankly than to try to give the erroneous impression that you are expert where you are not.

As to compensation, a good rule of thumb is to ask for twice whatever you are offered. And, of course, you should obtain reimbursement for your travel and local expenses.

When you accept outside work, you will suddenly acquire a dual allegiance, to your own institution and to a private company. It is common to be asked to sign a confidentiality form, and in any case, you should never accept two outside positions at the same time with companies in the same line of business.

By convention, academics are usually allowed full ownership rights to the articles and books they write, even when they are doing their publishing in order to fulfill tenure or other institutional requirements. But the issue is more complicated when it comes to patents on inventions made in a university laboratory. You should consult the responsible officers in your university's administration for the applicable rules. Sometimes the ownership of patents is assigned to the academic laboratory rather than to the inventor, providing the university with a significant source of income. One of the Max Planck Institutes in Germany, in the Ruhr Valley, has been nearly self-supporting for many years from a patent on the extraction of caffeine from coffee by supercritical carbon dioxide. In France, a chemistry institute at the National Center for Scientific Research (CNRS) accrues royalties from the manufacture of taxotere, an anticancer drug.

Whatever its merits—and it remains a subject of much debate—the Dole-Bayh Act of 1982 retroceded ownership of inventions funded by federal money in the United States to the universities in which research (or application) has taken place that has led to practical innovations. Supporters argue that this piece of legislation has been a major factor in the growth of the economy and in the creation of jobs in recent years.

10 Family, Gender, and the Personal Side of Academic Life

How has the choice of an academic career affected your family life?

John Goldsmith: This is a very complicated matter. My case is a bit unusual, but then most cases are, at least viewed from close-up. I'm married, and have been for eighteen years. We have three kids, one from a prior marriage. Both my wife and I were junior academics—assistant professors, both of us in linguistics—when we got married. We made one major geographical move not too long after we were married, and the upshot of the move was that I had a job at a better university and my wife did not. Several years later she obtained an academic job in a related, but different area, computer science, and found after a couple of years that she did not like the job enough to want to keep it. A few years after that, she was offered an extraordinarily attractive position as a researcher in private industry, which required that we relocate to the Pacific Northwest. For the last few years, we've been back and forth between the Pacific Northwest and the Midwest. Most of the backing and forthing has been mine; I've racked up enormous numbers of airplane miles, and jointly we've spent a lot of money on maintaining two homes in two cities.

But we're both very attached to our jobs, and there has so far seemed to be no way that either of us could obtain anything approaching an equivalent job close to where the other one of us works. It's been hard, but for the most part, all of us (kids and adults) have had a very good time of it, and as far as this peripatetic lifestyle goes, I don't think any of us regrets the decisions we've made. We are, to the contrary, grateful that our salaries have been generous enough to permit us to do this.

And our employers (a university in my case, a software company in my wife's) have shown considerable flexibility in making unusual arrangements. Still, the arrangements have often meant the one or the other of us being a single parent for days, and sometimes for weeks, at a stretch. None of us likes that, and since neither my wife nor I have mastered the skill of being in two places at the same time, the one of us that's the single parent at any given time feels a good deal more torn between the calls of work and kids than we'd like to, or than we ought to, frankly.

We have not gone in for large amounts of babysitting or in-house child care. I know a number of academics, and I read in the papers about a lot of two-career couples who employ full-time nannies at home who can arrive early in the morning and be available through suppertime. For various reasons, that approach has not appealed to us (or even been a viable option, most of the time). So we've simply struggled over the years, and things do tend to get easier over time.

Has it been worth it? I hardly know how to think about answering the question. One of the very worst sides of academia is how difficult it is—virtually impossible, really—to find a job in one's discipline in a specific geographical area. You have to be willing to take a job wherever it may turn out to be. Viewed from up close, that's just a fact of life, but when you compare academia to other job tracks available to a talented young person—becoming a doctor, a lawyer, a computer programmer—this is most definitely a down side. I mentioned earlier that a few farsighted universities have made special provisions for hiring pairs of married academics, locked into the so-called two-body problem. This is a start, but it's just a drop in the bucket, and I frankly don't see a solution in sight at the moment. In my own case, I suspect that if I had taken the nonacademic route in life, I would have always regretted it and missed the intellectual freedom of exploration that I have had in the career that I actually chose. But another career would have made most job-related issues a lot easier, I also suspect.

John Komlos: I agree—the thrill of discovery, and the freedom to communicate those ideas to our students and peers, is what makes academics tick, by and large. The major obstacles to fulfillment for those who choose not to remain single are that career mobility is invariably tied to geographical mobility for most of us and that geographical mobility is not always gentle on family life. I chose to do a fair bit of moving around—from Chicago to Vienna, Austria, back to Chapel Hill, North Carolina, on to Pittsburgh and Munich, Germany. This kind of frequent relocation puts stress on all family members. For instance, having children change school systems frequently is not easy on them by any means. Even without moving around, it is difficult to allocate adequate time to the members of the family unit because of the heavy professional demands on our time. In this regard, being an academic is similar to being a doctor or a lawyer. If you've committed seventy hours a week to your profession as a single academic and think you can maintain that pace even with a family, you are bound to be disappointed. Children and spouse will demand some quality time, and if they do not get it from you, they will feel neglected and deprived. You will eventually be unhappy as well, and divorce or separation is both costly and frustrating. So you need to think through these issues and make your academic and family plans accordingly. We fortunately postponed having children until rather late in my career so that I no longer needed to worry about tenure while changing diapers or flying kites. Still, it did not come easily to me to dedicate a chunk of time every day to the children, but I learned how to do that, and am much happier for it.

Penny Gold: My husband and I met and married in graduate school in the early 1970s. We had things all planned out as to how we would take turns getting jobs, but life doesn't always work out as planned. I was on the job market first, and my husband followed me to two positions (one temporary, one tenure-track) while he continued to work on his dissertation. He ended up taking an administrative job at my institution, which has meant that we've been able to live in the same place for most of the time—very nice indeed, although it also meant an abandonment of his academic goals. And since administrators work straight through the year and can't take long leaves (even unpaid ones), we have had to be apart when I have been away from home for grants and sabbaticals. Some of this is not bad. In one long stint, we found that if we could see each other at least two weekends a month and called each other on the phone most days, we still felt very much in touch. In fact, we especially enjoyed our chunks of time together in that period of separation because we put aside work for those few days a month and did more together than we would have if we'd been living in the same house.

But it doesn't work the same way when children are in the picture, and although we've spent a couple of summers and a year commuting since the adoption of our child fifteen years ago, the stress on the family of living in two places is much greater than when just two adults were involved. There are grants I don't consider applying for because they would take me too far away, for too long. I'm not sure how I would have handled this had children come earlier in my career. I intended to get pregnant as soon as my dissertation was completed, but, again, life didn't work out as planned. Instead, after a year or so, I began extended infertility tests and treatments (a stress factor in the lives of any number of academic women I know). We also signed on with an adoption agency, and eight years later a child arrived in our home. So I began child rearing with the security of tenure, a book recently published, and a husband with a flexible schedule (at that point in a graduate program and working part-time for the college). I kept working full-time and managed work and family fairly well for some years. Especially in the first couple of years (blessed with a child who slept predictably and for long stretches), I was able to work for large blocks of time while at home with the baby, and I felt it a great privilege not to have to use eight or nine hours of child care early on. I can arrange my teaching schedule so that I can see my son off for school in the morning (afternoon is more difficult because of 4:00 committee meetings and lectures). For me, the hardest time came with junior high, when after-school care disappears and when the emotional challenges of parenting are—in my experience—much greater than in the early years. Kids' problems in adolescence and the teen years can't be solved with a hug and calming words. For the last three years, I have cut back to a two-thirds teaching schedule in order to be able to be at home when school lets out.

While my own post-tenure delay in adding a child to my life was involuntary, many academic women purposely try to time childbearing for a time when it will least affect their professional work—or their colleagues' perception of their professional work. This often means trying to time delivery for the early summer or postponing children entirely until after tenure. Needless to say, precision timing doesn't always succeed, and too long a delay works against a woman's declining fertility. For women, personal concerns about how to successfully mesh family and children with work are exacerbated by the awareness that many of one's colleagues are wondering just that. And since the pregnancy is carried visibly, in public, for at least the last few months, the concern has plenty of time to express itself. I've not heard similar concern expressed when a male colleague's wife is pregnant, even in the cases of couples who plan to share equally the responsibilities of child care.[1]

John Goldsmith: In my case, one of the most difficult lessons to learn about mutual accommodation between work and family life was that it was possible to live a year at a time, by which I mean that a series of short-term solutions can be just as good as a single solution that endures for the same length of time. Life is a sequence of years, months, days; it is a sequence of breaths. The choice of an academic career offers certain kinds of flexibilities, as we have seen, and when these flexibilities can be used to solve family problems or to provide partial solutions, then we should use them.

The flexibility of the academic schedule is wrapped around a core of inflexibility: that core is the hours during which your courses are scheduled. There are few reasons acceptable for canceling a class. If you are home sick in bed, that's one; but in general, having a child home sick in bed is not a valid reason to cancel a class. Cancel an appointment, yes, or office hours. (And why is it that children seem to get sick or a snow day is called in the school system on just those days that you have, besides two classes, a key appointment with the dean that you had to wait two weeks for, an interview with your department's favorite choice for a job opening, and a committee meeting in which a proposal you've been working on for months will be discussed?) If you are the parent on whom the responsibility falls for taking care of a sick child, you should have a back-up or emergency plan to make it possible to get to your class. So the good part is that much of your day is flexible and you don't have a manager (in most cases) with whom you must check in or clear it, but for certain fixed hours of the week, you simply must be in class, and sometimes other responsibilities are difficult to postpone, even for a day.

The flexibility doesn't end there, to be sure. You can bring a child to your office when you want without clearing it with anyone, and it's up to you and yours whether you get any work done under those circumstances—some people really do have babies who can sleep for hours in their mom's or dad's office. You've got time during the summer and in late December to spend with the family if you wish—though it is unlikely that your spring break will coincide with kids' school vacation, another child-care nightmare. You can arrange to stay home in the mornings and work later at night if that's necessary or works out better for you.

Penny Gold: One other thing: so often we think in terms of conflict between family life and professional life. And with the enormous demands on our time made by our institutions and our own expectations of ourselves, that conflict is understandably a shaping paradigm for family-professional interaction. But I have also found that parenting has enriched my life as a teacher. As I've mentioned before, parenting has made me take time away from my work, which is a good thing. Even more positively, learning how to be a parent has taught me much about how to be a teacher. No one teaches us in graduate school how to motivate students or how to enlist their cooperation. But learning about a two-year-old's need for at least limited autonomy taught me much about college students' parallel need. I prescribe much less now in my courses and instead structure in choices. And having learned firsthand from child rearing that positive feedback is more effective than negative, I try to supply that in critiques of student writing as well. Both parenting and teaching are about helping young people learn how to do things on their own, and I've found advice books for parents more helpful on this topic than most guides for college teaching.

Are there any special issues for people who share an appointment or teach in the same institution?

Penny Gold: Couples working within the same institution have the great advantage of no commuting problems. But they have another problem that can put its own stress on a relationship: it is easy for work to pervade one's whole life, since you're always in the company of someone else with whom you can hash out issues about work. The dinner table, evenings out, even vacations—it takes a special effort to put the job aside and talk about other things. And with both people at the same job location, it's likely that most of one's friends will come from there as well, further reinforcing the focus on work. Given a job where it's already the case that work can take up all available discretionary time, it can help one's sanity to find other activities and social networks outside of the college or university community.

What is the extent of discrimination in academia?

John Komlos: Frankly, I have not seen any overt *or* covert discrimination along gender, racial, or ethnic lines. So far as I am concerned, these are nonissues. After all, women now play a very significant role in academia, and that could not have come about if hostility toward them would be overwhelming. I have, however, seen favoritism by which a president, for example, had a friend appointed to a faculty position without following affirmative action guidelines. In addition, there are plenty of anecdotes about the experience of academics before our generation, and there are still some faculties in which certain cohorts are more homogenous than one would expect them to be if there had been no discrimination sometime in the past.

John Goldsmith: I'd have to say that I have not seen any examples of overt discrimination myself either, but I recognize that both John and I are young (well, relatively young: postwar baby boomers), white, and male. We've both made an effort in this book to limit the advice and opinions we offer to those areas where we have some personal experience; this is not a research essay on the status and structure of academia, after all.

But my experience does include hearing some hair-raising stories, of which I'll share one. A very senior academic of my acquaintance, by now much-lauded and widely recognized in her field, has told me of an experience she had when she was a young academic at a very well known college, where one would have thought the following experience to be impossible. I'll refer to her as Professor X. The time was nearly thirty years ago.

The college was small enough to have a number of plenary faculty meetings during the year, and at one final spring meeting, two items were brought to the faculty's attention. They were both petitions from graduating seniors. One involved extending a deadline by several months for a student who had been extremely ill during her junior year; the other was a matter of waiving the foreign language requirement for seniors who had failed their elementary languages courses several times. (Of course, the issues were more complicated than I'm describing, but the actual questions at hand only set the stage for the comment to come.) Professor X had been at the college for no more than a year or two, and she spoke in favor of extending the deadline for the first student on simple humanitarian grounds; nonetheless, the motion to extend was voted down. On the matter of the language requirement, the faculty (to Professor X's surprise) voted to waive it entirely for several undergraduates. Feeling an imbalance between these two decisions, Professor X—a very junior and (inside, at least) nervous young professor—stood up and made a plea for equity: surely they should also treat the first student humanely. The president of the college listened to her statement and then dismissed it with what he undoubtedly meant to be taken as a bit of lighthearted humor: "See? I told you we should never hire a woman!"

A remark like that would be unimaginable today, I think. American society has changed and continues to change. And that anecdote doesn't even prove discrimination as such existed at the college in question; Professor X had been hired there, after all. But empirical studies do show that academia still has a good distance to go before it can feel satisfied with itself. It was only very recently[2] that an internal report at MIT came out—it was widely publicized in the press—in which MIT acknowledged that there had been, and continued to be, significant differences in the way male and female faculty were treated there. To its credit, MIT has published much of this material on the Web site; one can read there, for example, in the introductory paragraph of the faculty report on the status of women faculty in science at MIT:

> In contrast to junior women, many tenured women faculty feel marginalized and excluded from a significant role in their departments. Marginalization increases as women progress through their careers at MIT. Examination of data revealed that marginalization was often accompanied by differences in salary, space, awards, resources, and response to outside offers between men and women faculty with women receiving less despite professional accomplishments equal to those of their male colleagues. An important finding was that this pattern repeats itself in successive generations of women faculty.[3]

Penny Gold: Part of the reason that the MIT report came as a surprise to many (though not, I suspect, to most women in academia) is that most discrimination in academia—including concrete differentials in things such as salary and lab space, as documented at MIT—did not, most likely, result from overt discrimination. That is, it's unlikely there were conversations in which someone said: "Let's give Professor X a lower raise because she's a woman." But that doesn't mean that discomfort with and hostility or prejudice toward women and minorities aren't played out in myriad ways in the hiring process and in day-to-day interactions on the job, and these forces can contribute, even if unintentionally, to key decisions about the merits of individuals. The extent of such discrimination is less today than twenty-five years ago, but is still felt. Both women and minority professors experience the more intense scrutiny that comes from being "different." It gets very wearing.[4]

It's true that, as John Goldsmith says, certain kinds of remarks "would be unimaginable today." But this doesn't necessarily mean that the sentiments have entirely disappeared—only that the climate has changed enough that the people who still feel this way judge that they should not say such things publicly. I consider such restraint a significant improvement. But it's very different from my dream environment, in which everyone has equal access—and the real means to equal access—to the privileges of our profession and no one thinks it should be any different. It goes without saying, of course, that these issues are not confined to academia—but neither is academia a haven from them. Here are some of the ways in which debilitating prejudice concerning women—the group with which I'm most familiar—manifests itself in the academy.

1. *Hiring.* Search committees routinely sort through more than a hundred applications for any advertised position. Finding "the best" candidate in such a pool, when many candidates are fully qualified and virtually all come with rave recommendations, is an unscientific task. The committee meeting in which candidates are sorted is an arena in which the personal interests, anxieties, and prejudices (of all sorts) are not far below the surface of talk about who would be the most successful teacher/scholar. At a place like Knox, not in a prime urban location, talk can venture into the game of "We shouldn't waste an interview slot (or an offer) on this person because they wouldn't stay here." I can't remember ever hearing this argument used for a man. If a woman is single, some of my colleagues fear she will leave because of the difficulty of finding a potential mate in this small city. And then if she's married, they worry about what her spouse will do. Knox has had several male hires leave because their wives were unhappy in this location—yet I've never heard it mentioned in a search that we should be concerned about hiring a married man—or a single one.

The impressions a search committee gets from a woman's dossier are sometimes tainted by comments of recommenders about personality, style of dress, and physical appearance, qualities less likely to be noted for a man. And even if a candidate has been discreet about marital status in her own materials, a well-meaning, but unthinking, recommender can open the door to concerns by mentioning spouse issues.

2. *Student expectations.* Women often experience a different range of expectations from students than do men. Students may expect more personal attention from women. Women who are amenable to this expectation may end up spending many extra hours dealing with students' personal problems in addition to their academic ones. Women who are resistant to this expectation may be more harshly judged than a male professor who keeps a distance from students. Another area of difference is the diminished professorial authority when the body exercising it is female rather than male.[5] I sometimes wonder, for example, if students are more likely to challenge a grade given by a female professor than by a male. Both on

campus and in the outside world, some people still experience disjunction in seeing a woman as "professor." I routinely have had people ask me in wonderment if I have a Ph.D. after I've told them I've been teaching college for more than twenty years—something I'm quite sure they would not experience as disjunctive if I were a man.[6]

3. *Daily life on campus.* Personal style, dress, and personality are differentially scrutinized in men and women, by students as well as by colleagues. It's old news, for example, that behaviors that would seem properly "assertive" in any self-respecting man may well be construed as "aggressive" in a woman. Dress is an arena that continues to be noticeably gendered, despite the informality of the times and the prevalence of "unisex" garments. Men have standard uniforms that can be worn, whether for teaching or for professional conferences and interviews, ranging from a jacket and tie to jeans and a sweater, and no one will raise an eyebrow. For women, however, every morning is a new clothing choice, and each choice has a range of not-always-predictable consequences. Too sexy? Too frumpy? Too "masculine"? What you can be sure of is that people are noticing. For many years, I avoided wearing close-fitting or revealing clothing in order to discourage roving eyes in male observers. It's only now that I'm in my fifties—and no longer, in our culture, a prime sexual object—that I feel free to occasionally wear leggings or a neckline below my collar bone.

4. *Attitudes about affirmative action and discrimination.* A couple of other common attitudes can contribute to the undermining of confidence. If it is perceived by colleagues that your appointment was an "affirmative action hire," you may be subject to the opinion that "the only reason" you got the job was because you are female, black, Hispanic, or some other minority. This will usually not be expressed to you directly, but can still be felt, and it is demoralizing. And this will be thought by some no matter how stellar your credentials. To succeed in the face of such an attitude can mean piling up more accomplishments than might be needed for a less noticeable new hire. Another debilitating attitude holds that there is no discrimination in academia and that anyone who perceives such is just whining or looking for excuses to cover up her own failings. The entry of women and minorities into the profession has, indeed, threatened the dominant position of white males, so it is understandable that defensive attitudes like these would have developed. They contribute to an invisible, yet felt, layer of hostility that makes life that much more challenging for some of us in the academy.

John Komlos: I have not heard of hostility directed at women in the academy. However, it is clear that academic appointments are not made alone on the basis of counting how many words one has published. The criteria used are overwhelmingly academic, but it goes without saying that the extent to which an individual fits into a particular social and academic culture inevitably enters into the calculus. Such factors are based on second-guessing certain aspects of one's future actions based on character assessment and family situation. Will that person really commit to living here for an extended period of time? Will she be collegial? Will she and her family be happy in the particular environment? If you are an avid mountain biker, will you be happy with an appointment in Nebraska? All such questions are in some sense extraneous, but still unavoidable, because such factors do have an effect on overall performance within the academic unit. However, this phenomenon is not confined to women. I have seen such criteria applied to men as frequently as to women. Perhaps they were not always the same set of criteria, but analogous ones.

For someone, like myself, who had the ill fortune of having lived under two different kinds of dictatorships before finding refuge in a country with well-functioning democratic institutions and whose life itself was threatened at birth by virtue of having parents belonging to a "pariah" religious minority, the identification with the disadvantaged comes more or less automatically. Hence, I find academia's record of discrimination vis-à-vis women, those of African ancestry, and religious and ethnic minorities both unfortunate and reprehensible, and its recent amelioration welcome. Yet early in my career, when I found myself at an unexpected and distinct disadvantage in job applications for being suddenly classified as a white male, I admittedly did not particularly think that justice was being served. So I am probably not being politically correct in asserting that I am too much of an advocate of meritocracy in academia to be a true believer in such policies as affirmative action and reverse discrimination. Yet I had absolutely no problem in advocating hiring an alleged homosexual for a particular job because I thought that he happened to be well qualified for the position. I believe that no one should be at an a-priori disadvantage in a job application and that the interests of the academy should transcend any other considerations. We should make sure that the academy is equally welcoming to everyone. That means that whenever we are on a search committee, we should do our best not to discriminate along extraneous dimensions. But it seems to me that reverse discrimination is not helpful in fulfilling the ethic to which we aspire because it contradicts the very notion of equality that we would like to propagate.

Penny Gold: It is also possible to disagree on what constitutes "the interests of the academy," and this contributes to making the issue of affirmative action controversial. Affirmative action policies have been a crucial—indeed, a determining—factor in the advances the academy has made in the hiring of women and minorities. They have pushed search committees to look harder for a range of candidates (gone are the days when tenure-track positions could be filled by phone calls to colleagues at a few institutions) and to consider enhanced diversity within a department or institution as one of the many elements to achieve in a particular hire. I'm sure there have been instances when "more qualified" white males were rejected in favor of a female or person of color. But many of these cases are complicated by the fact that in the highly competitive job market of the last twenty-five years, there are large numbers of highly meritorious people competing with each other and many factors can go into a final decision. It used to be that part of being "best qualified" was to be as much as possible like the people already in the department, ending up in the homogeneity that we've remarked on earlier. Now, in some cases, the inclination is in the other direction. My own experience undoubtedly influences my thoughts on this issue, as John Komlos's does his. I went on the job market in 1975–76, and I'm sure that some of the interviews I got were influenced by search committees wanting to look at female candidates. Perhaps gender was also a factor in my being hired at Knox. Some people may have thought that the "only" reason I got the job was because I was a woman. I'd like to think it also had to do with the quality of my training, recommendations, and research.

Is there anything you'd like to say about the debate about "political correctness"?

John Komlos: There is a fundamental cultural change that is spreading through academia with an ideological purpose. "Political correctness," as it is called, advocates an orthodox liberal view on such political-cultural issues as affirmative action, sexual orientation, women's liberation, and minorities. Though almost all academics agree with its basic tenets and agree that they address legitimate concerns, some do not feel particularly comfortable about being prescribed a package in total. It seems to some that the movement has been taken to an extreme in that peer pressure is often so strong that members of the academy are intimidated from expressing their true beliefs from sheer fear of being branded an outsider. I would argue that such pressure can be inimical to free speech itself.

Penny Gold: It's true that a generation of academics whose intellectual and political understandings were shaped by the social movements of the 1960s and 1970s (civil rights, antiwar, and feminist) has had an important impact on academic life. But I don't see this impact as the result of a monolithic "movement" or as an orthodoxy that has taken control of the academy. From my experience, "political correctness" serves as a scare word that fosters accusation rather than the debate that we continue to need. The political and intellectual positions represented in the academy are highly diverse, and we should try to hear the multiplicity of voices rather than brand each other as being on one side or another of an artificial divide.

How do you see issues regarding sexual harassment in the academic workplace?

John Goldsmith: This is an enormous and difficult area, far larger than the space that we can devote to it, and I don't think I'm among the best placed people to take it on. I would like to mention just a couple of points relating to subjects that we have been discussing.

First, let's look again at the relationship between advisor and graduate student. When we discussed the subject of mentoring, I emphasized the guru-student nature of that relationship. I don't want to blow this completely out of proportion, but one must be prepared (both as a graduate student and, more important, as an advisor) for the academic equivalent of oedipal conflicts and of something like the phenomenon of transference that psychoanalysts talk about: oedipal conflicts in the sense that there can be (on either side) occasional flashes of competition, jealousy, and even hostility between advisor and student, and transference in the sense that (genders being appropriate) advisors and advisees may start to think that they have a very special, personal, and intimate human relationship going that may lead to something other than good research.

I'm not going to say much more about the conflicts that I've labeled oedipal between mentor and student, except to note that fortunately most of this comes out after the student has completed the Ph.D. (and is, indeed, no longer a student). Former students need to prove that they are now able to stand on their own two intellectual feet, and they may well become extremely aware of the intellectual or personal limitations of their former mentor. I have no advice to give on this point, except to note that it is useful to know how common a sentiment this is, and how human it is as well.

The other phenomenon is more insidious in a sense, since it can lead to a strong emotional relationship between mentor and student, which, in turn, can lead to other things. It should be noted that many successful marriages have been the result of romances between mentor and student, but my strong impression is that this occurs in a remarkably small proportion of cases. Of course, successful marriages arise in only a remarkably small proportion of social relationships of any sort. In my opinion, and I suspect that most academics agree with me on this point, a serious emotional relationship can arise between advisor and student only at the cost of the student's research and professional development and, as a matter of general policy, should be strictly avoided.

But it's very important to have some grasp of the mechanisms at play. The professor is likely to be very intelligent, perhaps brilliant, and is someone that the student looks up to as a real role model. This kind of admiration can feed one's ego, and, of course, attentions from one's teacher and role model are flattering, in turn, from the student's perspective. Student and professor may even go to the same conferences or research meetings and have dinner together. But they had better leave it at that!

John Komlos: To paraphrase former President Jimmy Carter, you can sin in your heart:[7] I do not think there are any earthly laws against that. However, within our culture, intimacy—even consensual intimacy—between academics with asymmetric power is not only seen as "unprofessional," but also categorized as being almost incestuous. Yet such occasions arise frequently because of close working relationships or, as Henry Kissinger is reputed to have asserted, because of the aphrodisiacal nature of power, and professors do possess considerable power. Authority figures, in other words, might call forth erotic feelings in some students. So be forewarned—you might well notice that some students are coming to your office hours a little bit too frequently. Body language often says more than actual words. You should leave the door to your office open at all times and beware that the slightest innuendo or double entendre can lead to painful public consequences, which include not only embarrassment, but dismissal as well. In addition, you lose your independence to a considerable extent and open yourself up to being blackmailed. Taking such risks concerning your career and family cannot possibly be worth it. At times, however, it is exactly the excessive risk that some find attractive. People regrettably act in inappropriate ways out of motives that no one, including themselves, can truly understand.[8] I remember a law professor who was dismissed for stealing an item from a store worth less than ten dollars! Such actions cannot be discussed within the realm of the rational.

Be that as it may, sexual harassment has an extensive literature, and I see no need to go into it at great length here. Our recommendation is simple: stay clear of it, regardless of your gender. I see no fundamental difference between academia and the outside world in this respect. Regardless of the setting, if it does come your way, common sense is usually the best reflex to rely on. Equally important, bear in mind that all universities now have procedures in place to deal with all kinds of infractions from fraud in research to sexual harassment, plagiarism, discriminatory practices, and so forth. My experience is that they tend to be slow, cumbersome, and rather ineffective. You will probably choose to make use of these mechanisms only in the most extreme cases as the very last resort. Most of the time, you should rely on your own judgment, tempered by your moral fortitude and values, to develop common-sense approaches to the problems.

Penny Gold: The troubled territory of sexual relations in the academy looks different from the perspective of someone who's gone through academic life in a female body. In my experience, it is more frequently male professors who use the power of their position to make suggestive remarks or to "come on" to young women than it is students who try to seduce their professors. Virtually all academic women I know experienced such remarks or seductive behavior from professors when they were students, and it can continue into one's teaching career as an element in the differentially powered relationships between senior male and junior female faculty. The male professor's seduction of lovely college students continues to be a positively regarded trope in contemporary fiction and film. This popular sanctioning of professor/student relationships is part of a wider cultural approval for "December/May" relationships where it's the male who is the older one in the couple, as well as of the general cultural sexualization of women. It's not easy to develop and sustain an image of oneself as an intellectual and as an accomplished scholar when your teacher/colleague is looking at your breasts or making suggestive comments.[9] The sexual objectification of female students (and colleagues) has been pervasive in the academy. I am hopeful that new generations of professors are more sensitive to this issue and less likely to engage in behaviors that undermine the self-confidence of women.

John Komlos: I do not think it is particularly useful to argue about which gender, or race, or ethnic minority has been more prone to commit improprieties. I think that it is wise counsel to be conscious of the risks involved in doing so, regardless of the group to which you happen to belong.

Penny Gold: Another issue is consensual relations between faculty and students. There is not always a clear line between sexual harassment and consensual relations, but it's important to know the basic difference. Virtually all places of employment have explicit sanctions against sexual harassment. Consensual relations, on the other hand, while sometimes explicitly discouraged, are rarely punished and are often tolerated or even welcomed by the community. Just look around at the faculty of any college or university, and count up how many of the marriages are between male faculty and former students. The reason that the line isn't always clear, and the reason that some places discourage even consensual relations, is because the nature of consent is warped by the power differential between teacher and student and because the establishment of a sexual relationship with a student will necessarily complicate, and perhaps compromise, that student's academic situation.

John Komlos: Insofar as professors have considerable power over the lives of individuals, the possibility of inappropriate action is extensive. The abuse of power, of course, also comes in other guises besides sexual ones. A thesis advisor who makes career-threatening remarks, for instance, in order to discourage the publication of a paper that might be vaguely injurious to his Nobel Prize aspirations, in my mind, does not act essentially differently from one who expects sexual favors in return for approving a dissertation, though the former may not be punishable by law, as is the latter. All in all, it is perhaps worth reiterating that American academia, all its flaws notwithstanding, has done a better job of integrating women and minorities into its mainstream than many other institutions, such as the political system, for example, and accomplished this with relatively little conflict or antagonism. Though you may not be entering the Land of Oz, the academy's tolerance of "otherness," its willingness to nurture, and its commitment to altruistic higher ideals are more widespread than in other large institutional structures within our society.

11 | Conclusion

John Komlos: We have presented this overview of the academic life in the hope of helping you decide whether to embark on such a career and, if you have already entered, helping you to succeed and prosper within it. The more realistic your expectations are and the more credible the information you have is, the more rewarding your career decisions are likely to be. Is this the right career path for you? The answer to that question entails knowing not only about academia, but also about yourself. Do you know your potential? Can you develop skills for assessing what that potential actually is? Are you sure of your likes and dislikes? Do you know what motivates you? Will you change your own mind, or will you try to change the views of others? These are extremely difficult questions because they entail thinking about yourself in possibly new ways. You need to determine how others see you and to consider how their view fits in with yours. If the two sets of views agree, then you can use that as a basis of further action. If, however, they do not, then you need to ask why, and how you can bring the two views into congruity.

The academy has a very special place in society. It is, as it were, the caretaker of our civilization, that is to say, our values and our intellectual treasures. At the same time, by producing the next generation of intellectual, political, business, and other leaders, it influences profoundly the evolution of society. It would be desirable if the people attracted to it were cognizant of this responsibility and had the spiritual foundation to uphold and advance these traditions. In my opinion, the North American system of higher education is the best in the world, and will remain so for a long time, partly because, in the main, it was able to attract that kind of people. Though we tend to take this for granted, not all educational systems are capable of doing that. The outcome depends on a delicate balance of rewards, disincentives, and institutional structure, including the competitive selection process.[1]

That ideal, however, needs to be tempered by the reality that higher education is very big business, subject to the same kinds of pressures found in the corporate world and, in the case of state-financed institutions, the political one as well. You will need considerable spiritual resources to know when to uphold an ideal and when, and the extent to which, to compromise. This is incredibly difficult, and you should not expect ready-made recipes on how to approach the challenges that lie ahead. I have often debated with myself what Galileo or Copernicus would have done in certain circumstances and tried to hold myself to such imaginary standards, but it was not always possible, or always helpful. The degree to which moral standards can be maintained in face of the exigencies of the moment is a problem as old as humanity, and we have little choice but to grapple with essentially the same ethical issues that our ancestors did. However, it seems important to me that we do grapple with them and do not resort to prepackaged answers.

In addition, you need to weigh the fact that the academic job market has been plagued by (or blessed with, depending on your point of view) an oversupply of potential entrants in many fields, possibly because of a lack of accurate information. The academic life is less glamorous than it seems from the outside. Alas, it is not a life of contemplation. Though there are chunks of time that one can set aside for unrestrained thinking, that is only one aspect of the career. It is a life of nurturing, but it is also one of contending with students who are unprepared for your classes and who are interested in pursuing their small advantages in order to obtain their diplomas and move on as quickly as possible. It is about collegiality, but also about difficult colleagues. It is about freedom of thought, but also about adhering to administrative directives as well as peer pressure. It is a life with lots of drudgery and limited financial rewards. Yet, for a large majority of those who make academia their career, it provides much—even if intermittent—satisfaction. And when students mature and prosper, one does have the feeling of having made a contribution.

While it is true that there is a myriad of external factors over which you have little or no control, it is also the case that a realistic assessment of both your aptitudes and the workings of academia will improve your chances of success, especially if you are able to match your aspirations to your talents and what academia will expect of you. Academia is as competitive as any other profession; in some respects, it is more so. And scholars themselves are not moved exclusively by ideas and altruism. Prestige, respect, power, and, yes, money all play a role in their motivation as well, to varying degrees. The academic world has its own unique set of challenges. How you face those challenges—determining to which you should respond and which are best left to others—depends on you alone.

Penny Gold: At the same time that we have been discussing strategies to give you logical, rational guidelines for success in academia, I'm also very much aware of how much of one's journey in life is out of one's control. You may find the graduate school you think perfect for your talents and interests, but you may not get accepted there. You may know that the best kind of teaching position for you would be at a small liberal arts college, but the only job offer you get is at a large state university. You may have had the good fortune to find a position at just the right kind of institution for you, but your spouse or partner is unable to find a job in the same area; you eventually move to an institution that is not a first choice for either of you, but that has offered you both jobs. So, while we encourage you to learn as much as you can about yourself and your institution in order to make productive, rational decisions, I would also advise you to cultivate an attitude that allows you to make the best of an imperfect situation. There will be many of these to cope with in the course of your career! Make the most of the situation that you're in, even while you may be looking to move elsewhere. Institutions are one of the intersecting worlds within which we act and influence others. In what ways might life in this place contribute to your own personal development, and what is the contribution that you can make to this world of academia in the forty or so years that you will be a member of it?

John Goldsmith: I'd like to make one final personal comment that relates to the thrust of this book as a whole. I feel some concern that our comments to young academics might increase their risk aversion—and, in fact, my real worry is that academics are already too averse to taking intellectual risks. This aversion shows itself in decisions to adopt intellectual frameworks or fashions for one's work, regardless of whether one is convinced that the intellectual merits of the case have been made. I fear that the more one emphasizes the difficulties of an academic career, the more a rational young person will opt for career decisions that will simplify matters, in general, and facilitate publication, in particular.

So my final observation is this: there is a higher calling beyond one's personal success that an academic career entails. Research and teaching involve an effort to attain something that goes beyond the conventions of our contemporaries. I'd like to call that something Truth with a capital T to acknowledge that I'm being just a touch ironic in labeling it so simply. How one carves out and distills Truth varies tremendously across disciplines, but some kind of feeling about it—one part reverence to two parts thrill—ought to be sitting in an academic's soul. We must not lose sight of that.

We have explained a number of things to you that you ought to know in order to make informed choices and decisions in your academic career. But there may come times (there will come times) when a rational and informed person sees self-interest and the interests of Truth diverging, be it ever so slightly. I hope that our explanations of how the system works will not encourage you to choose the interests of your career over those of Truth. If you're not so sure how you'd make such a call—maybe some other line of work would be best for you. Otherwise, we'll look forward to seeing you on campus.

We wish you the best of luck—and great success in your career.

Appendix 1

The Administrative Structure of a University

John Goldsmith: Whether you are a student or a faculty member, you need to know something about the nature and structure of the institution that you are a part of. While the details and the terminology will vary from one institution to another, there are general principles regarding how they are set up, and it will be helpful to outline them briefly.

First of all, at the top there is a president and a board of trustees. These people make the final decisions on all hard questions, many of which may affect the average professor's life only indirectly. The president is the chief executive officer and, as such, may be less involved in the details of everyday academic decisions than others ranked below him on the hierarchy. At Harvard, I understand, the president personally presides over the tenure decision for every single faculty member,[1] but that is relatively unusual, certainly for a large university. Most presidents are heavily involved in the external aspects of the life of the university, of which the most important considerations are financial, and a big part of that is fund raising. Ultimately, they must make sure that their universities will continue to receive sufficient financial support, and they must make large-scale decisions, like whether to expand the student body on campus, to turn their college coeducational, to establish a law school, or to shut down the library school. But the day-to-day life of the university is more likely to be in the hands of the next person down in this hierarchy.

There is no single name for the office of this person just below the president. It may be the provost, it may be the vice president in charge of academic affairs, or it may be the dean of faculties. This person is most likely, though, to make the final decision on faculty matters, like how to handle difficult tenure cases, or what to do when a senior professor gets an outside offer and is sorely tempted to leave, or whether a department should be allowed (or encouraged) to make an offer to an outstanding professor from a rival university. This person makes the lion's share of the decisions regarding the ways in which resources are distributed across competing constituencies inside the university. For our purposes and to be concrete, let's suppose that this person is called the provost.

Below the provost on the academic hierarchy will typically come a raft of more or less coequal deans, and how these deans relate to one another varies considerably from one campus to another. There may be one dean in charge of undergraduate instruction, typically called the dean of the college; there will certainly be separate deans in charge of each professional school (law, business, medicine). There may be separate deans for various subparts of traditional teaching and research, such as arts and sciences, or humanities, or physical or biological sciences.

Of course, not all deans are necessarily equal in terms of their privileges and resources. Some will have the final say in hiring decisions in their units; others may not. At some institutions, the graduate dean or deans have no say in the matter; in others, it is the dean of the college who plays at best an advisory role in hiring. Deans of this sort are often called "academic deans," and they are themselves typically tenured professors in a department of the university. An important decanal appointment may require selection of someone from outside of the particular university, though more often the dean is chosen from within the university. The dean will typically have some administrative experience, often as chairman of a department or perhaps as associate dean.

The status of deans in the larger administrative system of the university is a difficult, and downright touchy, question, one that has recently even made it into the court system. If we carry over the "management-labor" distinction from the capitalist business world into the world of academia, where do we find the managers? The students might claim that the labor is performed by them and that the faculty as a whole are managers, but that view can hardly hold water. The only other sensible cut lies in calling the administration—deans and associate deans, together with the provost and the president—"management" and letting the rest of the faculty be "labor." Is this an accurate picture?

While it is an unfortunate fact of academic life that in some universities there is some truth to that picture, it does not hold in the healthy and well-functioning college or university. The academic administration is composed of men and women whose values have been formed during their years as professors teaching and doing research; when they are done with their tenure in office as dean—after three, five, or ten years—they will return to being a professor, in most cases. If for no other reason, they will therefore have to continue their research (and, to some extent, teaching) during their term as dean so that they may fit back into life as a professor.

There are other administrators at most universities, however, that are called "deans," though they are not academic deans. These positions are often filled by people with doctoral degrees, but without regular academic appointments, and typically the nonacademic dean has no job to return to if and when she is relieved of her duties in that position. The various positions of dean of students (graduate and undergraduate) are often of this sort.

The most vexing question is whether deans (and their associated administrators) ultimately have a different set of interests than mere professors do. In general, the answer is "no," though when a dean finds her interests do diverge from those of her faculty, that is often a sign of a serious problem. Perhaps the single most striking difference between a decanal position and that of teaching professors is that the dean must constantly be seeking to balance conflicting claims on a limited amount of resources, financial or otherwise. Professors often find themselves in the position of asking for funds or other resources from deans or outside agencies, but it is relatively rare that they find themselves in the position of having a pool of resources that several groups are competing for, presenting strong and compelling cases to spend more money than is available. That, though, is the situation that a dean typically finds herself in. These tough choices require some considerable judgment in order to compare the relative value for the university as a whole that will flow from making one set of choices rather than another. To some extent, this means performing a task different in style from that expected of most professors, and to some extent, this may require a sort of larger perspective not expected of professors. But if done properly, it does not require a different set of interests and values from those of the (may we say it?) rank-and-file professoriat.

Reporting to the deans are the chairs of each department. The chair is generally chosen by the department, subject to the approval of the dean; in some cases, it is the dean who directly appoints the chair after consulting individually with the members of the department. In rare cases, if a consensus is difficult to reach within the faculty, a chair can be brought in from another department or even hired from another institution. How much power the chair has depends on the department, on the university, and on her personality and style, but generally the chairs do wield considerable power. Even if the dean is in a position to reverse a decision made within the department (on tenure, for example), the dean's information generally comes from and through the chair, and that is considerable power right there.

At most universities, salaries for members of the department are determined by the dean in consultation with the chair. This system is certainly not universal. In some universities, the chair determines each year's raises, with the dean taking a more distant supervisory role; in others—at Harvard, for example—it is the dean, and the dean alone, who determines the amount of the raise.[2] The chair of a department does many other things as well, involving budget allocations (who gets what discretionary money), report writing (what have the various faculty members been up to this year? how have recent alumni fared in the job market? why does the student lounge require a new set of chairs?), direct involvement in hiring practices and perhaps student recruitment, and the mentoring of untenured faculty in many cases. At times, she must also become confessor and confidante to faculty and students who have serious problems that are affecting their abilities to work productively in the department. The chair will usually get a course reduction to perhaps as little as half of the course load of the other faculty members, but chairing well is a job that demands full-time attention.

The heart of the university consists of the professors, who compose the faculty of the various departments. Faculty are generally divided into three ranks: (full) professors, associate professors, and assistant professors. In virtually all cases, full professors have tenure and assistant professors do not; at most universities, associate professors may or may not have tenure because, while an assistant professor who receives tenure will always be promoted to associate professor, it is not uncommon for promotion to that position (though without tenure) to come one, two, or three years earlier than the awarding of tenure.

Most universities hire assistant professors on what is called a "tenure track," meaning that they will be considered for an appointment with tenure at the end of a certain period, typically at the beginning of the sixth year. A few universities (of which Harvard and Yale are the most notorious in this respect) make their junior appointments with no presumption, and often with very little possibility, of tenure. There, when a senior position becomes available, through retirement or departure, a search is typically conducted to find the best candidate available, regardless of person's place of present employment.

There is not a great deal of difference, from an official or a structural point of view, between a full professor and a tenured associate professor. In general, the salary of the full professor may be higher, but that will be due in large part to the fact that the full professor has been on the job longer. Nonetheless, promotion to full professor involves a detailed review of a candidate's dossier and an evaluation based on research, service, and teaching. What questions govern the evaluation behind promotion to full professor? In some respects, it is a recognition that the person has continued to mature significantly beyond the work that was done at the time that tenure was offered.

We might take a stronger criterion for promotion to be this, though this makes sense primarily in the context of the research university: that promotion to full professor is a recognition of the significant role that the person plays in defining the central questions that concern her field of research. We have observed that the award of tenure (typically going hand in hand with promotion to associate professor) is based on the judgment that the person has demonstrated her ongoing willingness and ability to contribute substantively to the central questions of her field, just as the award of a Ph.D. shows that the student has demonstrated her capacity to make at least one significant contribution. There is thus an increasingly strong set of criteria for each passage: the Ph.D. demonstrates the ability to make a single contribution, tenure marks an ability to continue to make similar contributions, and promotion to full professor marks the ability not only to contribute answers within the domain of research, but also to succeed in the more difficult task of defining the questions.[3]

I might add that this explication of the meaning of the three familiar academic ranks is my own and that, though I have been asked to prepare letters for a good number of promotion dossiers to full professor, I have rarely been given any explicit statement of just what a full professor ought to have demonstrated. It usually is left rather undefined in practice.

Many professors are simultaneously members of more than one department at many universities. These joint appointments, however, often mask the quite different nature of the appointments. More often than not, only one of the appointments plays any role in budgetary considerations, and it is virtually always the case that a person's teaching and service responsibilities to a given department are directly related to the proportion of her salary that comes from the budget of that department. If Smith has an appointment in the French department, the English department, and the psychology department, but her salary comes 50 percent from French and 50 percent from English, then she may expect her teaching load to be evenly split between courses in French and courses in English. By virtue of her appointment in psychology, she may participate in the affairs of that department, teach a course there on occasion, and work with students there, but the expectations are considerably lower for such an appointment.

A professor whose salary comes entirely from a single department is considered to be "1 Full Time Equivalent," or 1 FTE, there; a professor who is half in a given department is said to have only 0.5 FTE there; and a department that adds up its members will normally add up only its FTE, not everyone who has an appointment of one sort or another. In this way, a department may have 10 FTE or less (for example) and still have 20 or more official members, members who may, indeed, participate and vote in important decisions of the department.

Committees by and large have a bad reputation on campus among professors. All too often they waste the time of the professors who have volunteered, or been chosen, or been elected, to serve on them, discussing *ad nauseam* issues that might just as well be decided administratively.

But this bad reputation is not entirely deserved for several reasons. First of all, quite a few faculty committees serve good functions and produce results that do matter—results that could not be produced in another, more administrative fashion. Second, the work is often quite instructive for the professor; it can open her eyes to sides of the university and its functioning that she had never seen before. And third, it is an excellent opportunity to meet colleagues in other departments and divisions, which is both interesting in itself and serves other important long-term goals, like getting to know colleagues from more distant parts of the college or university.

One important committee function involves overseeing tenure and promotion decisions. While these decisions are ultimately made by the dean, provost, and president, they are made at virtually all universities with the advice of at least one committee composed of faculty outside the candidate's own department. In some universities, this committee serves throughout the academic year, reviewing all candidates for tenure and promotion in the given year, while at other universities, ad hoc committees are set up for each promotion or tenure case.

Academic administrators were once graduate students and junior faculty, too. From their point of view, they are not that different from the human beings they were at that point. Above all, remember (if you are a faculty member) that they are your colleagues and they should be treated as such. If that is not clear enough, it may be worthwhile spelling it out: chairs, deans, and their administrative colleagues should not be conceived of as bosses or as parents.

One point to bear in mind, as one gazes up the administrative tree, is that although the person a step or two above may seem to have a good deal of power (especially when you are asking them for something), the situation is more complex. From the other person's point of view, their power is greatly circumscribed by all those even higher up the academic hierarchy; it is always salutary to remember that wherever one happens to be at the moment (i.e., holding the rank of graduate student or assistant professor), one possesses considerably more freedom and privileges than others in lower positions on the hierarchy; it is all too easy to forget this and, in effect, take one's own power for granted. In short, the person of whom one may need to ask things will—surprise!—most likely not feel like she is in a qualitatively different position, a qualitatively superior position.

Penny Gold: While it is certainly true that administrators have less power than faculty tend to think they do, there really are differentials. The person who sets the agenda for a meeting has more power than the people who suggest agenda items. The person who controls a budget—and the budgeting process—has more power than the people making requests. The person who speaks from their position as a dean has more authority than one or another faculty member speaking within a group. When the dean encourages or supports a new idea—whether verbally or with money—that idea has a much better chance of being institutionalized than if the dean opposes or ignores it. The best administrators are truly leaders of their institutions, cultivating and nurturing excellence in a variety of ways. But they have a good deal of choice in which ways get a "yes" and which get a "no." In the long run, if the choices they make are widely perceived as bad ones, faculty can sometimes gather their collective authority and force the resignation or firing of an administrator, but that is an extreme measure, and usually happens only after years of desperation.

John Goldsmith: Raises in a given year are generally based on a guideline percentage increase (3 or 4 percent, perhaps, or less) that will be given to all faculty members in the absence of specific reasons to go above or below this guideline. It may be up to the chair, then, to determine in each individual case whether the professor's work in the past year was especially good or especially poor, and that guideline figure may then be adjusted in view of that decision. Other factors may be taken into consideration other than simply the quality of work in the past year. If a person's salary is inequitably low, the chair and the dean may undertake to give the person a raise based on that consideration alone. For example, if starting salaries ("entry level salaries") in a specific field are rising at 6 percent a year and raises over the past few years have averaged 4 percent a year, then a fourth-year assistant professor may be making less than a first-year assistant professor, or an associate professor may not be making more than a few thousand dollars more than a newly hired assistant professor. These are generally taken to be matters of equity, to be resolved by distributing the money for raises in a way that may give professors with lower salaries a higher percentage raise than the professors with higher salaries.

One large exception to the picture I have just sketched is the University of California system, in which salaries are fixed to a specific salary scale, with several particular salary grades established for each academic rank (assistant professor, associate professor, full professor). Everyone gets raises automatically as the entire scale shifts upward (a matter of state politics or of inflation, depending on how you wish to look at it), and also as one is promoted from one salary grade to the next, a mini-promotion that may take place every two to four years.

Professors at public universities are employed by the state (or the city) government and thus have a number of things in common with public servants—such as discovering that their salaries are matters of public record. Just as we can easily find out the salary of the governor or mayor, so, too, is the salary of a professor at Indiana University or at Rutgers a matter of public record. Finding out is typically a matter of going to the right office, either at the university or in the state house, but since the information is in principle public, it is typically reproduced and widely circulated, sometimes by the faculty union if there is one. The salaries of professors at private universities, on the other hand, are by no means public knowledge and are quite confidential. The prevailing ethos generally prohibits people from discussing their salaries with their colleagues, but that is one of those unwritten laws that not everyone recognizes.

By and large, the kinds of salary raises that we have discussed up to now are raises that keep up with inflation, but not a whole lot more. The most significant salary raises are the result of that most difficult of subjects—the outside offer, which is the subject of chapter 9.

Here are some recent statistics on average salaries that give us a good sense of where salaries currently stand:

Public Universities	
Professor	$69,924
Associate professor	$50,186
Assistant professor	$42,335
All	$55,068
Other Public Four-Year Institutions	
Professor	$61,076
Associate professor	$47,850
Assistant professor	$39,544
All	$48,566
Private Universities	
Professor	$84,970
Associate professor	$56,517
Assistant professor	$47,387
All	$65,405
Other Private Four-Year Institutions	
Professor	$57,089
Associate professor	$44,186
Assistant professor	$36,325
All	$44,504
Two-Year Colleges	
Public	$43,295
Private	$31,915

SOURCE: From the *Chronicle of Higher Education* at *http://chronicle.com/free/almanac/1998/nation/nation.htm#colleges*.

Appendix 2

Policies on Parental Leave
and Shared Positions

Parental Leave Policy at Knox College

The official parental leave policy, as stated in the Knox Faculty Handbook, *gives in concise form the essence of the leave policy worked out by the Executive Committee of the college in 1990. The dean has implemented the policy in accord with the guidelines developed by the Executive Committee. Both documents are presented below. Knox's academic year consists of three ten-week terms.*

PARENTAL LEAVE

The College's health plan allows six weeks of sick leave with pay. In interpreting this policy as it affects academic obligations, the College recognizes the special nature of faculty obligations on the term system by granting a birth-giving parent one term of leave with pay, or a two-course reduction in teaching responsibility. For fathers or non–birth giving parents the policy is a one course reduction in teaching responsibility.

CHILDBIRTH LEAVE AND PARENTAL LEAVE FOR FACULTY
(EXECUTIVE COMMITTEE DOCUMENT, APRIL 2, 1990)

Childbirth leave: A childbirth leave is comparable to other medical or disability leaves, and is intended to provide a woman time to recuperate physically from childbirth. Given her particular health circumstances (vaginal birth versus caesarian, complications or not), she might need more or less time, as could be ascertained by her physician. Some women also need time off from work before the birth, again depending on particular circumstances. Any such time is directly related to the physical condition of pregnancy and childbirth, and so is comparable to any other kind of medical needs (some of which are gender specific, like prostate surgery). Current health insurance covers such medical leaves. Length of the child-birth leave will be *six weeks at full pay* for a "normal" childbirth; more time will be given when medically needed.

Parental leave: This leave is meant to provide a parent time to focus on the needs of a new child and to have some respite from work in order to rearrange life to accommodate both child and work. Such a leave is not contingent on physical disability from childbirth and so is available to all parents: that is, adoptive mothers and all fathers, as well as birth mothers. Length of the leave will be *five weeks at full pay*.

Ways in which parental leave may be taken:

1. As five weeks of full time leave. Combined with six weeks of childbirth leave, this would result in one full term of leave.
2. As ten weeks of half-time leave, thus the teaching of one course instead of two.
3. As five weeks of full-time leave, with another five weeks taken without pay, resulting in one-term's effective leave.

Details of how a parental leave will be taken will be worked out between the parent, the department, and the Dean. In the case where both parents of a child work for the College, a five-week parental leave may be taken by both.

Shared Position Policy at Grinnell College

Two persons who are both members of the Grinnell College faculty are able to share a single faculty position. By creating shared positions, the College has responded to those consistent employment challenges in-curred by academic couples in small communities such as Grinnell. Both individuals sharing a position have full faculty status. The College benefits by attracting faculty to the College who might not otherwise be able to accept a position at Grinnell College. By having two persons in a single faculty position, the College also may gain curricular flexibility.

Because of the contractual differences between shared positions and single full-time positions, shared-position issues must be carefully considered both for current holders of shared positions and for candidates applying for faculty positions at Grinnell on a shared basis. This document presents a discussion of these issues.

1. Persons considering a shared-position application for an advertised faculty position must decide prior to the on-campus interview of the applicant pool if they wish to apply separately for the full-time position or together for a shared position. The College will honor their choice. For shared-position candidates, both candidates must be ranked near the top of the applicant pool to be offered a shared position.

The College will also consider converting a single full-time appointment to a shared-position appointment. The department should present a proposal to the Dean that indicates how the conversion would benefit the College and that presents evidence for excellence in teaching, scholarship, and potential service on the part of the candidate. The Dean will take the proposal to the Executive Council for its recommendation. The Executive Council will decide whether the proposal is sufficiently compelling and recommend whether the College should proceed with its normal hiring procedures.

2. The College will not require one member of a shared position to teach full time during an approved family or medical leave granted to the other partner. However, in the event that one of the individuals holding a shared position resigns or is unable to continue his or her teaching duties for a period of time extending beyond an approved medical or other leave of absence, the other individual in the shared relationship must assume teaching duties up to the equivalent of one full-time position. For example, if one individual in the shared-position relationship suffers a long-term disability or resigns, the other individual in the shared-position relationship must assume the full-time position. To fulfill this obligation, shared-position faculty must have expertise in the same or closely allied academic discipline or subdiscipline and must hold appointments in the same academic department.

3. As regular, continuing members of the Grinnell College faculty, shared-position faculty have the same duties, obligations, responsibilities, and privileges as outlined in *The Faculty Handbook* for all regular faculty. Thus, shared-position faculty have the same performance expectations for teaching and scholarship as full-time faculty and have the same contract and promotion review schedules and procedures as full-time faculty. Service expectations for the shared position should be the same as for a single regular faculty position. Each faculty member in a shared-position rela-

tionship is separately considered for contract renewal and for promotion and tenure. They may each apply for support for attendance at an annual professional meeting and for grant board support according to the guidelines in *The Faculty Handbook.*

4. Since the current full-time teaching schedule at Grinnell College is five courses or course equivalents per year, a full-time shared-position schedule is five courses per year. Each faculty member in a shared position shall teach at least two courses per year unless given permission to teach fewer courses by the Dean of the College.

5. Currently each shared position carries a base salary associated with the position rather than two base salaries respectively associated with each individual in the shared-position relationship. For appointments made after September 1, 1994, each individual will have a base salary. Having individual base salaries allows the College to make appropriate merit salary increments and to develop shared-position appointments with individuals who have different experience or academic rank. The College will make salary payments to each individual according to one of two methods.

Method one. Salary payments will be made to each of the faculty members at their respective prorated salary. That is, if the faculty members teach respectively three and two courses in a given year, each will receive three-fifths and two-fifths of their respective individual base salary. Each additional course is compensated at one fifth of the respective individual base salary.

Method two. Salary payments will be made to each of the faculty members at the prorated average base salary of the shared position faculty members. That is, if the faculty members teach respectively three and two courses in a given year, each will receive three-fifths and two-fifths of the average base salary calculated from the two individual base salaries. Each additional course is compensated at one fifth of the average base salary.

With either method, if one faculty member assumes the full-time position, the base salary of this faculty member will be his or her individual base salary.

Shared position faculty must choose method one or method two at the time of appointment. Subsequently, at the conclusion of every fifth year of service at the College, they may elect either method of salary allocation for the next five years.

Regardless of the method of salary allocation for the shared position, if the shared position members have approximately equal teaching duties, current College policy permits the College upon the request of both members of the shared position to allocate 1/2 of the sum of their actual salaries to each member of the shared position. In this case, each member would receive the same salary for the year.

6. Shared-position faculty members qualify for those benefits described in *The Faculty Handbook*. Since shared-position faculty members share full faculty positions, benefit waiting periods for all shared-position faculty members will be those for full positions rather than for part-time positions.

7. Each faculty member in a shared position is eligible for a sabbatical leave in accordance with *The Faculty Handbook*. The College will base the compensation during this sabbatical period on the average number of courses taught per year calculated from the previous six years of teaching, excluding unpaid leave periods.

8. All full-time, regular faculty are eligible to apply for Senior Faculty Status (SFS) [a transitional status available to faculty between the ages of sixty-four and seventy] according to the guidelines stated in Part II. Section X. of *The Faculty Handbook*. During the period of a shared position, each faculty member separately accumulates time toward the fifteen-year SFS eligibility requirement with each year of service counting as one of the fifteen years required for SFS eligibility.

Upon meeting the SFS eligibility requirements, a member of a shared position may propose moving to SFS. While both members need not propose to move to SFS at the same time, the College may ask the other member of the shared position for a commitment to a specific timetable for retirement or moving to SFS prior to approving the request of the proposing member.

The total SFS compensation for the shared position member proposing to move to SFS will be calculated as described in *The Faculty Handbook* but pro-rated at a rate equal to his or her average FTE yearly course load during his or her career at the College as a holder of a single full-time faculty position or a full-time shared position. For example, under the current SFS 55% compensation policy, a member of a shared position who has taught an average of four courses each year (80% FTE) while at Grinnell may propose moving to SFS with annual compensation of 80% of 55% of the faculty member's base salary in the shared position.

When one member of a shared position moves to SFS, the second member assumes a full-time teaching position. Subsequently, upon meeting the SFS eligibility requirements, this person may propose moving to SFS using the same compensation rules as described in the preceding paragraph.

If the shared position converts to a single position prior to either member moving to SFS, the position converts to a single position and the holder of this position falls under the SFS guidelines that pertain to a full-time member of the faculty as described in *The Faculty Handbook*.

As stated in Part II.X.E of *The Faculty Handbook,* the College re-serves the right to re-evaluate its position at any time concerning the offering of the SFS option or withdraw from offering it as the College deems necessary. If such adjustment or withdrawal should occur, those faculty members who have been granted the option will be continued under the plan as specified in their SFS appointment agreement with the College.

Appendix 3

Tables

Table 1 Academia as Employer: Total Employment in Four-Year and Two-Year Institutions, 1997

	Four-Year Institutions	Two-Year Institutions
Administrative	125,000	29,000
Faculty	683,000	320,000
Full-time	460,000	115,000
Part-time	223,000	205,000
TA/RA	219,000	4,000
Nonfaculty professional	425,000	49,000
Total professional	1,452,000	402,000
Clerical, service, technical	755,000	166,000
Total employment*	2,207,000	568,000

SOURCE: U.S. Department of Education, National Center for Education Statistics, Integrated Postsecondary Education Data System, "Fall Staff" survey, 1997, NCES 2000-164, tables A-2 and A-3. Available at *http://www.nces.ed.gov/pubsearch/pubsinfo.asp?pubid=2000164.*
*Does not include less-than-two-year institutions with employment of 33,353.

Table 2   Distribution of Annual Faculty Salaries, 1997

Salary (Thousands of Dollars	Percentage of Faculty	
	Full-Time	Part-Time
< 10	2.6%	74.4%
10–24.99	5.6	18.1
25–39.99	34.4	4.2
40–54.99	31.0	3.3
55–69.99	14.5	
70–84.99	6.1	
85–99.99	2.1	
100 <	3.7	
Total	100.0	100.0

Table 3   Median Salaries in the Sciences and Social Sciences by Highest Degree, Age, and Employment Sector, 1997 (Thousands of Dollars)

Major/Age	Business	Private Four-Year College-University	Government
Master's Degree			
Computer/Math			
< 30	50	22	—
30–39	61	37	56
40–49	70	35	60
Social Sciences			
< 30	30	13	—
30–39	42	34	41
40–49	50	40	48
Doctorate			
Computer/Math			
< 30	72	40	—
30–39	76	45	68
40–49	87	55	83
Life Sciences			
< 30	50	25	—
30–39	60	35	39
40–49	75	55	62
Physical Sciences			
< 30	58	25	—
30–39	65	39	50
40–49	80	55	72
Social Sciences			
< 30	31	37	—
30–39	55	40	52
40–49	75	50	58

SOURCE: National Science Foundation, Division of Science Resource Studies, 1997 Scientists and Engineers Statistical Data System, table F-3. Available at *http://srsstats.sbe.nsf.gov/preformatted-tables/1997/DST1997.html.*

Table 4   Median Salaries of Full-Time Faculty by Rank and Gender, 1974 and 1997 (1998 Dollars)

	Full Professor	Associate Professor	Assistant Professor
	Men		
1974	$66,000	$50,000	$41,300
1997	68,200	50,500	41,900
	Women		
1974	$58,300	$47,500	$39,500
1997	60,200	47,100	39,400

Table 5   Distribution of 1992–93 Bachelor's Degree Recipients Enrolled for an Advanced Degree in 1997

Degree Program	Percentage
Master's program	66
MBA program	10
Other professional program	14
Doctoral program	10

SOURCE: U.S. Department of Education, National Center for Education Statistics, *Life after College: A Descriptive Summary of 1992–93 Bachelor's Degree Recipients in 1997, with an Essay on Participation in Graduate and First-Professional Education*, 1999, NCES 1999-155, by Alexander C. McCormick, Anne-Marie Nuñez, Vishant Shah, and Susan P. Choy. Available at *http://www.nces.ed.gov/pubsearch/pubsinfo.asp?pubid=1999155*.

Table 6   Financing an Advanced Degree, 1997 (Percentages)

Type of Financing	Type of Degree			
	Master's	MBA	Professional	Doctoral
Loan	20	18	53	25
Grant	12	5	5	28
Grant and loan	6	7	13	8
Campus job	5	0	1	14
Employee benefits	4	18	0	1
Other	3	7	1	4
No aid	50	45	26	21

SOURCE: See table 5.

Table 7   Estimated Time Distribution for Full-Time Faculty per Week (Hours)

	Typical	Range
Teaching in class	8	3–16
Class preparation	19	15–40
Office hours	1	1–6
Research/scholarship	12	5–40
Administration/service	11	0–15
Outside consulting	1	0–20
Total	52	50–80

SOURCE: Typical figures from U.S. Department of Education, National Center for Education Statistics, National Study of Postsecondary Faculty, 1993. Available at *http://www.nces.ed.gov/pubs99/digest98/d98t227.html*, table 227. Range figures are conjectures by authors.

Table 8   Publishing Schedule of a Typical Academic

Year 1	Submit article #1	Start revising thesis	
Year 2	Submit article #2	Revise and publish article #1	Continue revising thesis
Year 3	Start new project	Revise and publish article #2	Submit thesis
Year 4	Submit article #3	Continue new project	Publish thesis
Year 5	Submit article #4	Publish article #3	Tenure deliberations begin
Year 6	Submit article #5	Publish article #4	Tenure decision

Notes

PREFACE

1. We have little to say about professional schools directly, such as schools of nursing, business administration, law, and so forth. Nonetheless, graduate students in those areas who are interested in pursuing careers in academia should find much in this book that will be broadly applicable to them.

2. Their numbers have been increasing greatly: of 170,000 graduate students in science and engineering in 1993, 43 percent were foreign. Amy Magaro Ruvin, "Foreign Influx in Science Hurts Americans' Recruitment," *Chronicle of Higher Education*, 14 July 1995, International Section, A33. Sixty percent of economics Ph.D.s are now granted to nonnationals of the United States.

3. For an insider's view on the University of Chicago's traditions, see Edward Shils, ed., *Remembering the University of Chicago: Teachers, Scientists and Scholars* (Chicago: University of Chicago Press, 1991).

4. Just to give one example, there are no studies on which methods of directing dissertations yield the best results.

5. See, for example, Richard M. Reis, *Tomorrow's Professor: Preparing for Academic Careers in Science and Engineering* (New York: IEEE Press, 1997).

6. For an international comparison of academic systems and their evolution, see Burton R. Clark, ed., *The Academic Profession: National, Disciplinary, and Institutional Settings* (Berkeley: University of California Press, 1987).

7. Melanie Gustafson, ed., *Becoming a Historian: A Survival Manual for Women and Men* (Washington, D.C.: American Historical Association, 1991); Emily Toth, *Ms. Mentor's Impeccable Advice for Women in Academia* (Philadelphia: University of Pennsylvania Press, 1997). See also Penny Gold's response to Toth's book: "Giving Advice to Women in Academe: Where 'Ms. Mentor' Goes Wrong," *Chronicle of Higher Education*, 1 May 1998, B7. Penny also edited a faculty-written guide, *Survival/Success Guide for Knox Faculty;* this guide, while geared to local circumstances, contains much that is of general use. It is available on the World Wide Web at *http://www.knox.edu/knox/knoxweb/faculty/guide*.

8. Critical, even cynical, voices abound. See, for example, Stanley Fish, "The Unbearable Ugliness of Volvos," in *English Inside and Out: The Places of Literary Criticism*, ed. Susan Gubar and Jonathan Kamholtz (New York: Routledge, 1993).

9. I regret that higher education has become such a big business, but it is a natural economic evolutionary process. With nearly 3 million employees, it could hardly

be run like a family enterprise. I also find it regrettable that college tuition has skyrocketed: more than doubled in real terms since the mid-1950s. C. T. Clotfelter, *Buying the Best: Cost Escalation in Elite Higher Education* (Princeton, N.J.: Princeton University Press, 1996); E. Larsen, "Why Colleges Cost Too Much," *Time*, 17 March 1997, 11; U.S. Department of Education, *Digest of Education Statistics* (Washington, D.C.: Government Printing Office, 1997).

CHAPTER ONE

1.   Jules B. LaPidus, president of the Council of Graduate Schools, writes ("Why Pursuing a PhD Is a Risky Business," *Chronicle of Higher Education*, 14 November 1997, Opinion Section, A60) that the decision to enter graduate school is the responsibility of the student: hence, the student has to face up to the consequences of his decision. However, I would argue that that view overlooks the fact that students do not have all the information they need to make an informed rational judgment about their prospects. Beginning graduate students typically do not have a good way of predicting how well they will do relative to the rest of their cohort upon completion of their program. That is probably one of the main reasons why there is an endemic overproduction of Ph.D.s.

2.   The Bureau of Labor Statistics has an abundance of information available on its Web site *(http://www.bls.gov)* and in its two publications, the *Monthly Labor Review* and *Occupations Outlook Review*.

3.   Data pertain to men; women earned about $1,000 less on average.

4.   "Letter to the Editor," *Perspectives* 37, no. 8 (November 1999): 12.

5.   Darnton continues: "As department chair, he . . . fought to create what we modestly refer to as the greatest history department in the country. . . . The man we knew and loved was gentle and generous. . . . Why did he go out of his way to have lunch with inconsequential visiting firemen and unimportant junior lecturers? Why did he read and correct endless drafts of papers by colleagues in fields far removed from his? . . . He was a one-man employment agency, finding jobs in places where his students never dreamed of applying. He was their literary agent, too, guiding their work into his inside track at *Past and Present* and the Oxford University Press. . . . He . . . recalled that 'the experience [at Oxford] taught me the importance of sheer factual information—erudition, if you like—in the cut-throat struggle for survival in the life of learning'" (pp. 44–45).

6.   Detailed information on salaries by educational attainment in the sciences and social sciences can be found at *http://srsstats.sbe.nsf.gov*.

7.   This does not reveal the whole story, however, because the ranges in salaries differ by much more. In 1998, the top annual salary of an economist going into an academic job immediately after graduate school was $128,000, but the equivalent in business was fully 33 percent higher: $170,000.

8.   That, of course, means that half of the candidates take longer than five years after the master's degree to complete.

9.   *http://www.irs.ustreas.gov/prod/tax_stats/ind.html.* The number of millionaires in the United States was 1.3 million in 1994, and nearly 1 percent of the adult population in California, New York, New Jersey, and Florida.

10. We will return to this matter in chapter 9. Suffice it to say for now that such threat of leaving your home institution is practically the only way to raise your salary substantially because your college/university might well meet the salary offered in order to keep you from moving. If it fails to do so, you can then raise your salary by accepting the outside offer. Becoming chair of a department usually does not raise your salary meaningfully unless this is part of an outside offer. Another way to increase your salary is to go into academic administration—for example, by taking on the assignment of a deanship later on in your career.

11. The Web site *(http://www.nextwave.org/survey)* has much other information, including salaries, career guides, and other features—mostly for scientists, but of considerable interest to other scholars as well. College graduates in the early 1990s were unemployed only 1.9 percent of the time and those holding advanced degrees 1.6 percent of the time. That is to say, graduates were unemployed only seven days out of the year on average.

12. *Perspectives* 37, no. 8 (November 1999): 3.

13. Nonreporting in 1991 was only 32 percent. *Perspectives* 37, no. 1 (January 1999): 24.

14. *Occupational Outlook Handbook, 1998–99 (http://www.bls.gov/oco/ocos066. htm).*

15. A word of caution: this is not universally true. Some friends have told me their situation is not at all parallel to what I describe. Other colleagues in France, by contrast, point out that professors there don't even *have* offices, so they have no other place to work except at home or in the cafés. But the croissants are better there.

16. There's a lot to discuss about this in connection with having a family, but we'll hold off on that until chapter 10.

17. In the laboratory sciences, experiments might well have to be carried on during the summer months as well.

18. It is quite useful to read the newsletters of professional organizations in order learn about the discipline in general. See, for example, *Perspectives* (newsletter of the American Historical Association, *http://www.theaha.org*). Some organizations, however, such as the American Economic Association, do not publish a newsletter. A perusal of the *Chronicle of Higher Education* will also give you a sense of academic life. It has an extremely useful electronic databank accessible at *http://www.chronicle.org*. Do be sure to check out *http://chronicle.com/jobs*, where you can find a lot of resources on jobs in academe, and also *http://chronicle.com/jobs/book shelf.htm*, which has information on books on job searches and other aspects of academic life.

19. See the journal *Alternative Life Styles*.

20. We shall return to this issue with a whole chapter (8) devoted to it because that decision marks your entry into the senior ranks of the profession.

21. Educational services contributed $61.5 billion to gross domestic product in 1997 (as compared to $85.0 billion produced by the motor vehicles manufacturing sector).

22. On the difficulties of publishing articles in economics that eventually became

classics, see Joshua S. Gans and George B. Shepherd, "How Are the Mighty Fallen: Rejected Classic Articles by Leading Economists," *Journal of Economic Perspectives* 8 (1994): 165–79. Of course, we do not know how many potential classics ended up unpublished.

23. I discuss examples of such in "'A Teacher Is Either a Witness or a Stranger,'" in *The Role of Advocacy in the Classroom*, ed. Patricia Meyer Spacks (New York: St. Martin's Press, 1996), 260–70.

24. For an intriguing analysis in which professional training and work conditions can also militate *against* independent thinking (a necessary component of institutional change), see Jeff Schmidt, *Disciplined Minds: A Critical Look at Salaried Professionals and the Soul-Battering System That Shapes Their Lives* (Lanham, Md.: Rowman & Littlefield, 2000).

25. Degrees were granted by nearly 1,800 institutions of higher education. When interviewed in 1993, fully 85 percent of this cohort actually responded that they expected to obtain an advanced degree sometime in the future. By 1997, however, the share among the 1993 graduates declined to 72 percent. Yet only a minority actually acted on their desire to obtain an advanced degree: 41 percent of the graduates had applied for admission, and of these, an amazing 87 percent were accepted into a program. *Life after College: A Descriptive Summary of 1992–93 Bachelor's Degree Recipients in 1997, with an Essay on Participation in Graduate and First-Professional Education*, NCES Statistical Analysis Report NCES 1999-155, Alexander C. McCormick, Anne-Marie Nuñez, Vishant Shah, Susan P. Choy, MPR Associates, Inc., Paula R. Knepper Project Officer (Washington, D.C.: U.S. Department of Education, Office of Educational Research and Improvement, National Center for Education Statistics, 1999).

26. Distribution of 1992–93 bachelor's degree recipients who enrolled for an advanced degree by field of study:

Education	21.5%
Business/management	18.1
Health sciences (including medicine)	15.5
Social science	9.7
Engineering/math/computer science	8.5
Law	8.1
Art/humanities	8.1
Science	5.6

Chapter Two

1. Useful information can be found on the Web page of the Council of Graduate Schools, "dedicated to the improvement and advancement of graduate education" *(http://www.cgsnet.org)*. The council has many publications relevant to various aspects of graduate education. Information pertinent to graduate students is available not only at the departmental level of all universities, but at times also at the university level; see, for example, *http://www.mit.edu/activities/gsc* and *http://www.harvard.edu/~gsc* for the Graduate Student Councils of MIT and Harvard Uni-

versity, respectively. A 1995 report on doctorate programs by the National Research Council, National Academy of Sciences is available at *http://www.nap.edu/reading room/books/researchdoc.*

2.   The graduate school is a particularly Anglo-Saxon institutional form and is the backbone of American excellence in scholarship. Continental European countries are just beginning to think seriously about emulating it.

3.   Joining an Internet discussion group could be useful in giving you insights on the general outlines of academic life. On economic history, look at *http://www. eh.net.* It has links to interesting sites. Over a hundred humanities and social science discussion networks can be accessed through *http://www.h-net.msu.edu.* Also look at the Web page of the American Council of Learned Societies at *http:// www.acls.org.* It has links to many important scholarly societies in America.

4.   In technical terminology, your forecast errors about yourself should not be correlated with one another over time. If they are, that means you are probably not using some of the information available to you.

5.   You will not have much time to earn money during the academic year, since most students in doctoral programs attend classes during weekdays. The distribution of attendance in advanced programs in 1997 was as follows:

Program	Weekdays	Weeknights	Weekends
Master's	40	56	4
MBA	22	77	1
Professional	95	5	0
Doctoral	89	11	0

6.   See note 25 of chapter 1 above.

7.   For historians, this information is published by the American Historical Association in an annual compendium, *Directory of History Departments,* which lists pertinent information on more than seven hundred departments in North America, including valuable data on who completed the graduate program, the title of their dissertation, and their employment. You might need to do some research to find the relevant publication in your field.

8.   In 1998, there were 2,500 Ph.D.s granted by history departments. In contrast, in 1992, there were about 9,300 students entering graduate school in history. So the average ratio of Ph.D. students entering to those graduating is close to 1 in 4, or 25 percent. This is not a precise indicator of the dropout rate in doctoral programs, insofar as many students must be entering graduate programs with the intention of getting only an M.A.

9.   Useful data on education are provided by the National Center for Education Statistics *(http://www.nces.ed.gov).* According to its projections, the number of doctoral degrees granted annually will reach 50,000 during the course of the first decade of this millennium, up from about 44,000 during the 1990s. Other relevant information can be found at *http://www.cpst.org* (Commission on Professionals in Science and Technology), *http://www.ams.org* (American Mathematical Society), and *http://stats.bls.gov* (Bureau of Labor Statistics).

10.   The *Newsletter* of the Cliometric Society has published regular articles on the

careers of prominent economic historians. See also such books as Michael Szenberg, ed., *Eminent Economists: Their Life Philosophies* (New York: Cambridge University Press, 1992).

Chapter Three

1.   This is a matter of great importance that we've already mentioned and will return to in the next chapter.

2.   I prefer the analogy of "frontier" to that of the often used "cutting edge" because the latter implies that the boundary separating knowledge from ignorance is precisely defined. This is seldom the case. Rather, the boundary seems to me to be fuzzy, discontinuous, multifaceted, and constantly changing directions. Moreover, there is spontaneous creation of knowledge even in areas that were previously not thought of as being on the "cutting edge."

3.   I remember how difficult it was to get an appointment with my mentor. At times, he even forgot appointments. But I do recall vividly how much I benefited from our conversations when I finally did catch up with him.

4.   The dissertation committee usually consists of four professors, not all of whom need to be from the same department or even the same institution. The other readers play a much smaller advisory role than the first reader; their expertise is generally peripheral, but still crucial to your success. If you have an interdisciplinary emphasis in your research, it is advisable to have a representative of the other discipline sit on your committee.

Chapter Four

1.   ABD (All But Dissertation) is not an official designation. It means that the person in question has completed all coursework and has taken all examinations, but did not finish the thesis.

2.   We are not going to discuss the mechanics of writing a dissertation. See, for instance, Lawrence F. Locke, Waneen Wyrick Spirduso, and Stephen J. Silverman, *Proposals That Work: A Guide for Planning Dissertations and Grant Proposals,* 3rd ed. (Newbury Park, Calif.: Sage, 1993); Kjell Erik Rudestam and Rae R. Newton, *Surviving Your Dissertation: A Comprehensive Guide to Content and Process* (Newbury Park, Calif.: Sage, 1992); and Soraya M. Coley and Cynthia A. Scheinberg, *Proposal Writing* (Newbury Park, Calif.: Sage, 1990).

3.   Of those who were enrolled in a doctoral program in 1997, only a half had started on their thesis four years after graduating from college. The breakdown in the various programs is as follows:

Program	Thesis in Progress	Completed	Not Required
Master's	27	7	25
MBA	12	6	43
Doctoral	52	5	8

These data have their limitations because they do not reveal when the student started the program. But the information does give us some idea of the progress of college graduates within four years after receiving their first degree. For example, 5 percent of those in a doctoral program in 1997 had completed their thesis requirement at that point. To be sure, 40 percent had not started yet.

4. The University of Michigan Dissertation Abstract Database can be found at *http://www.umi.com.*

5. The National Science Foundation supports research in a number of social science areas, including sociology, political science, economics, law, statistics, and management (for doctoral research as well). See *http://www.nsf.gov/sbe/ses/start.htm.*

6. You might state, "I do not have the foreign trade figures for Liechtenstein, but they probably do not exceed on a per capita basis those of Switzerland, given the similarities in socioeconomic structure of the two countries. Therefore, I increased the European totals by 0.5 percent in order to account for the absence of data for Liechtenstein." Period. You have provided an interim solution to the problem and offered an intuitive way of dealing with the order of magnitude of your error. If, on the other hand, you impulsively take the next month to find the exact figures in order to complete your dissertation on recent trends in European international trade, you will have made a mistake, and you might well jeopardize its timely completion. Of course, the case would be different if your dissertation were on economic growth of the handful of tiny countries in Europe.

CHAPTER FIVE

1. You should not limit yourself to American journals.

2. Note also that there are many ways to be unprepared. Detail does matter: for example, make sure you know how to operate the overhead projector before you begin your lecture. It can be embarrassing to fumble with switches and might make you nervous. If you are depending on written notes, staple them together beforehand in the proper order so that you will not find yourself with a misplaced sheet halfway through your presentation.

3. I served as the coordinator of the economic history sessions for the Social Science History Association in 1993 and organized twelve sessions with about fifty participants, but received only one request from a graduate student to be included in the program. I would have been quite willing to give others priority over established scholars in order to help them gain some experience.

4. So does the Cliometric Society, for example, for economic historians.

5. I remember how disappointed I was at the first conference I attended. I had just published a four-page comment, and no one seemed to have taken notice of it.

6. For advice on how to write a prospectus for publishers, see Robin Derricourt, *An Author's Guide to Scholarly Publishing* (Princeton, N.J.: Princeton University Press, 1996).

7. Natural scientists might have an on-site interview without an interview at the annual national meeting.

8. Some people may perceive marriage to be a plus for men, as is the assumption

of the writer of a letter of recommendation I read recently; he described a male candidate as having "a charming and devoted wife and a delightful baby son." Needless to say, the word "husband" doesn't substitute easily in such a line.

9. As a rule, the interview takes place in a hotel room, which is usually a bedroom—and hence was not designed for a formal interview. So be prepared for some awkward situations.

10. Emily Toth, *Ms. Mentor's Impeccable Advice for Women in Academia* (Philadelphia: University of Pennsylvania Press, 1997), 27, 36. Jane Lubchenco, a professor at Oregon State University, agrees with me on candor, but advises sharing information on your spousal situation early in the process (if your spouse is also an academic) to facilitate finding two jobs ("Advice for Academics Who Are Members of Two-Career Couples," *Chronicle of Higher Education,* 26 May 2000, B12).

11. The program "Preparing Future Faculty" at the University of Minnesota is but one indication of this tendency. See its Web site at *http://www.preparingfaculty.org.* See *Perspectives* 37, no. 1 (January 1999): 1. You might also consult Stephen D. Brookfield, *Becoming a Critically Reflective Teacher* (San Francisco: Jossey-Bass, 1995).

12. Diagrams are preferable to tables because of the ease of comprehension.

13. There is a discussion of this in the *Chronicle of Higher Education,* which can be found at *http://chronicle.com/colloquy/98/fashion/background.htm.* What do they say? "[W]hat about good looks [and dress]? Can such things tip the scales in a job interview, weaken a bid for tenure, or keep you off the A list on the conference circuit? Many professors say they can, although there is quibbling over the reasons why." They quote Emily Toth, whose book, *Ms. Mentor's Impeccable Advice for Women in Academia,* talks about many human sides of academia. The *Chronicle's* colloquy series also opens the door to a wide range of issues, like the pros and cons of dating academics. See *http://chronicle.com/colloquy/99/dating/background.htm.*

14. Oddly enough, I have gotten an offer every time that something unexpected happened during my job talk. It must have an effect on the way the audience perceives me or my talk. At my Munich job talk, a professor in the audience stood up at the beginning and demanded that I give it in German. Well, the agreement with the dean was that I would give my talk in English, and it would have been disastrous for me to switch languages at the last minute. So I just waited until the professor and the dean had talked it out for a long five minutes in front of an overflow audience of at least fifty people. For some reason, I thought it was so hilarious that I chuckled through my whole lecture and even forgot an important equation, without anyone seeming to notice.

15. All these conversations may be weighed after your visit and can count as much as your more public, formal presentation. They can even help make up for the latter if it was weak: "I know she didn't answer all the questions at her talk very well, but she was great when I was asking her about her research one-on-one."

16. I felt that the query was too personal and that they should not need that kind of a evidence to decide whether they wanted me or not. I thought they should make an independent judgment on my abilities.

17. If you teach at a local college as a graduate student, your affiliation with your

university will override any disadvantage that would otherwise attach to such employment. However, the situation changes if you accept a temporary position after you have completed your graduate program. In that case, the most recent affiliation dominates as the one setting your market value. Hence, if you do not aspire to teach at a junior college in the long run, you had better not accept such a position after you have received your Ph.D.; work instead in a nonacademic position for a year.

18. A symposium on job opportunities for economists is published in the *Journal of Economic Perspectives* 13, no. 3 (Summer 1999): 115–56. The references there are pertinent to many other disciplines as well.

19. For what it feels like being chosen in a field of 185 applicants for a tenure-track position in English, see Robin Wilson, "A Job Search Revisited: Graduate Student Tracked by Chronicle Lands a Position," *Chronicle of Higher Education,* 11 March 1998, Daily News Section. Her difficulties in finding a job the previous year can be found in Robin Wilson, "A Graduate Student's Job Search Leads Her Far Afield," *Chronicle of Higher Education,* 25 April 1997, Faculty Section, A10.

20. Sabbatical policies vary substantially across institutions, but they generally entail granting the academic a semester off from teaching with full pay about every seven years in order to give him the opportunity to devote that time to intensive reading and research. Sabbaticals can be taken away from the home institution, and with the help of some grant money, one might be able to extend it to a full year of leave. This can obviously play a crucial role in the development of a research project.

21. Thanks to Anne Houtman and Natalie Adolphi for their advice about shared appointments, from the initial application to on-the-job issues.

22. In one history department, the original position was divided into two half-positions in order to be able to give jobs to both spouses. This was an interim, but useful solution. Subsequently, both positions were upgraded as soon as other positions became available in the department.

23. A variant of this scenario is receiving an invitation for an on-campus interview from Stanford University after having accepted the offer from Iowa State. It seems to me that in this case it is easier to decline the invitation and stick with your commitment because the improvement in your position is uncertain. In this case, one would have to weigh the possible gains against the possibility that you do not receive the Stanford offer and alienate the future colleagues at Iowa State for having considered reneging on your commitment to them.

Chapter Six

1. The traditional institution of tenure is being questioned currently because it is seen by many administrators as not sufficiently cost effective. The number of part-time faculty in history departments has increased by some 20 percent since 1986. *Perspectives* 37, no. 1 (January 1999): 24.

2. For example, after I accepted an offer, I received welcoming letters from several of the senior faculty members of the department, and these happened to be the very same people who, as I subsequently found out, had the most influence on major decisions taken.

3.   Suppose one wants to achieve A, but it is either too controversial or contrary to local custom. But suppose that both A and C are subsets of B. Then people often find it easier to argue for C in order to accomplish their goals—particularly if C is also a subset of D. One can argue for C as in D, and then, at a future date, one can switch the dialog to C as in B. Once one has accomplished B, then it is possible to shift focus to another subset of B, such as A. If this sounds complicated on paper, it is even more so verbally during a controversial meeting when several such arguments might be floating around.

Or consider a colleague who wants to support Jones, let's say, for a position open in the department, but initially argues for Smith. After awhile, she changes her mind and supports Jones with the remark that although she was originally for Smith, she now sees the advantages of Jones, and if she can change her mind, so can others. You may not be able to see through such strategic maneuvers unless you pay close attention and keep track of the way colleagues argue over time.

4.   Quoted in "A Crusade against Cronyism or a Breach of Collegiality?" *Chronicle of Higher Education*, 7 July 2000, Faculty Section, A12.

5.   Much of the substance of my comments here is taken from *The Success/Survival Guide for Knox Faculty*, 3rd ed. (2000), 14, 41–42, which I wrote jointly with several of my Knox colleagues: Natalie Adolphi, Heather Hoffman, Carol Horowitz, Lynette Lombard, and Elizabeth Carlin Metz. I thank them for their permission to use this and other scattered material drawn from the *Guide*, and even more for the pleasure of working with them on that project.

6.   Arcadius Kahan, my first dissertation advisor at the University of Chicago, was a workaholic who passed away from heart failure at the age of sixty-two. Knut Borchardt, whom I replaced at the University of Munich, retired due to heart problems also at the age of sixty-two.

7.   For an analysis of gender and institutional life, applicable well beyond the business world it describes, see Rosabeth Moss Kanter, *Men and Women of the Corporation*, 2nd ed. (New York: Basic Books, 1993). For a trenchant analysis of the family/work conflict, with proposals for policies and legal initiatives that would eliminate this conflict, see Joan Williams, *Unbending Gender: Why Family and Work Conflict and What to Do about It* (New York: Oxford University Press, 2000). And to learn about an organization working for such change, visit the Web site of the College and University Work/Family Association: *http://www.cuwfa.org.*

8.   John J. Siegfried and Wendy A. Stock, "The Labor Market in New Ph.D. Economists," *Journal of Economic Perspectives* 13, no. 3 (Summer 1999): 115–34.

9.   No wonder that the more belligerent voices in academia are coming from students of English. For the point of view of a postmodernist English professor, see Terry Caesar, *Writing in Disguise: Academic Life in Subordination* (Athens: Ohio University Press, 1998). In 1994, 10 percent of Ph.D. recipients in English and in foreign languages were unemployed, and, in addition, in English, 7.8 percent of new Ph.D.s found employment outside of academe, while in foreign languages, 12.2 percent did so. "Unemployment Rate for Language Ph.D.s Hits 10-Year High," *Chronicle of Higher Education*, 12 January 1996, Personal & Professional Section, A15. Of the 1995–96 Ph.D. recipients in mathematics, 9.4 percent were unemployed in September 1996. The unemployment rate declined from the previ-

ous year's record high of 14.7 percent. Denise K. Magner, "Job Market for Ph.D.s Shows First Signs of Improvement," *Chronicle of Higher Education*, 31 January 1997, Faculty Section, A8. The unemployment rate continued to decline among new doctoral recipients in mathematics to 6.8 percent in 1996 – 97, the lowest such figure since 1990. "Unemployment Rate Drops for New Mathematics Ph.D.s," *Chronicle of Higher Education*, 9 January 1998, Faculty Section, A14.

10. A. Sanderson, V. C. Phua, and D. Herda, *The American Faculty Poll* (Chicago: National Opinion Research Center, 2000); the report is available at *http://www.norc.uchicago.edu/online/tiaa-fin.pdf.*

CHAPTER SEVEN

1. In addition, teaching questions are often appropriate for posting on subject-centered lists. The disciplinewide teaching lists are better for general issues of methodology, while the subject-centered lists are better for questions about specific teachable material.

2. This workshop is offered every summer and is open to professors from all kinds of institutions. I highly recommend attendance; your institution may well pay for the cost of the workshop out of faculty development funds. For more information, see the description on the GLCA Web site: *http://www.glca.org/cdt.*

3. This kind of approach is described in detail in Lawrence Lovell-Troy and Paul Eickmann, *Course Design for College Teachers* (Englewood Cliffs, N.J.: Educational Technology Publications, 1992).

4. Your colleagues' syllabi can help you in assessing your students' capabilities. Economics syllabi for all subfields have been published for many years now by Ed Tower of Duke University (Chapel Hill, N.C.: Eno River Press). Markus Wiener Publications puts out collections of syllabi in various fields of history.

5. For a directory of lists of discussion groups in the humanities and social sciences, see the H-Net Web site: *http://www.h-net.msu.edu.* Another excellent source for a wide variety of teaching issues is "Tomorrow's Professor": *http://sll.stanford.edu/projects/tomprof/newtomprof/index.shtml.*

6. For example, economic historians have an H-teach discussion group. One can subscribe at *http://eh-net.edu.*

7. Alan Brinkley, *The Chicago Handbook for Teachers: A Practical Guide to the College Classroom* (Chicago: University of Chicago Press, 1999). Some disciplines have journals devoted to teaching that can provide important insights: see, for example, *Journal of Economic Education.*

8. Some books to begin with: Wilbert J. McKeachie, *McKeachie's Teaching Tips: Strategies, Research, and Theory for College and University Teachers*, 10th ed. (Boston: Houghton Mifflin, 1999); Robert Boice, *First-Order Principles for College Teachers: Ten Basic Ways to Improve the Teaching Process* (Bolton, Mass.: Anker, 1996); Jane P. Tompkins, *A Life in School: What the Teacher Learned* (Reading, Mass.: Addison-Wesley, 1996); bell hooks, *Teaching to Transgress: Education as the Practice of Freedom* (New York: Routledge, 1994). And one article on strategies for discussion that I find newly helpful each time I re-read it: Peter Frederick, "The

Dreaded Discussion: Ten Ways to Start," *Improving College and University Teaching* 29 (1981): 109–14. Some disciplines have journals devoted to teaching that can provide important insights: see, for example, *The History Teacher.*

9.   For this point, see C. J. Guardo, "Designing Curricula for Imaginary Students," *Liberal Education* 71 (1986): 213–19.

10. Arthur Levine and Jeanette S. Cureton, *When Hope and Fear Collide: A Portrait of Today's College Student* (San Francisco: Jossey-Bass, 1998). It can also be helpful to learn something about the cognitive and moral development of college-age students. The source of much recent thinking about the influence of personal development on student learning is William Perry, *Forms of Intellectual and Ethical Development in the College Years* (San Francisco: Jossey-Bass, 1998; originally published 1970).

11. I've been helped by books by Peter Elbow, such as *Writing without Teachers,* 2nd ed. (New York: Oxford University Press, 1998). Your institution's writing center will have many other recommendations.

12. A useful compendium of ideas on assessment of student work is Thomas A. Angelo and Patricia K. Cross, *Classroom Assessment Techniques: A Handbook for College Teachers,* 2nd ed. (San Francisco: Jossey-Bass, 1993).

13. At Knox, we receive a computer printout once a year that shows us how our grades in the past year compare with the grades given those same students by other instructors. It's a convenient way to get a quick, rough assessment of how in line I am with general practice at the institution. If your institution does not do this, you might inquire if such a tabulation could be added to the duties of the registrar.

14. Admittedly, one might ideally aim to set standards just a little bit above average for pedagogical reasons, so that students need to stretch a bit to attain your expectations, but even that is likely not to be easy. Remember that in our academic culture, education is, in the main, what economists call a "consumption good," being purchased in much the same way as any product in the marketplace. You deliver this service, and, in a sense, you are responsible for customer satisfaction. In turn, the customer pays the tuition and expects to be well served by the expenditure. Moreover, the parents of the customers control the political power in the case of state universities, and they expect something for their tax dollars, namely, a diploma for their children, even if its worth is deflated over time. Because there is a lag between the deflation in the value of a diploma and its realization by the outside world, it does not meet as much public resistance as it would otherwise.

15. Herbert Simon, a Nobel Prize–winning psychologist, named the process "satisficing" in opposition to optimizing. Herbert A. Simon, "Rational Decision Making in Business Organizations," *American Economic Review* 69 (1979): 493–513.

16. According to George Loewenstein, a professor at Carnegie-Mellon University, "[W]inning a teaching award is frequently a leading indicator of denial of tenure." "Because It Is There: The Challenge of Mountaineering . . . for Utility Theory," *Kyklos* 52, no. 3 (1999): 339. On a sad case of an English professor who was denied tenure the same time as he won the Teacher of the Year Award (in an unidentified college in upstate New York), see Sascha Feinstein, "Some Lessons about the Spirit of Teaching and Academe's Political Burdens," *Chronicle of Higher*

Education, 16 January 1991, Opinion Section, B2. Of course, the lesson here is not that you shouldn't try to be a good teacher, but rather that if you are at an institution that requires publication for tenure, a teaching award will be no substitute.

17. Tough graders are, of course, not always and inevitably the best teachers.

18. "More than three-quarters of the almost 2,000 students . . . surveyed at nine large public institutions in 1993 admitted to one or more instances of serious cheating on tests or examinations, or to having engaged in serious academic dishonesty on written assignments." Donald L. McCabe and Patrick Drinan, "Toward a Culture of Academic Integrity," *Chronicle of Higher Education,* 15 October 1999, Opinion and Arts Section, B7.

19. According to an Associated Press report, a Northwestern University associate provost said that "plagiarism is our most prevalent form of academic dishonesty." There are now some ways to combat plagiarism through the Internet, for about $1 per paper. See *http://www.plagiarism.org.* The program successfully caught 45 students in a class of 300 in a Berkeley neurobiology class in 1999. See *http://enquirer.com/editions/1999/11/26/fin_web_site_sniffs_out.html.*

20. William Thomson, "The Young Person's Guide to Writing Economic Theory," *Journal of Economic Literature* 37 (March 1999): 157, 182.

21. Laurel Richardson, *Writing Strategies Reaching Diverse Audiences* (Newbury Park, Calif.: Sage, 1990); chapter 8 is about academic writing.

22. For helpful advice on this and much else related to book publishing, see Robin M. Derricourt, *An Author's Guide to Scholarly Publishing* (Princeton, N.J.: Princeton University Press, 1996).

23. I recommend William Strunk and E. G. White, *Elements of Style,* 4th ed. (Boston: Allyn & Bacon, 2000), for good advice on readable prose style.

24. See *Arts and Humanities Citation Index, Social Science Citation Index,* and *Science Citation Index.*

25. Some publications of national organizations devote a volume to report the proceedings of the annual meeting. These issues are often not refereed, but the screening occurs by having the paper accepted for presentation at the meeting.

26. Thomson, "The Young Person's Guide," 182.

27. But always do keep a copy of the original version for reference.

28. Of course, this ought not be interpreted as license to disregard the scholarly requirements of accuracy, thoroughness, objectivity, and honesty.

29. Do not forget that you will have plenty of time to polish the article while it is under consideration, or even thereafter—it is possible to make minor changes after copyediting, and even at the time you are reading the page proofs. The process of publication often takes as long as a year after acceptance. So do not hold up the initial submission of the article for long.

30. To be more precise, for the 1998 volume of *American Economic Review,* for instance, the modal time to rejection was four to five months, with a third of the articles taking longer, and 14 percent taking longer than nine months. The acceptance rate was 8 percent. See frontispiece to vol. 89 no. 4 (1999).

31. Refereeing is a time-consuming and rather thankless process, so it is a won-

der that it works as well as it does. I am somewhat reluctant to mention this because it may give you an incorrect impression of the way the refereeing process usually works, but the longest it has taken me to receive a referee report was two years!

32. In one case, I ran into the same referee on submissions to three different journals, and his appreciation of the paper did not increase over time. There are some people in such strategic positions that they are obvious referees for a paper on a certain topic. The only thing I could do on the fourth round was to send the article to a journal as far away from the presumed person's field as possible.

33. Editors have considerable discretion in choosing referees. Insofar as they have known the referees for an extended period of time, they have a sense of what their opinion is likely to be. Hence, they can influence what kind of reading your article is likely to receive.

34. For a reflection on this behavior by academic reviewers, see Amy Hackney Blackwell, "Reviews of Journal Manuscripts: Nasty, Petty, Arrogant," *Chronicle of Higher Education*, 2 June 2000, B10.

35. Joshua S. Gans and George B. Shepherd, "How Are the Mighty Fallen: Rejected Classic Articles by Leading Economists," *Journal of Economic Perspectives* 8 (1994): 115–79.

36. For example, in the case of the present volume, collaboration made sense to us because we were able to bring our own varied experiences to the project.

37. Usually, they should appear in the order of decreasing contribution to the project, though in some disciplines the idea for the project carries additional weight. In case of equal contribution, an alphabetical order is usual. Some journals impose a policy of listing authors in alphabetical order, regardless of any other factors.

38. In turn, you will be expected to go to their presentations at conferences, and if you cannot make it for some reason, though you are there, you might want to explain and apologize.

39. See footnote 24.

40. See Derricourt's *An Author's Guide to Scholarly Publishing* for further advice about the prospectus.

41. Presses frequently pay referees in kind by giving them an option to choose a couple hundred dollars' worth of books free of charge and consequently see the consecutive refereeing procedure as a cost-saving device.

42. You will receive about ten complimentary copies of your book. You should also explore the possibility of translating the manuscript and publishing it abroad by actively looking for foreign publishers. Although this will not bring you much in the way of accolades in America, the cost in terms of effort in doing so is not excessive, and it might well be worthwhile pursuing the option. It can introduce you to other academic worlds and help you obtain invitations or visiting positions at foreign universities.

43. The overhead rate varies from university to university, but when one submits a grant proposal with a certain budget, an additional amount (in the area of 25 to 50 percent) is added on by the university for what is called "overhead." This money is given by the granting agency to the university, which uses it to pay for utilities, space, and so on.

44. Many universities have a research office worth consulting for advice. They also have useful guides for writing research proposals.

Chapter Eight

1. I have written one or two letters like that myself. One of them was for someone whom I really didn't like and whose professional worldview I didn't like either. But this person's publications were remarkably good and intellectually interesting—all that they should have been. I was honest in my letter about my personal reservations (which, I also explained, were fundamentally irrelevant) and about my professional judgment that the publications in question were of very high quality. It was undoubtedly amusing to the dean who received the letter, and I daresay carried more positive weight than a letter that was nothing but praise.

2. The American Association of University Professors (AAUP) has important information available on tenure and related issues on its home page: *http://www. aaup.org.*

3. For the sad case of Karen Sawislak, who was denied tenure, although the department recommended that she be granted tenure twenty-four to zero and she had written a well-received book published by the University of Chicago Press, see her article, "Denying Tenure: Who Said Anything about Fairness?" *Chronicle of Higher Education,* 17 September 1999, Opinion and Arts Section, B4. In his letter to Ms. Sawislak, Stanford University President Gerhard Casper suggested that the unanimous vote of the department was not the sole criterion for the decision of the administration and, furthermore, agreed with the interpretation that the question of tenure ought not be framed "in terms of whether a candidate 'deserves' or has 'earned' tenure." Rather, he sided with those who argue that there is a predictive element to granting tenure, in the sense that future scholarly performance is also legitimately at stake.

4. George Loewenstein, "Because It Is There: The Challenge of Mountaineering . . . for Utility Theory," *Kyklos* 52, no. 3 (1999): 338.

5. The interested reader may consult the *Chronicle of Higher Education* at *http:// chronicle.com/colloquy/98/tenure/background.shtml:* "Contracts Replace the Tenure Track for a Growing Number of Professors; Colleges Say Alternatives to Lifetime Job Security Are Needed to Control Costs and Assure Flexibility."

6. In fact, you should educate yourself about the AAUP long before tenure time and consider joining. This organization advocates for faculty on a wide variety of issues.

7. Contesting a tenure denial is almost always a time-consuming and painful experience. The odds are not high for winning a case, but it does sometimes happen. Sometimes a monetary settlement is gained, even if restitution of one's job is not. For a number of controversial cases, see Robin Wilson, "Women Lose Tenure Bids despite Backing from Departments; Some Female Academics See a Pattern in the Difficulties They Face at Top Universities," *Chronicle of Higher Education,* 6 June 1997, Faculty Section, A10.

CHAPTER NINE

1.   Gallaudet University is chartered by the U.S. Congress, but operates as an independent institution, with some members of its board of trustees appointed by Congress.

2.   One can hire administrators, too; the analogy to business in the profit-making center cannot be entirely discounted.

3.   A colleague of mine told me that when, in his callow youth in his first academic appointment, he was made an outside offer, he knew for sure that he was going to accept it, but decided to negotiate with his current institution because he was entirely inexperienced in the ways of academia and negotiation. He felt it was an important life skill—and one that cannot be developed elsewhere. Frankly, I'm not sure what to make of that argument.

CHAPTER TEN

1.   For these and many other issues related to academia and family life, see Constance Coiner and Diana Hume George, eds., *The Family Track: Keeping Your Faculties while You Mentor, Nurture, Teach, and Serve* (Urbana: University of Illinois Press, 1998).

2.   See, for example, the front-page article by Kate Zernike in the *Boston Globe* of 21 March 1999, currently available on the Web at *http://www.edc.org/Womens Equity/edequity/hypermail/0156.html.*

3.   "A Study on the Status of Women Faculty in Science at MIT: How a Committee on Women Faculty Came to Be Established by the Dean of the School of Science, What the Committee and the Dean Learned and Accomplished, and Recommendations for the Future": *http://web.mit.edu/fnl/women/women.html.* See also Robin Wilson, "An MIT Professor's Suspicion of Bias Leads to a New Movement for Academic Women," *Chronicle of Higher Education,* 3 December 1999, Faculty Section, A16.

4.   For some personal accounts by women in academia, I recommend *Wise Women: Reflections of Teachers at Midlife,* ed. Phyllis R. Freeman and Jan Zlotnik (New York: Routledge, 2000), a collection of essays by twenty-seven female academics; Gail Griffin, *Calling: Essays on Teaching in the Mother Tongue* (Pasadena, Calif.: Trilogy Books, 1992); and idem, *Season of the Witch: Border Lives, Marginal Notes* (Pasadena, Calif.: Trilogy Books, 1995). Also helpful on understanding gendered interactions is Deborah Tannen, *Talking from 9 to 5* (New York: William Morrow, 1994). Tannen's book is about workplaces of all kinds, but she is a professor herself, and examples from academia figure throughout the book.

5.   On differential evaluations of males and females, see Tannen, *Talking from 9 to 5,* chapter 6, especially page 193. One study on assessments of authorship, especially relevant to academic judgments, is Michele A. Paludi and William D. Bauer, "Goldberg Revisited: What's in an Author's Name?" *Sex Roles* 9 (1983): 387–90.

6.   See JoAnn Miller and Marilyn Chamberlin, "Women Are Teachers, Men Are Professors: A Study of Student Perceptions," *Teaching Sociology* 28 (2000): 283–

98. Such experiences happen higher up the academic ladder as well. Several female provosts report that "they have encountered prejudices, if unconscious ones, during their careers. Some recall being mistaken for the dean's wife or stopped by the security force for parking in the provost's spot." Kit Lively, "Women in Charge," *Chronicle of Higher Education,* 16 June 2000, A35.

7.   Paraphrasing Matthew 5:28.

8.   In 1994, James B. Maas, a psychologist, "had harassed four female students who claimed that he had touched them inappropriately and made sexual comments. To punish him, the university said the harassment finding could affect the professor's raises and promotions for five years." Alison Schneider, "Cornell U. Professor Loses Lawsuit Challenging Harassment Finding," *Chronicle of Higher Education,* 17 December 1999, Faculty Section, A19. "A Macomb Community College (Detroit) professor with a fondness for four-letter words will have another chance to use them in the classroom. . . . [He] was suspended in February after a female student lodged a sexual-harassment complaint against him (*The Chronicle,* February 26). The professor's language was 'dehumanizing, degrading, and sexually explicit,' she wrote." "Federal Judge Rules College Must Reinstate Foul-Mouthed Professor," *Chronicle of Higher Education,* 10 September 1999, Faculty Section, A14. The head football coach at the University of Alabama at Tuscaloosa was fined $360,000 and had his contract reduced from five years to three years after he admitted to an improper relationship with a university employee. The university paid the employee $350,000 to settle her accusation of sexual harassment. Welch Suggs, "U. of Alabama Fines Football Coach for Sex Harassment," *Chronicle of Higher Education,* 3 September 1999, Athletics Section, A85.

9.   Sexual fantasies and desires may also enter into relations between female professors and male students, but because of the general disdain with which older female–younger male relationships are held in our society, these are less likely to take the form of actual relationships than is the case for male professors and female students. Same-sex attractions, with their own distinct patterns with respect to age differences, contribute a further layer of complexity to the sexual geography of academia.

CHAPTER ELEVEN

1.   This is by no means the place to do a comparative analysis of educational systems. Suffice it to say that too much pecuniary reward probably can be as detrimental as too little. While this is by no means obvious, the high reward systems attract more ambitious and pragmatically oriented people. In North America, such people would be more likely to go into the highly competitive segments of our business world.

APPENDIX ONE

1.   Henry Rosovsky, *The University: An Owner's Manual* (New York: W. W. Norton, 1991).

2.   Some schools organize their departments with a "head" rather than a chair or

director, and the head of a department is typically given stronger unilateral powers than a chair. In some cases, the head may make appointment decisions without the majority support of the faculty of the department (a situation I find difficult to imagine, to be honest).

3. In addition to the professors, associate professors, and assistant professors, there may be lecturers, senior lecturers, research assistants, research associates, part-time appointments, and adjunct appointments in the department. An adjunct appointment has merely a casual relationship with the department. She may have an appointment in another department or a full-time position outside of the university.

APPENDIX TWO

1. Thanks to Dean Jim Swartz of Grinnell College for sharing this policy.

Bibliography

Allen, Michael W. *Authorware Academic User's Guide: Version 3.5 for Use with Macintosh and Windows.* Upper Saddle River, N.J.: Prentice-Hall, 1996.

Anthony, Rebecca, and Gerald Roe. *The Curriculum Vitae Handbook: How to Present and Promote Your Academic Career.* 2nd ed. San Francisco: Rudi, 1998.

Association for Women in Science. *Cultivating Academic Careers: AWIS Project on Academic Climate.* Washington, D.C.: Association for Women in Science, 1997.

Benjaminson, Peter. *Publish without Perishing: A Practical Handbook for Academic Authors.* Washington, D.C.: National Education Association, 1992.

Blaxter, Loraine, Christina Hughes, and Malcolm Tight. *The Academic Career Handbook.* Buckingham, England: Open University Press, 1998.

Bloom, Dale F., Jonathan D. Karp, and Nicholas Cohen. *The Ph.D. Process: A Student's Guide to Graduate School in the Sciences.* New York: Oxford University Press, 1998.

Blum, Laurie. *Free Money for Graduate School: A Directory of Private Grants.* New York: Holt, 1990.

Boice, Robert. *First-Order Principles for College Teachers: Ten Basic Ways to Improve the Teaching Process.* Bolton, Mass.: Anker, 1996.

Boufis, Christina, and Victoria C. Olsen. *On the Market: Surviving the Academic Job Search.* New York: Riverhead Books, 1997.

Breneman, David W., and Ted I. K. Youn. *Academic Labor Markets and Careers.* New York: Falmer Press, 1988.

Brennan, Moya, and Sarah Briggs. *How to Apply to American Colleges and Universities: The Complete Manual for Applying to Undergraduate and Graduate Schools in the United States.* Lincolnwood, Ill.: VGM Career Horizons, 1992.

Brinkley, Alan, Betty Dessants, Michael Flamm, Cynthia Fleming, Charles Forcey, and Eric Rothschild. *The Chicago Handbook for Teachers: A Practical Guide to the College Classroom.* Chicago: University of Chicago Press, 1999.

Caesar, Terry. *Writing in Disguise: Academic Life in Subordination.* Athens: Ohio University Press, 1998.

Cantor, Jeffrey A. *A Guide to Academic Writing.* Westport, Conn.: Greenwood Press, 1993.

Caplan, Paula J. *Lifting a Ton of Feathers: A Woman's Guide for Surviving in the Academic World.* Toronto: University of Toronto Press, 1993.

Carnegie Foundation for the Advancement of Teaching. *A Classification of Institutions of Higher Education.* Princeton, N.J.: Carnegie Foundation for the Advancement of Teaching, 1994.

Clark, Burton R. *The Academic Life: Small Worlds, Different Worlds.* Princeton, N.J.: Carnegie Foundation for the Advancement of Teaching, 1987. (Available from Princeton University Press, Princeton, N.J.)

————, ed. *The Academic Profession: National, Disciplinary, and Institutional Settings.* Berkeley: University of California Press, 1987.

Coiner, Constance, and Diana Hume George, eds. *The Family Track: Keeping Your Faculties while You Mentor, Nurture, Teach, and Serve.* Urbana: University of Illinois Press, 1998.

Cornford, Francis Macdonald. *Microcosmographia Academica, Being a Guide for the Young Academic Politician.* Chicago: University of Chicago Press, 1945.

Derricourt, Robin. *An Author's Guide to Scholarly Publishing.* Princeton, N.J.: Princeton University Press, 1996.

Dilts, David A., Lawrence J. Haber, and Donna Bialik. *Assessing What Professors Do: An Introduction to Academic Performance Appraisal in Higher Education.* Westport, Conn.: Greenwood Press, 1994.

Fairweather, James Steven. *Faculty Work and Public Trust: Restoring the Value of Teaching and Public Service in American Academic Life.* Boston: Allyn and Bacon, 1996.

Falk, Gerhard. *The Life of the Academic Professional in America: An Inventory of Tasks, Tensions and Achievements.* Lewiston, N.Y.: E. Mellen Press, 1990.

Fisher, Shirley. *Stress in Academic Life: The Mental Assembly Line.* Buckingham, England; Open University Press; Bristol, Pa.: Society for Research into Higher Education, 1994.

Frederick, Peter. "The Dreaded Discussion: Ten Ways to Start." *Improving College and University Teaching* 29 (1981): 109–14.

Freeman, Phyllis R., and Jan Zlotnik, eds. *Wise Women: Reflections of Teachers at Midlife.* New York: Routledge, 2000.

Frost, Peter J., and M. Susan Taylor, eds. *Rhythms of Academic Life: Personal Accounts of Careers in Academia.* Thousand Oaks, Calif.: Sage, 1996.

Gold, Penny S. "'A Teacher Is Either a Witness or a Stranger.'" In *The Role of Advocacy in the Classroom,* ed. Patricia Meyer Spack. New York: St. Martin's, 1996.

Griffin, Gail B. *Calling: Essays on Teaching in the Mother Tongue.* Pasadena, Calif.: Trilogy Books, 1992.

————. *Season of the Witch: Border Lines, Marginal Notes.* Pasadena, Calif.: Trilogy Books, 1995.

Guardo, C. J. "Designing Curricula for Imaginary Students." *Liberal Education* 71 (1986): 213–19.

Gustafson, Melanie, ed. *Becoming a Historian: A Survival Manual for Women and Men.* Washington. D.C.: American Historical Association, 1991.

Hansen, Kristine. *A Rhetoric for the Social Sciences: A Guide to Academic and Professional Communication.* Upper Saddle River, N.J.: Prentice-Hall, 1998.

Harris, Muriel. *The Writer's FAQs: A Pocket Handbook.* Upper Saddle River, N.J.: Prentice-Hall, 2000.

Heiberger, Mary Morris, and Julia Miller Vick. *The Academic Job Search Handbook.* 2nd ed. Philadelphia: University of Pennsylvania Press, 1996.

Higgins, Jerry D., and John W. Williams. *Academic Preparation for Careers in Engineering Geology and Geological Engineering.* Sudbury, Mass.: Association of Engineering Geologists, 1991.

Higham, Robin D. S. *The Compleat Academic: An Informal Guide to the Ivory Tower.* New York: St. Martin's, 1974.

hooks, bell. *Teaching to Transgress: Education as the Practice of Freedom.* New York: Routledge, 1994.

How to Get into Graduate School. Livingston, N.J.: Newsweek, Inc., and Kaplan Educational Centers, 1997.

Howe, Barbara J. *Careers for Students of History.* Washington, D.C.: American Historical Association, 1989.

Isaac, Alicia. *The African American Student's Guide to Surviving Graduate School.* Thousand Oaks, Calif.: Sage 1998.

Jensen, Jane McEldowney, and Lisa D'Adamo-Weinstein. *Piecing It Together: A Guide to Academic Success.* Boston: Allyn and Bacon, 1999.

John Minter Associates. *JMA Guide to Identifying Comparable Academic Institutions.* 3 vols. Boulder, Colo.: John Minter Associates, 1993.

Jordan, R. R. *English for Academic Purposes: A Guide and Resource Book for Teachers.* Cambridge, England: Cambridge University Press, 1997.

Judge, Harry George. *American Graduate Schools of Education: A View from Abroad: A Report to the Ford Foundation.* New York: Ford Foundation, 1982.

Kaplan, Max. *One Life: The Free Academic.* Madison, N.J.: Fairleigh Dickinson University Press, 1998.

Keith-Spiegel, Patricia. *The Complete Guide to Graduate School Admission: Psychology and Related Fields.* Hillsdale, N.J.: Erlbaum, 1991.

Keller, Peter A., ed. *Academic Paths: Career Decisions and Experiences of Psychologists.* Hillsdale, N.J.: Erlbaum, 1994.

Kennedy, Donald. *Academic Duty.* Cambridge: Harvard University Press, 1997.

Lanks, Karl W. *Academic Environment: A Handbook for Evaluating Employment Opportunities in Science.* 2nd ed. Washington, D.C.: Taylor & Francis, 1996.

———. *Academic Environment: A Handbook for Evaluating Faculty Employment Opportunities.* Brooklyn, N.Y.: Faculty Press, 1990.

Leape, Martha P., and Wilson Hunt Jr. *Choosing an Academic Career: A Discussion of Graduate Study and Fellowships with Special Information for Minority Students.* Cambridge: Harvard University, Office of Career Services, 1993.

Levine, Arthur, and Jeanette S. Cureton. *When Hope and Fear Collide: A Portrait of Today's College Student.* San Francisco: Jossey-Bass, 1998.

Lewis, Lionel Stanley. *Scaling the Ivory Tower: Merit and Its Limits in Academic Careers.* New Brunswick, N.J.: Transaction Publishers, 1998.

Lightman, Marjorie, and William Zeisel, eds. *Outside Academe: New Ways of Working in the Humanities: A Report on the Conference "Independent Research Institutions and Scholarly Life in the 1980s."* New York: Institute for Research in History and Haworth Press, 1981.

Lodge, David. *Changing Places: A Tale of Two Campuses.* London: Secker and Warburg, 1975.

————. *Small World: An Academic Romance.* New York: Warner Books, 1984.

Lovell-Troy, Lawrence, and Paul Eickmann. *Course Design for College Teachers.* Englewood Cliffs, N.J.: Educational Technology Publications, 1992.

Luey, Beth. *Handbook for Academic Authors.* 3rd ed. Cambridge: Cambridge University Press, 1995.

McKeachie, Wilbert J. *McKeachie's Teaching Tips: Strategies, Research, and Theory for College and University Teachers.* 10th ed. Boston: Houghton Mifflin, 1999.

Montagu, Ashley. *Up the Ivy; Being Microcosmographia Academica Revisited, a True Blue Guide on How to Climb in the Academic World without Appearing to Try, by Academicus Mentor.* New York: Hawthorn Books, 1966.

Moxley, Joseph Michael. *Publish, Don't Perish: The Scholar's Guide to Academic Writing and Publishing.* Westport, Conn.: Greenwood Press, 1992.

National Center for Education Statistics, Association for Institutional Research, and American Association of State Colleges and Universities. *Integrating Research on Faculty: Seeking New Ways to Communicate about the Academic Life of Faculty: Results from the 1994 Forum.* Washington, D.C.: U.S. Department of Education, Office of Educational Research and Improvement, 1996.

Nelson, Carey, and Stephen Watt. *Academic Keywords: A Devil's Dictionary for Higher Education.* New York: Routledge, 1999.

Newhouse, Margaret. *Cracking the Academia Nut: A Guide to Preparing for Your Academic Career.* Cambridge: Harvard University, Office of Career Services, 1997.

Oshima, Alice, and Ann Hogue. *Introduction to Academic Writing.* 2nd ed. White Plains, N.Y.: Longman, 1997.

Paludi, Michele Antoinette, and Richard B. Barickman. *Academic and Workplace Sexual Harassment: A Resource Manual.* 2nd ed. Albany: State University of New York Press, 1998.

Perry, William. *Forms of Intellectual and Ethical Development in the College Years.* San Francisco: Jossey-Bass, 1970; reprint, 1998.

Peterson's Compact Guides. *Graduate and Professional Schools in the U.S.* Princeton, N.J.: Peterson's, 1998. CD-ROM.

Phelan, James. *Beyond the Tenure Track.* Columbus: Ohio State University Press, 1990.

Preece, Roy A. *Starting Research: An Introduction to Academic Research and Dissertation Writing.* London: Pinter Publishers; New York: St. Martin's, 1994.

Reis, Richard M. *Tomorrow's Professor: Preparing for Academic Careers in Science and Engineering.* New York: IEEE Press, 1997.

Research and Education Association. *REA's Authoritative Guide to Graduate Schools: Detailed Profiles of Over 500 Graduate Schools in 60 Fields of Study.* Piscataway, N.J.: REA, 1997.

Rheingold, Harriet Lange. *The Psychologist's Guide to an Academic Career.* Washington, D.C.: American Psychological Association, 1994.

Richardson, Laurel. *Fields of Play: Constructing an Academic Life.* New Brunswick, N.J.: Rutgers University Press, 1997.

Rittner, Barbara, and Patricia Trudeau. *The Women's Guide to Surviving Graduate School*. Thousand Oaks, Calif.: Sage, 1997.

Rosovsky, Henry. *The University: An Owner's Manual*. New York: W. W. Norton, 1990.

Rossman, Mark H. *Negotiating Graduate School: A Guide for Graduate Students*. Thousand Oaks, Calif.: Sage, 1995.

Schenck, Mary Jane Stearns. *Read, Write, Revise: A Guide to Academic Writing*. New York: St. Martin's, 1988.

Schmidt, Jeff. *Disciplined Minds: A Critical Look at Salaried Professionals and the Soul-Battering System That Shapes Their Lives*. Lanham, Md.: Rowman & Littlefield, 2000.

Shearmur, Jeremy. *Scaling the Ivory Tower: The Pursuit of an Academic Career*. Fairfax, Va.: George Mason University, Institute for Humane Studies, 1995.

Sherrill, Jan-Mitchell, and Craig A. Hardesty. *The Gay, Lesbian, and Bisexual Students' Guide to Colleges, Universities, and Graduate Schools*. New York: New York University Press, 1994.

Shrier, Diane K. *Sexual Harassment in the Workplace and Academia: Psychiatric Issues*. Washington, D.C.: American Psychiatric Press, 1996.

Silva, Anjalika I. *Employment Guide for Foreign-Born Chemists in the United States*. Washington, D.C.: American Chemical Society, Department of Career Services, 1997.

Stelzer, Richard J. *How to Write a Winning Personal Statement for Graduate and Professional School*. 3rd ed. Princeton, N.J.: Peterson's, 1997.

Straughn, Charles T., and Barbarasue Lovejoy Straugh. *Lovejoy's Guide to Graduate School Programs in Humanities and Social Sciences*. New York: ARCO, Simon & Schuster Macmillan, 1997.

Taylor, Peter G. *Making Sense of Academic Life: Academics, Universities, and Change*. Philadelphia: Open University Press, 1999.

Thomson, William. "The Young Person's Guide to Writing Economic Theory." *Journal of Economic Literature* 37 (March 1999): 1, 157–83.

Tompkins, Jane P. *A Life in School: What the Teacher Learned*. Reading, Mass.: Addison-Wesley, 1996.

Toth, Emily. *Ms. Mentor's Impeccable Advice for Women in Academia*. Philadelphia: University of Pennsylvania Press, 1997.

Tsang, Reginald C., and William Oh, with the assistance of Lynda L. Price. *Beginning an Academic Medical Career: Research, Writing, Speaking*. Philadelphia: Hanley & Belfus, 1993.

Turabian, Kate L. *A Manual for Writers of Term Papers, Theses, and Dissertations*. 6th ed., revised by John Grossman and Alice Bennett. Chicago: University of Chicago Press, 1996.

U.S. Information Agency. *U.S. Academic Explorer Computer File: A Guide to Higher Education in the United States*. Washington, D.C.: U.S. Government Printing Office, 1996. Laser optical disc.

U.S. News and World Report. *America's Best Graduate Schools*. Washington, D.C.: U.S. News and World Report Inc., 1994–97.

Walker, John Henry, III. *Thinking about Graduate School: A Planning Guide for Freshman and Sophomore Minority College Students.* Princeton, N.J.: Educational Testing Service, 1973.

Williams, Joan. *Unbending Gender: Why Family and Work Conflict and What to Do about It.* New York: Oxford University Press, 2000.

About the Authors

John A. Goldsmith is the Edward Carson Waller Distinguished Service Professor in and former chair of the Department of Linguistics at the University of Chicago. He received a bachelor's degree with honors in philosophy, mathematics, and economics from Swarthmore College in 1972 and a doctoral degree in linguistics from the Massachusetts Institute of Technology in 1976. He taught for eight years at Indiana University and has held visiting appointments at McGill University, Université du Québec à Montréal, University of California at San Diego, and Microsoft Research. He is the editor of *The Last Phonological Rule* (Chicago: University of Chicago Press, 1993), *The Handbook of Phonological Theory* (Cambridge, Mass.: Blackwell, 1995), and *Phonological Theory: The Essential Readings* (Malden, Mass.: Blackwell, 1999); author of *Autosegmental and Metrical Phonology* (Oxford: Blackwell, 1990); and coauthor of *Ideology and Linguistic Theory* (London: Routledge, 1995). He has been a Mellon Faculty Fellow at Harvard, was a finalist for *Discover Magazine's* 1997 Technology Award, and has received research grants from the National Science Foundation and the American Council of Learned Societies. In 1995, he was awarded a faculty prize at the University of Chicago for excellence in graduate teaching. He is married to the linguist Jessie Pinkham, who works at Microsoft Research in Redmond, Washington. They have three children, ages 24, 16, and 8.

John Komlos is professor of economics, chair of the Institute of Economic History, and former chair of the Department of Economics at the University of Munich. He received doctoral degrees in history and economics from the University of Chicago in 1978 and 1990, respectively. He has taught at the University of Pittsburgh, has held visiting appointments at Duke University,

the University of Vienna, and at the Vienna School of Economics, and was a postdoctoral fellow at the Population Center of the University of North Carolina at Chapel Hill. He has received grants or fellowships from Fulbright, the American Council of Learned Societies, and the National Science Foundation, and has directed summer seminars for college teachers for the National Endowment for the Humanities. He has written a number of books, including *The Habsburg Monarchy as a Customs Union: Economic Development in Austria-Hungary in the Nineteenth Century* (Princeton: Princeton University Press: 1983) and *Nutrition and Economic Development in the Eighteenth-Century Habsburg Monarchy: An Anthropometric History* (Princeton: Princeton University Press, 1989), and has edited a number of books as well, including *Stature, Living Standards, and Economic Development: Essays in Anthropometric History* (Chicago: University of Chicago Press, 1994). He is a leading proponent of the new field of anthropometric history, which explores the impact of economic processes (such as industrialization) on the well-being of the human organism. He is married to Liliane Komlos and has two sons, ages 10 and 5.

Penny Schine Gold is professor in and chair of the Department of History at Knox College, where she is also chair of the Gender and Women's Studies Program. She received a bachelor's degree in history *cum laude* in 1969 from the University of Chicago and a doctoral degree in medieval studies from Stanford University in 1977. She has also taught at the University of Cincinnati and has had visiting appointments at the University of Iowa and the University of Chicago. She is the author of *The Lady and the Virgin: Image, Attitude, and Experience in Twelfth-Century France* (Chicago: University of Chicago Press, 1985), co-editor of *Cultural Visions: Essays in the History of Culture* (Amsterdam: Rodopi, 2000), and is writing a book for Cornell University Press entitled *Making the Bible Modern: Children's Bibles and Jewish Education in Twentieth Century America.* She has held a National Endowment for the Humanities Fellowship and been a senior fellow at the Institute of the Advanced Study of Religion at the University of Chicago. She was the first Knox College recipient of the Sears-Roebuck Foundation Award for Teaching Excellence and Campus Leadership in 1988 and was also awarded the Caterpillar Faculty Achievement award in 1999. Her husband, David Amor, is Director of Foundation and Corporate Relations at Knox College. They have a son, age 15.

Index